DANCING MAN

DANCING MAN

A Broadway Choreographer's Journey

Bob Avian

with Tom Santopietro

UNIVERSITY PRESS OF MISSISSIPPI / JACKSON

The University Press of Mississippi is the scholarly publishing agency of
the Mississippi Institutions of Higher Learning: Alcorn State University,
Delta State University, Jackson State University, Mississippi State University,
Mississippi University for Women, Mississippi Valley State University,
University of Mississippi, and University of Southern Mississippi.

www.upress.state.ms.us

The University Press of Mississippi is a member of
the Association of University Presses.

First printing 2020
∞

Library of Congress Cataloging-in-Publication Data available
LCCN 2019046220

Hardback ISBN	978-1-4968-2588-9
Epub single ISBN	978-1-4968-2697-8
Epub institutional ISBN	978-1-4968-2698-5
PDF single ISBN	978-1-4968-2699-2
PDF institutional ISBN	978-1-4968-2700-5

British Library Cataloging-in-Publication Data available

FOR PETER P. AND MICHAEL B.

CONTENTS

ACKNOWLEDGMENTS

I would first like to thank my co-author and good friend Tom Santopietro, without whom this book would not have seen the light of day. His prodding and insistence upon putting pen to paper made this book a reality. His enthusiasm and talent are boundless.

A huge debt of thanks goes to my publisher Craig Gill, who led me so adroitly through the process of creating a memoir. Additional thanks to Craig's associate, Emily Bundy, for her first-rate help with a myriad of details, as well as to copy editor Peter Tonguette for his time and dedication. A special thanks to Pete Halverson for his jacket design and to illustrator Ken Fallin, whose theatre caricatures beautifully enhance this book.

To my agent Malaga Baldi, thank you for finding exactly the right publisher in the University Press of Mississippi. Your guidance through the entire process cannot be overestimated.

My gratitude as well to the professional photographers Bob Deutsch, Paul Kolnik, Anthony Timiraos, Michael Le Poer Trench, and the late, great Stephen G. Jennings, whose work has added so very much to this book.

Lots of love and hugs to my old pals Patti LuPone and Cameron Mackintosh, who agreed to look at early drafts and then encouraged me with their endless support.

I send gratitude as well to Adrian Bryan-Brown and Heath Schwartz for their help in spreading the word, along with Jordan Nettles, Courtney McCreary, and Steve Yates.

And for all their guidance and help, I thank my friends, family, and colleagues, including my sister, Laura Nabedian; Jane Austin; Natasha Dennison; Marti Stevens; Michael Keller; James Vandernoth; Ron Madelbaum and Bill Miller; Stanley Steinberg; Josh Johnston; Philip Rinaldi; John and Nan Breglio; Gemma Allsopp; Megan Gorman; Barbara A. Callahan; Brig Berney; and Dan Kaufman.

Lastly, but most importantly, to my husband and best friend Peter Pileski, whose unconditional love and endless support help me more than I can convey.

THE LEADING LADIES

Carol Lawrence	*West Side Story*
Anna Maria Alberghetti	*Carnival!*
Chita Rivera	*Zenda*
Barbra Streisand	*Funny Girl*
Betty Grable	*Hello, Dolly!*
Mary Martin	*Hello, Dolly!, Jennie, and I Do! I Do!*
Katharine Hepburn	*Coco*
Elaine Stritch	*Company*
Alexis Smith	
Dorothy Collins	
Yvonne De Carlo	*Follies*
Sada Thompson	*Twigs*
Michele Lee	*Seesaw*
Donna McKechnie	*A Chorus Line*
Dorothy Loudon	*Ballroom*
Jennifer Holliday	
Sheryl Lee Ralph	
Loretta Devine	*Dreamgirls*
Diana Rigg	
Julie McKenzie	*Follies* (London)
Lea Salonga	*Miss Saigon*
Patti LuPone	
Glenn Close	
Betty Buckley	
Elaine Paige	
Diahann Carroll	*Sunset Boulevard*
Julie Andrews	
Carol Burnett	
Kathie Lee Gifford	*Putting It Together*
Lucie Arnaz	
Maria Friedman	
Joanna Riding	*The Witches of Eastwick*

DANCING MAN

CHAPTER ONE

KATHARINE HEPBURN, *COCO*, AND A BIG SMASH FLOP

Summer 1969

KATHARINE HEPBURN, I'VE JUST DISCOVERED, CAN'T SING AND SHE SURE can't dance. Which is a big problem, since she's starring in *Coco*, the most talked-about musical of the Broadway season. And why is this particular problem of concern to me? Because I'm the associate choreographer of the show, working alongside my best friend Michael Bennett, who is fresh off a Tony nomination as choreographer of the Broadway smash hit *Promises, Promises*. On this, the very first day of pre-production rehearsal, we're excited and even in awe of the great Kate—for precisely ten minutes. And then Michael and I look at each other and realize there's an elephant in the room: the legendary Katharine Hepburn doesn't have a musical bone in her body. Michael and I can read each other's thoughts: We're in trouble. Big trouble.

The show is already sold out for the first three months of its run, and there is two million dollars, the biggest budget in the history of Broadway, riding on the line. On this particular day, we wanted to start work on "The Money Rings Out Like Freedom," a montage we've conceived of Coco Chanel's rise to the top of the worldwide fashion industry, complete with twenty-four models and constantly spinning turntables, all of it anchored by Kate/Coco singing and dancing center stage. But, if Kate can't walk in time to music, how are we going to stage this mammoth number?

What exactly had brought us to this juncture? Well, we were two ambitious young men—I was thirty-two to Michael's twenty-seven—and we had eagerly signed on for the show, both of us excited by the chance to work with an impressive roster of A-listers: composer André Previn, librettist and lyricist Alan Jay Lerner, designer Cecil Beaton, and Kate Hepburn herself.

Once we had agreed to work on the show—Michael would choreograph and I would assist him, just as I had done on *Promises, Promises*—we met with Alan Jay Lerner at his elegant house in Oyster Bay, Long Island, in order to discuss the shape of the show. Alan proposed putting portions of the show on film: key moments from Coco Chanel's life would unroll on giant screens, the film footage bleeding into live presentation as the elegant Chanel models stepped through the screen while the film footage faded away. An interesting idea but one Michael nixed quickly. Film footage meant weeks and weeks of expensive pre-production, resulting in numbers being frozen months in advance, even as we continued to work on the show. There would be no room for the changes every musical endures on the way to opening night, and Michael and I also knew that film footage would detract from the live performers. *Coco* was supposed to focus on one thing and one thing only: Katharine Hepburn live and in person singing a Previn/Lerner score with a thirty-three-piece orchestra conducted by the eminent Robert Emmett Dolan.

Michael and I were in agreement about nixing the film footage, but then we were in agreement about most things. We had been best friends, roommates, and kindred spirits ever since meeting on the international tour of *West Side Story* back in 1960. When Michael started his rise to the top of Broadway as the Tony-nominated choreographer of his very first show, *A Joyful Noise*, and followed that by signing to choreograph *Henry, Sweet Henry*, he said to me: "Come dance in the chorus of *Henry, Sweet Henry* and be one of my assistant choreographers." The show only ran for three months, but our working relationship made perfect sense. I wasn't cautious with Michael; I knew him so well that I could tell him exactly what I thought. In effect I seemed to instinctively assume the role of his editor. Michael was a more mercurial personality than I, and ambitious though I was, I did not possess Michael's burning intensity. I didn't want to be Michael, and he didn't want to be me. That's what made our decades-long relationship, from *Coco* and *Company* to *A Chorus Line* and *Dreamgirls*, work so well. We'd finish rehearsal, go home to our apartments, and call each other to discuss the day's work. And at the end of this first day with Hepburn, we were on the phone for hours, both laughing and trembling.

It's not that we came to this pre-production unprepared. Far from it. We had met with Cecil Beaton in London, where he presented us with his daring idea to have the climactic "Always Mademoiselle" number presented entirely in red. He then sent us hundreds of sketches of the dresses, pants, and pieces of costume jewelry that would figure in "The Money Rings Out Like Freedom." This was Cecil Beaton of *My Fair Lady* fame—we were in great hands, or so we thought.

We had flown to Paris to meet with Coco Chanel herself, and she and Michael hit it off so well that Michael stayed on for two weeks, observing her painstaking attention to detail while she hemmed, pinned, and scrutinized every garment that left her shop on the Rue Cambon. In typical Michael style, he had seduced Coco—if not literally, then emotionally, sweeping her up into his world just as Coco herself seduced Michael with her genius. And she was a genius. Both Michael and I experienced moments when we thought, "We're watching Coco Chanel at work—we can't believe it!" Coco spoke a little English, we spoke a little French. Somehow we communicated.

The story making the rounds on Broadway was that when the producers and writers were preparing the show, Coco Chanel herself was asked whom she wanted to star in her life story and she replied: "Hepburn"—meaning Audrey, not Katharine. True or not, here we were one week before full company rehearsals started, and our star was proving herself unmusical, devoid of rhythm, and totally out of her element.

We went to work.

Michael gave Kate little marching steps to carry her from one side of the stage to the other. What we quickly found out was that even these rudimentary movements proved difficult for her. What she did have, however, was star presence to burn, extraordinary acting ability, and a fierce work ethic. The question was how to find a way to make those gifts shine.

To top it all off, in her frightened state Kate proved contrary in the extreme, automatically contradicting whatever direction Michael gave her. If Michael said to her, "I think you'll enter from upstage right," Kate would say "Oh, no, no, no—I can't do that. I'll come in from downstage left." Finally, we hit on a solution to the problem: if we wanted Kate to enter from stage right we'd say, "It might be nice if you'd enter from stage left," and she'd do the exact opposite.

Michael simplified every single step. During "The Money Rings Out Like Freedom," as Coco musically explains her success and innovations, we decided to sit her on the lip of the stage, leafing through a scrapbook as the models came to life. Michael kept encouraging Kate and finally we achieved a breakthrough. No, she still couldn't sing or dance, but when she broke down in tears—"I don't know what gives me the goddamn nerve to think I can do this"—we realized that she not only felt vulnerable, but would finally start trusting us to protect and guide her.

Kate understood just how much was riding on her shoulders and in typical fashion took no prisoners. She happened to live in a Turtle Bay brownstone next door to Stephen Sondheim, who was composing his landmark score for *Company*. Steve liked to work late at night, composing through the early hours of the morning. "Early to bed, early to rise" Kate was having none of it, and would lean out of her windows and bang a broom against the side of his house while barking "Stop making all that noise!"

Director Michael Benthall had assembled a terrific supporting cast, with George Rose as Coco's business manager and Rene Auberjonois (who went on to win a Tony for Best Featured Actor in a Musical) as Coco's fashion rival, but Benthall was out of his element shepherding this gigantic musical. Having worked with him in the past on *The Millionaress*, Kate had personally chosen Benthall as the director, but when he attempted to direct her in a scene, she would simply direct the scene herself. As soon as a scene required moving more than a handful of people around the stage, he ran scared, often retreating to the men's room for a slug of gin. Michael Bennett then took over the staging of the show for all intents and purposes, but he was scared as well. When we walked to the theatre for our first run-through, we tried to calm ourselves by telling each other optimistically, "Just think—we'll be the first people ever to watch Katharine Hepburn sing on Broadway!"

Unlike typical musicals, which rehearse in bare-bones studios, we had rehearsed on the stage of the Mark Hellinger Theatre from day one because of the complex fashion numbers. We needed the real set with its revolves and concentric turntables. Most of the creative team was perched in the orchestra for the first run-through, but Michael and I had parked ourselves in the mezzanine; we wanted the full perspective, the best place from which we could gauge the effectiveness not only of the musical numbers, but also of the few remaining film sequences depicting the important men in Coco's life.

The house lights dimmed, and at the end of the overture the stage lights came up on the gargantuan Cecil Beaton set, at which point our worst fears were confirmed. The set was big, clumsy, and beige. Make that *very* beige—and extremely difficult to light.

The show began, but after just a few minutes we whispered to each other: "Oh my God—this is awful!" There was no other word for it. By the end of the run-through, we were downright depressed but we plowed ahead. We had no choice. We knew what we could change and what we couldn't. Michael conferred with lighting designer Tom Skelton about brightening up the set. We simplified, cut, restaged, and in a few days' time made it through our first public preview. It wasn't very good, but the theatre was packed. Everyone in the business was there to assess Hepburn in her musical debut.

The massive turntable set—which revolved from workshop to Coco's apartment, complete with dozens of models gliding on and off the turntables—now worked most of the time, but Kate's lack of musical ability leapt out at even the most casual viewer. If your star can't sing or dance, how do you create theatre magic?

And yet some sequences actually worked very well. We were happy with our three big production numbers, and those numbers seemed to carry the audience along through the lumbering book scenes. Kate was terrific in the big sequence at the end of act one which covered the week leading up to her big comeback collection. This montage showed Coco working at fever pitch, and each revolve depicted a different day: one day the office was in an uproar, the next showed Coco sewing and fitting models, and the frenzied activity continued throughout all seven days. All that time Michael had spent at Chanel's apartment and workshop resulted in this entertaining sequence, and Kate pulled it off very well because she was acting instead of dancing or singing. This Coco Chanel may have spoken more like a New England school marm than a Parisian couturiere, but at preview after preview, the audience seemed happy just to be in her presence. So delighted were they with Hepburn that they actually seemed happiest when, during one matinee, the turntable broke and Kate came out to explain the entire comeback montage. The audience was now being addressed directly by Kate herself and they were nothing short of ecstatic.

The big production numbers were in good shape, but we realized that we needed to make the evening glossier so that the show wouldn't come to a screeching halt with every transition. We were maneuvering a lot of people around the set—twenty-four young women, the most beautiful on Broadway—as well as a male dancing chorus and a singing chorus. We succeeded in speeding things up, but we couldn't get around the fact that the basic material was mediocre. Although Previn and Lerner were giants in their fields, this show did not rank among their better works. As the weeks of previews stretched on, Michael began to get more and more depressed. We kept thinking, "We're staging the biggest show in town—and it's a turkey." Finally, during the last ten days before opening, Michael could barely bring himself to show up at the theatre. Even though we were satisfied with our contribution, he was just too upset over the state of a musical that could have presented us with major career opportunities as the biggest show of the season yet seemed to simply lumber around the Hellinger stage.

We made it to opening night in December of 1969, and the critics weighed in. Here's what Clive Barnes said in the *New York Times*: "I had always imagined that Devil's Island apart, there was no place I would rather not be in than Las Vegas. There were one or two moments in the first act [of *Coco*] when I began to wonder whether the verdict had been a little hasty." The *New York Times* was telling us that having to sit inside the Mark Hellinger Theatre constituted a form of torture, and guess what? The public couldn't have cared less. *Coco* sold out every performance for the eight months Hepburn stayed in the show. Each and every performance found the actors playing to standing room only, and at the end of the show audiences leapt to their feet, no matter how mediocre the product. These ovations were a tribute to Hepburn. A star is a star is a star, as Gertrude Stein might have said.

The critics did not pay much attention to the extraordinary work Michael had done, and if we were mentioned at all, it was in terms of "*Coco* unleashes a whirlwind of models" . . . Fortunately, Michael's work lives on in the "Always Mademoiselle" number, which was filmed for the Tony Awards and can be seen on YouTube. The packed houses continued, and Michael and I began referring to *Coco* as our "smash flop." This wasn't the show we envisioned, but audiences kept coming and the resulting royalties represented a very nice bonus.

It was fascinating to observe Kate, because while she carried herself like a star, she definitely did not behave in typical star like fashion. Her dressing room was as stark as an army barracks. She had a cot with a white sheet lying on top, and another white sheet hanging up to separate the room into two sections. On her dressing room table were a hairbrush, a comb, mascara, pancake, and lipstick. That's it. No other accoutrements.

Post-opening, we would stop by the theatre to check on the show and after the final curtain would go backstage to say hi to Kate. On one particular night, she had guests attending the performance, and when we all left the theatre together, she offered her guests a ride; the show always provided her with transportation to and from the theatre, and in typical Kate fashion, the car was a very unostentatious Plymouth sedan. No Cadillac limo for her. On this night, Kate had more guests than anticipated, and after they piled into the car, there was no room for Kate. Her solution? She asked the driver to pop open the trunk, whereupon she climbed into the trunk to be driven home! Michael and I ran over and hauled her out of the trunk instantly. We couldn't believe it. Well, that was Kate.

At the end of eight months, Hepburn left the show and was replaced by Danielle Darrieux, the French movie star. She was wonderful—a true Frenchwoman, she could sing, move gracefully, exuded chic and femininity—and no one cared. Following Hepburn in the show was like holding a parade on the 5th of July, and the show closed two months later.

Coco was so expensive to produce that even after months of sold-out performances, the production costs still hadn't been recouped, so Hepburn agreed to go out on tour to help the show pay back the investors. That showed us what a pro she was. The show sold out everywhere it played— they even had to put folding chairs inside the Dorothy Chandler Pavilion in Los Angeles. Kate delivered—big time.

Kate grew to love Michael. She could see how extraordinary his work was, and how prodigious his gifts. She actually became much easier to work with on the tour because she now trusted us, and the show was a finished product. She felt confident reproducing the work she had performed in New York. Of equal import, the show had actually provided Kate with a turning point in her life. She had always been a bit afraid of the audience. Would she measure up to their expectations? But on *Coco*, the audience showered her with such love that she realized it wasn't a competition— they loved her precisely because of who she was. On closing night in New York, the chorus filed past her one by one, each one handing her a rose until her arms were overflowing with long stem roses. She even made a curtain speech at the end of the show, telling the audience: "I cannot begin to thank you enough and I hope that you learn the lesson that I have learned—and that is, I love you and you love me. Thank you." Smart words from a smart lady.

One more note on *Coco*. During technical rehearsals, we hit a problem when it came to the multi-screen Panavision process showing Coco interacting with the men in her life. Coco's early love, Grand Duke Alexandrovitch, was played by Jack Dabdoub, a great guy with a terrific voice but not a romantic looking Grand Duke. The sequence wasn't working, but we wanted to keep Jack's magnificent singing. The solution came when André Previn, who had grown used to seeing me leap all around the stage demonstrating steps during rehearsals, said, "Let's re-film the sequence with Bob playing the role."

In a very short period of time, I had to learn how to precisely lip-synch the song and dialogue to Jack's recorded voice. I ran home and began practicing in front of the bathroom mirror. In no time at all, I was at the Paramount Studio in New York being fitted for wardrobe. The director of the film sequences, Fred Lemoine, came over and gave me the only bit of direction I was to receive—"Remember, when you raise an eyebrow, it's three feet on the screen"—and bam, just like that, we were filming.

The cameras rolled, and I nailed the lip-syncing. Start to finish, the entire shoot took only two hours. We went to dailies to see the finished product and everyone seemed very pleased. Everyone except me—I hated seeing myself on screen. I literally couldn't watch myself, and any time we came to the theatre to check on the show, I had to leave the theatre as soon as that film sequence started.

Watching myself thirty feet high on the screen? No way.

But I did think to myself, "Now if I could just keep Jack Dabdoub's voice . . ."

CHAPTER TWO

BEGINNINGS

WORKING WITH KATHARINE HEPBURN WAS NOT EXACTLY IN THE GAME plan while growing up in Manhattan as the son of Armenian immigrants. My parents had been displaced by the Turkish genocide, having moved first to Beirut, Lebanon, before emigrating to the United States.

In a fashion very typical of the times, my father, John Hampar Avedisian (I shortened the name when I began dancing professionally), came to the United States as a young man and worked for two full years before he traveled back to Beirut, where he announced to his family that he needed a wife. Their reply: "We know a nice family, the Keleshians, and they have a daughter, Esther. You can see her at church." My father went to church, and three weeks later my parents married: my father was twenty-eight and my mother sixteen. They took the boat to America, and before my mother turned seventeen she gave birth to my older brother, Jackie. Strange to us, perhaps, but that was their culture.

It was at this time that the Depression hit, and my parents, now living in Manhattan, struggled, with my mother working as a seamstress and my father as a chef. The family grew, and two years after the birth of Jackie, my sister, Laura, was born. Seven years after that, I was born on December 26, 1937. The Depression was ending and as the baby of the family—OK, I admit, as the spoiled youngest child—I was the beneficiary of those changing times.

I grew up on the streets of Manhattan's Upper West Side, and it was a lot easier to just hang out with friends on the streets in those days. Diversity ruled. My grammar school had lots of Puerto Rican students, and my high school, Charles Evans Hughes High School in the then Hispanic Chelsea neighborhood, had many African American students. My two best pals were black, and I was fortunate because my immigrant parents always nurtured my friendships. They simply had no predetermined judgments about race. Looking back on it all, there is no question that I thought I was very fortunate to grow up in this integrated situation. I was thrilled to live in the melting pot of Manhattan where I could attend theatre and go to museums. I especially loved the Hayden Planetarium at the Museum of Natural History. In this multicultural atmosphere, everything I could possibly want was at my fingertips.

My favorite activity was to go to the movies, especially musicals, and I spent hours at the Lowes Eighty-third Street Cinema, the RKO at Eighty-first Street, and at the Beacon Theatre on Broadway. I loved those lavish escapist entertainments, all of them produced on the grandest possible Hollywood scale. The sheer scope of those films enthralled me, which meant that it was quite a shock when I saw my first Broadway production; my sister had started going to the theatre and she helped talk my parents into taking me to see *Oklahoma!* at the St. James Theatre. I was eight years old and when the curtain went up on an old lady churning butter, I thought to myself, "This is it? Where are Gene Kelly and Judy Garland?"

Eight years old and already a critic.

The truth, of course, was that I was expecting to see one of those lavish movie musicals onstage. I actually found *Oklahoma!* disappointing except for the Agnes DeMille dance numbers. I loved watching those dancers—right there in the same room with me—because I already realized that I could dance. By the time I was ten or eleven, even with no training or technique, I knew I could pull it off. When my parents went out, I would push back the furniture, clear an open space, turn on the record player, and leap around the apartment. Boys weren't supposed to dance, especially not in Armenian culture, but I loved music, and I especially loved the freedom I found in dancing.

I wasn't the only member of the family with artistic inclinations: my brother Jackie had a real eye for color and he became a first-rate photographer who owned his own color processing lab. My sister Laura not only loved theatre and movies but also had a real talent for interior design and fashion. I think all of these artistic impulses came from my father's side of the family; my dad adored music and loved to dance.

At this point in my life, I still had absolutely no formal dance training. I knew I wanted to be a part of the performing arts but my desire had not yet coalesced into a career as a dancer. I played the piano, the trumpet, the string bass, and in high school joined the glee club and drama club. When it came time to consider college, my sister, who now lived outside of Boston, talked about Boston University and I thought, "Sounds good—and it's in a city." I applied and upon being admitted, declared a major in theatre education. I was killing two birds with one stone: I'd be taking theatre courses, which is where my interest lay, and education classes, which held much less interest but fulfilled the key component of pleasing my parents, who wanted me to have the security of a teaching degree. The truth is that my parents had some difficulty with the English language and I was able to manipulate them a bit as to why a degree in theatre education was a good idea. Even better as far as I was concerned, a major in theatre education held no requirement for science and math. I'd still be in college if I had to pass those subjects. I'm without question a right brain kind of guy.

As a freshman at BU, I took a movement course, one which involved the ABCs of movement: walking in rhythm, stretching, how to fall, and some basic technique. There was a girl in my class who was a great dancer, and she felt I had a gift. One day she said to me, "Come to my ballet school—we need boys." Aha! I started at the school, and after three months, I was teaching the youngest pupils.

I soon enrolled at the Boston Ballet School, a venerable institution headed by E. Virginia Williams, who quickly became my mentor and teacher. I took class for one month, at which point I said to her, "I love this, but I just can't afford it." She replied, "That doesn't matter. Just come." It was extraordinarily generous of her, and to pay my way I again began teaching beginners. At the same time, I also started performing with Virginia's company, which would soon form the nucleus of the Boston Ballet Company.

Each spring vacation during college I would come home and audition for summer stock companies. There were so many of them in the late 1950s that I'd receive several job offers and then pick whichever one seemed most appealing. I'd announce to my parents: "I got a job. I'm going to dance in summer stock." Their response to this good news? "When did you learn how to dance?!" They were thrilled I had a job every summer, but then they would add, "You're not going to do this forever, are you?" I thought, "Of *course* I am!"

Summer stock—outdoor tent theatres where a different musical was performed every week—was enormously popular back in the 1950s and early '60s; an entire circuit of music tent theatres sprang up in New Jersey, Massachusetts, Ohio, and Cape Cod. I liked theatres where we could perform a new musical every week; that held much more interest for me than traveling from theatre to theatre while performing the same show every week. With all that dancing, my technique became much stronger and my dance vocabulary expanded. I hadn't started dancing seriously until I was seventeen and that made a difference, but soon realizing that I was more of a character dancer than a pure ballet dancer, I was determined to make that difference work to my advantage.

In my senior year at BU, I was required to do some student teaching. I was only twenty years old, and thought I'd be teaching drama and speech at one of the private schools where most student teachers were sent. Instead, I was sent to a public junior high school where I was told to teach literature and grammar. Talk about ill-equipped. I could teach the books, but I didn't know what I was doing when it came to teaching grammar or syntax. I was instructing both seventh-graders, who were like children, and ninth-graders, who were like gangsters. I managed to stay one step ahead of the kids—but only one. Every day at ballet class, I'd ask the kids who were there, "What's a participle? Conjunctive? What's that? . . ." If my students asked me something I had no idea about, I'd trot out my all-purpose excuse: "I don't want to confuse you. We'll get to that in due time."

It wasn't just a matter of dealing with the kids; the BU education professors would come around and check out my teaching skills, and so would the tough Irish Catholic principal of the school. No question about it: those surprise visits ultimately proved much more nerve-wracking than any Broadway opening night.

I graduated in 1959 and knew one thing: I wanted no part of this teaching gig. My mentor, Virginia Williams, wanted to send me to an Opera Ballet Company in Germany. It was prestigious and a great classical ballet company—but I wasn't interested. I wanted to dance on Broadway!

The summer after my graduation, I worked at the Pittsburgh Civic Light Opera, and after Pittsburgh, I began auditioning for better jobs. I was improving as a dancer, started to get small roles, and knew that I wanted to do more than dance in stock. Fueled by my determination to dance on Broadway, I auditioned to become a replacement in the national tour of *West Side Story*. The audition went well and I was told, "We'll be calling you." I waited by the phone—one month, two months—jumping every time the phone rang. Finally the call came: "You have the job. Go to Chicago immediately." I was scared to death, but with that confidence available only to the foolish or the very young, I threw things into a bag, flew to Chicago, and started rehearsals as a Shark. I had been watching the show in New York but this was entirely different, and I had very few rehearsals in Chicago. The dance captain never actually rehearsed me. I taught myself the show, with the help of friends already in the cast.

I was thrown onstage very quickly, and as I faced the audience for the first time, a terrifying thought flashed through my mind: "I've never even rehearsed climbing over the cyclone fence in the rumble scene. What the hell am I going to do?" I ran for the fence, clawed my way up, flipped over, and with my fists clenched, landed on my feet. I was ready, and then all around me I heard the other male dancers whisper "Get him girls" as all the Jets attacked me. It was both hilarious and terrifying—fear had carried me through.

Our tour eventually returned to New York for the show's second run on Broadway. That run provided me with firsthand experience dealing with Jerome Robbins, who scared us all to death. He was a genius, but one tough guy. He came in to polish and clean up the show, and when he was conducting rehearsals we all wanted to remain out of his sight line, desperately trying to dance behind someone else. As the great set designer Boris Aronson once said: "Every show has a victim. It's very important not to be the victim." Jerry Robbins could be extremely cruel, breaking dancers down until they were in tears. He was very insulting, saying heartless things that came out of his own insecurity. His frustration, in his art and personal life, came out in attacks on his dancers, and it was a horror show to endure. But what a giant talent he was and his gift remained monumental.

On opening night of our return engagement on Broadway, Leonard Bernstein conducted the overture. Not the whole show—just the overture. It was, in a word, thrilling. I was dancing on Broadway in a show written by Arthur Laurents, Leonard Bernstein, and Stephen Sondheim, directed and choreographed by Jerome Robbins. I may have been young, but I knew enough to realize that it didn't get any better than that.

As the run in New York neared its end, I auditioned to be the Bernardo understudy for the upcoming international tour. I knew that I would be auditioning for Hal Prince, who was producing *West Side*, so I prepared diligently and nailed the audition. I would now dance in the chorus as well as understudy the role of Bernardo. After an eight-month run in New York we were to open an international tour in Israel. I loved the adventure of traveling around the world, but the tour would prove even more momentous for one all-encompassing reason: during rehearsals in New York, I met a fellow castmate, Michael Bennett, a seventeen-year-old high school dropout marked for greatness.

Michael was playing Baby John, and we had a mutual friend in the show, Audrey Hays. Audrey was my best friend in the show and we would hang out together. She played a Jet, and unfortunately, during rehearsals she became one of Robbins's victims; he attacked her by calling her a nightclub dancer, and routinely tried to belittle her. It was awful to witness—degrading and unnecessary.

We would go out after the show, staying out until all hours, and I realized that Audrey liked younger men. She had fancied Eliot Feld, who went on to create his own great ballet company, and I could see her eying Michael, who was seventeen to her twenty-eight. When Michael, Audrey, and I were among those chosen for the tour, which we rehearsed in Israel, quicker than you can say "West Side Story," Audrey set her cap for Michael and snagged him. In fact, it was really through Audrey that Michael and I first became friendly, and even though he was only seventeen years old, I could see that he was smart as a whip. I liked him right away, but wasn't yet aware of his extraordinary ambition. In hindsight, I realize that I was also, in fact, ambitious. I was never as ferociously driven as Michael, but in my own quieter way, I was always looking for the next opportunity, the next rung up the ladder.

The tour proved to be fascinating and a true learning experience, both professionally and personally. I never had a rehearsal as Bernardo and when I was told to go on, it was like being thrown into the deep end of the pool. I was scared to death, mostly about "Dance at the Gym" and "The Rumble." Somehow I made it through, but not without unexpected mishaps. During "The Rumble," I had to flash a knife, but on my first night, the blade fell off. There I was, supposedly this tough guy Shark, but holding an empty knife. No time to worry—I needed to catch up to the rumble . . .

While on tour, I was also made the Chino understudy, and once again had no rehearsal. I was thrown onstage without any advance notice, and stumbled my way through by literally learning each scene while the show was already in progress. While Maria was singing "I Feel Pretty," I was behind the set, script in hand, memorizing lines. Thank God we were in Paris since much of the audience didn't speak English and we used subtitles above the proscenium.

My world was expanding very quickly. Once we landed in Germany, we had to travel through East Germany in order to get to Berlin, and at every stop soldiers would come on board the train demanding to see identification and passports. This was August 1961, and it was like something straight out of the movies. During one day when we gave two performances, we could hear a lot of hubbub, even over the sound of the orchestra. When we emerged from the theatre, it was to find that the Berlin wall had been built! That's how quickly the wall went up. East and West Berlin were now divided. Frightening.

While we were in Germany, our pal Audrey was injured during one performance and sustained a concussion. She was taken to the hospital and was told that she had to stay there for several days, even though the tour was moving on to our next stop. Just like in an espionage thriller, Michael and I snuck into the hospital, crept down the hallway, packed Audrey's bags, carried her out of the hospital, and got her onto the train with the rest of the cast. There was no way we were leaving her behind. These were exciting but very scary times; it was the height of the Cold War, and here we were in Berlin, two chorus kids sneaking patients out of hospitals. I look back and wonder what the hell I was thinking . . .

We then returned to Paris, where we were scheduled to run for another month. It is said that the French don't particularly like musicals, but unlike most American musicals that open in France, *West Side Story* proved to be a huge success. By this time, the close-knit atmosphere of the show—the endless intrigues and personal gossip—had come to feel confining and I wanted a break, at least temporarily. I became friendly with a male cancan dancer from the Folies Bergere who would take me around town and drag me to all the undercover clubs. He'd tell me, "Just don't speak any English and you'll fit right in." These were hole-in-the-wall, tough clubs. Having grown up on the streets of Manhattan, I certainly was not a hayseed; I was sexually self-aware, and although I knew at an early age that I was gay, I found that the sophistication and freedom of Europe (and especially Paris) made for an even deeper acceptance of who I was.

I was growing up—and fast.

CHAPTER THREE

BROADWAY GYPSY

WHEN MICHAEL AND AUDREY RETURNED TO NEW YORK, THEY RENTED an apartment and lived together. Their break-up at the end of two years occurred at the same time that I was moving out of my parents' apartment on West Seventy-first Street, so Michael and I decided to rent a walk-up apartment together in Chelsea. The rent was $75 per month, and I remember thinking: "It's tough, but I guess I can afford to pay $37.50 per month on my own."

It was when we started rooming together that I first learned about Michael's ambition to become a choreographer. In the meantime, however, we were both performing in Broadway shows, with Michael dancing in *Subways are for Sleeping*, *Here's Love*, and on television series like *Hullabaloo*, the show on which he first met Donna McKechnie. Michael saw an opportunity to assist the *Hullabaloo* choreographer David Winters, grabbed it, and soon enough, he was on to the next level, choreographing summer stock.

After *West Side Story*, I had joined the national tour of *Carnival!*, a show directed and choreographed by Gower Champion, whose work I admired greatly. I was so keen to dance in a Champion show that even though Joe Layton, the choreographer of the new Richard Rodgers musical *No Strings*, had picked me first out of all the dancers auditioning for the show, I turned down that Broadway run so that I could work with Gower. On the face of it, my choice seemed like a strange one because I was turning down Rodgers, Layton, and Broadway for a show on the road. But—I really wanted to play one of those *Carnival!* roustabouts and experience Gower's choreography. When I finally saw *No Strings*, I realized that I had made the right decision; the dance ensemble was used simply as background in the show, while in *Carnival!* I had a definite role to play.

I then had my first opportunity to see Michael's choreography in summer stock, the show in question, coincidentally, being *No Strings*. I thought his work was sensational and I knew right away that he had it—and he knew he had it. Michael got along very well with James Hammerstein, the director of *No Strings*, and it was clear to both men that Michael was already on his way to being a full-fledged choreographer. By this time, Michael and I were no longer living together; he had started dating Larry Fuller, who went on to choreograph *Evita*, and he and Larry moved in together.

I had a sensational time on *Carnival!* Ed Ames, a lovely man with a beautiful voice and a terrific work ethic, was our leading man. Jo Anne Worley, a hilarious, great gal, played one of the featured roles, and Susan Watson, who was married to one of the dancers in the show, played the lead role of Lili. When the tour reached Los Angeles, Susan was replaced by the original Broadway star, Anna Maria Alberghetti, and Susan went off to replace Anna Maria in the Broadway production. Anna Maria was more delicate than Susan—we were never chummy, but she was magical in the role. She possessed the perfect qualities for Lili: she was vulnerable, a bit fragile, had a beautiful voice, and her Italian accent only added to her charm. It all made for a shimmering performance.

I stayed with the show for ten months, left the tour in Philadelphia, and headed back to New York. I auditioned for the new musical *Nowhere to Go But Up* and was happy for the chance to work with some creative heavyweights: director Sidney Lumet, choreographer Ron Field, and producer Kermit Bloomgarden of *Music Man* and *Death of a Salesman* fame. The libretto was written by James Lipton, who years later achieved fame as host of *Inside the Actors Studio*. Michael Bennett was also involved, billed as "Assistant to the Choreographer."

I was one of twenty-four dancers; there was no singing chorus. The show revolved around the exploits of Izzy and Moe, two federal agents during Prohibition who were played by Tom Bosley and Martin Balsam, both of them super guys. The cast also included Bert Convy, Dorothy Loudon, and Louise Lasser, who was fired out-of-town and replaced by Mary Ann Mobley. In other words, a quirky original ingenue was replaced by a former Miss America. Then again, no one has ever said show business is logical. Dorothy was tricky, nervous—but already possessed that larger-than-life personality that was to serve her so well years later as Miss Hannigan in

Annie. You had to be very careful around her because you never knew what would set her off. She was strikingly unpredictable.

We had a great time in rehearsal, headed to Philadelphia for our tryout, opened—and the show flopped. Big time. In came Mel Brooks to fix the show, but Mel turned the show into a cartoon, a musical stuffed with his style and lots of schtick. When Mel had finished his rewrites, the cast was summoned to hear him read the new script and we were, in a word, dumbfounded. What the hell was this? Act Two was suddenly a mere twenty-five minutes long. This was unheard of.

I was still rather green, never having done a show from scratch before. *West Side Story* and *Carnival!* were finished products by the time I joined them, and when you are in the midst of rehearsing a brand-new musical you lose perspective quickly; you're concerned with your own performance and doing a good job, hoping the powers that be will like you. But, untested as I was, I still understood that this new script definitely did not represent a step in the right direction.

The cast's collective state of nerves wasn't helped by choreographer Ron Field. He was a talented man who went on to big successes with *Cabaret* and *Applause*, but he had a temper, and like Jerome Robbins, when he grew frustrated with his own work he would take it out on the dancers. If he couldn't tell whether or not a number was working, his solution was to yell at the dancer, "You're doing it wrong!" I saw him destroy a couple of dancers that way, his anger at himself finding voice in hurtful comments hurled at the dancers.

We limped into New York where we kept rehearsing before opening at the Winter Garden Theatre on Saturday, November 10, 1962. The handwriting was on the wall: no one opens on a Saturday unless you want the review buried, and we did in fact close exactly one week later.

I was fortunate in that I landed another job very quickly, having heard that Jack Cole was auditioning dancers for *Zenda*, a musicalized version of *The Prisoner of Zenda*. Auditions held in New York were supervised by George Martin because Jack was on the West Coast, where *Zenda* would premiere before hopefully coming into New York.

The chance to dance in a Jack Cole show was irresistible. Like so many dancers, I viewed him as a god, someone who broke tradition and introduced innovations through his use of jazz-based choreography and the injection of overt sexuality into the dance numbers. When George hired me—along with Alan Johnson, Michel Stuart, and Eddie Gasper—I was thrilled and very quickly found myself on a plane to LA to start rehearsals.

This was a big show: there would be eighteen dancers, twenty-one singers, and the stars included Alfred Drake, Chita Rivera, Anne Rogers, and Carmen Matthews. The music was by the great Vernon Duke ("Dancing in the Dark"), the lyrics by Martin Charnin, and George Schaeffer, who went on to find such great success in television, was slotted to direct.

I walked into the rehearsal room and was instantly terrified by Jack Cole. We all were. His mouth was vicious and he would say the rudest things. His temperament was so volatile that Marc Wilder, who was the lead dancer as well as Chita's partner in her numbers, would get into screaming matches with Jack in the hall, and they would have to be physically separated. A great craftsman but a tyrant.

Progress was slow—we knew the show wouldn't be easy to put together, but after six weeks of rehearsal, we hadn't even finished a complete run-through. There was a big ballet in Act Two that was murder to dance and really tough on Chita; she was to be front and center throughout the number and it hadn't even been completed. Chita's back was against the wall, and all the kids in the show soon grew exhausted and fed up with Jack's methods.

We finally opened, at which point I realized that in dance terms the show basically consisted of the same two numbers Jack Cole choreographed for every one of his shows and movies: a waltz with lifts and jetes, and the sensual, jazzy "Heat Wave" type number most famously performed by Marilyn Monroe in *There's No Business Like Show Business*.

Zenda was a very opulent show; it was so big that we found ourselves literally climbing over the scenery in order to make our entrances, and we thought that with so much money on the line, we'd surely end up at the Mark Hellinger Theatre in New York after playing Los Angeles, San Francisco, and Pasadena. But, as we were nearing the end of our run in LA, we found out that the show wasn't going to come in to New York—it was too expensive. It was actually a more than decent show, but it just never fully jelled.

The mixed reviews in Los Angeles had sealed our doom. Even so, I still had a great time. Alfred Drake may have been pompous and never talked to anyone in the chorus, but Chita was Chita—in other words, delicious—and Anne Rogers, who starred in the first national tour of *My Fair Lady* and actually originated the Julie Andrews role in *The Boy Friend*, was a lot of fun. I loved performing, and my days and nights had a rhythm: I was expected onstage eight times per week to do what I loved—dance—and I was now getting paid well for it. I was a working Broadway dancer, and even though the fact that I was short held me back in some ways, in other situations it helped me land jobs. I was twenty-four years old and becoming known to the big choreographers. I sure didn't give teaching school another thought.

I loved the sense of camaraderie I shared with my fellow gypsies. It also felt great to work in an atmosphere where being gay was not a big issue. That said, the truth is that I had never felt any deep conflict about being gay. I was gay and content: end of story. I grew up in Manhattan, and unlike the difficulties faced by many who grew up in small towns back then, men who had to face the daily taunts of "queer" and "fairy," I had no sense of being alone. (Of course, given the easily observed activities of the two gay men who had an apartment directly across the street from me, I definitely knew I wasn't alone . . .)

I'm so grateful I was born in a big city like New York because I never felt ostracized. My parents never questioned me about it, but they were smart and understood; back in the 1950s and '60s, issues of sexuality simply weren't discussed, and my folks and I were fine with that. When I left home to go to college in Boston, I was fortunate to be living in another big city, attending a major university that had a progressive population. I found myself among many gay men and women in the college theatre department, and it all just seemed so natural to me. I had gay professors, and even in the Pat Boone-type conservative cultural climate that dominated the times, I could chat openly with these older gay men. I was then, and always have been, very open about my sexual orientation. It has never hindered me nor have I ever had to lie about it. I realize, of course, how fortunate I was to feel this comfortable in my own skin compared to others in the LGBT community. I used to go to the Stonewall bar and was actually there two nights before the famous riots in June of 1969. I remember hoping that the uprising was the start of a real movement and revolution, because I think coming out and obtaining equal rights is absolutely key. The more we come out, the stronger we are. If I ever feel discouraged about the political situation, I remind myself that I never thought marriage equality would actually happen. For all the distance we still have to travel, we have made enormous strides in the last fifty years.

Manhattan of course was more liberal than most anywhere else in the country, and since that was home, I headed back after *Zenda* closed on the

West Coast. En route, however, I made a nine-week detour to Las Vegas, where I danced in a Minsky's Burlesque show. There would be three weeks of rehearsals and a six-week run, for an old-fashioned "tits and feathers" show at the New Frontier Hotel. I'm glad I had that taste of a long-vanished, old-school Vegas, but what I remember most of all is that I have never worked so hard in my entire life.

Four of us, dressed in tuxedos, were to dance nonstop all over the stage while presenting the nude girls. We had to sing, dance, memorize patter, and do three shows per night, seven nights per week. I broke my nose in one show. By the end of the run, I was skeletal and exhausted. I felt no one in Vegas had ever been so lonely or blue. The money was very good but I had no life; I'd get home from the last show at 3:30 a.m., tape cardboard over the windows, crawl into bed, sleep late, and go back to work. I have no idea how I survived that schedule but I was very young and never turned down any work that came my way.

Those tits and feathers shows are long gone, as is the glamorous Sinatra-style Rat Pack lifestyle in Vegas. At the time, however, the action centered around tourists who were all dressed up for a night on the town, beautiful showgirls, wiseguys, and high rollers expecting action both at the table and away from it. Penny Singleton, who was the head of AGVA at the time, emphatically emphasized that the girls were only showgirls and that there could never be any extracurricular activities. The reality, of course, proved to be far different. The only girls hired were single and available, and it was expected that they would go into the casino and mingle with the high rollers. Nowadays Vegas is family-friendly, but back then it was strictly an adult playground.

At the end of nine weeks, I felt exhausted and homesick and headed back to New York. Through the grapevine I learned that the new musical *Jennie*, starring Mary Martin, needed a swing who could learn quickly. If given the job I would go into the show in exactly three days— and learn the numbers after! But first it was necessary to meet Mary and her husband and producer, Richard Halliday, for their approval. Mary and Richard always wanted a harmonious atmosphere backstage and made sure that the ensemble consisted of team players; I was surprised that they were concerned with knowing me—after all, I had just come off *Zenda*, where Alfred Drake never even spoke to members of the chorus. But Mary operated differently, and I quickly found myself in her dressing room, being interviewed by the star of *South Pacific, Peter Pan*, and *The Sound of Music*! Whatever I said worked, because I passed muster and quickly signed a contract.

I watched the show for two nights before I went onstage. I was completely unprepared; no one goes on with a mere two days of rehearsal, but I also knew that this job was not going to last a long time; the show had opened to bad reviews, and even with Mary in the lead, business was not great. Why sign on? Because they needed a dance cover and I could do the job. I knew I could learn a lot by watching the greats onstage, and Mary was one of the all-time musical greats. Her dedication was total, even on this flop of a show.

I may have only been with the show for a brief period of time, but that time was not without its major challenges. Loosely based on the life of the actress Laurette Taylor (the original star of *The Glass Menagerie*), *Jennie* opened with a scene set at a waterfall, with Mary outstretched on a tree limb while trying to save a baby. When the scene was over, the plan called for two of us to unlock and push that huge piece of scenery upstage. On my very first night, the end of the scene came but I couldn't disengage the waterfall; the stage manager had issued me very hurried instructions and the damn set wouldn't budge. After a seeming eternity, I finally unlocked the scenery and pushed it upstage. Following such a harrowing start, I figured that the next night I would get ahead of the action and start unlocking the set early. This time, the setpiece came apart so quickly that I was way ahead of Mary, and when I started to push the scenery upstage, Mary was still suspended over the waterfall, frantically calling out to me: "Wait, wait! Hold it, boys! I'm still here!"

I had neither a singing nor a put-in rehearsal, and quickly found myself onstage with no idea of what I was supposed to do. One of the chorus girls would whisper to me, "Stand over here—just follow me wherever I go," while I numbly shuffled along behind her as I moved my lips in a desperate approximation of what I thought the lyrics might be. Very quickly another actor dropped out of the show, and all of a sudden I was onstage in yet another role I didn't know. The dance captain would try to give me hurried instructions on the choreography, but it was hopeless—no one is capable of learning a show like that. In retrospect, I can't believe they put me on, but they were desperate.

The show opened on Broadway in October of 1963 to lethargic notices, and the already slim prospects were further undermined when President

Kennedy was assassinated one month later. No one was in the mood to go to a lighthearted musical, especially a mediocre one. When the closing notice went up, all I could think was: "Thank goodness." Mary was great, and I'd be reunited eight years later with my wonderful fellow cast member Ethel Shutta on *Follies*, but at the time my overwhelming emotion about the closing was one of relief.

Right after *Jennie* closed, Ron Field called me to come and audition for *Café Crown*, a musicalization of the play by H. S. Kraft. Kraft would be writing the book of the musical, Marty Brill the lyrics, and Albert Hague the music. The cast was first-rate: Theodore Bikel, Sam Levene, Tommy Rall, and a then-unknown Alan Alda. The director was Jerome Eskow, who had just had a big success off-Broadway. Right off the bat the die was cast by that decision: Jerome Eskow may have succeeded off-Broadway, but he was the wrong man for the job of directing a big Broadway musical. In fact, everything about *Café Crown* was wrong.

This glum play, set in a restaurant on Second Avenue in New York City, did not lend itself to musicalization. The people who hung out at the restaurant were not likely to burst into song and dance, so the numbers felt forced. The turgid atmosphere found onstage permeated backstage as well, because the stars, with the singular exception of Alan Alda, were cold and distant towards the chorus. To a certain degree I could understand why; they were totally consumed with learning their songs and dances while simultaneously dealing with the stress of constant changes to the script. The atmosphere wasn't helped by Ron Field's nasty putdowns and constant yelling at the dancers. But, as happened on virtually every show in which I danced, I still had a great learning experience.

Act Two contained a *King Lear* ballet—yes, you read that right—and I was completely at sea. Bonnie Walker, who has gone on to function as the ultimate re-creator of Jerome Robbins's choreography for revivals of *Gypsy*, would keep steering me around the stage, somehow making sure I landed in the right place. It was all a mess, and after nearly a month of previews, we opened at the Martin Beck Theatre on Friday April 17, 1964, and closed the next day. I was beginning to get a complex: I'd been in four shows in the span of one year—*Nowhere to Go But Up, Zenda, Jennie,* and *Café Crown*—and they were four big flops.

But my luck was about to change. Enter *Funny Girl*—and Barbra Streisand.

CHAPTER FOUR

FUNNY GIRL, HELLO, DOLLY!, AND I DO! I DO!

FUNNY GIRL HAD OPENED ON MARCH 26, 1964, TO REVIEWS THAT IM-mediately established Barbra Streisand as the new queen of Broadway. There were twenty-three curtain calls on opening night, and every superlative you could think of was thrown her way. Barbra was the toast of New York, and the show grew into a big hit.

Immediately after the show opened, they let a chorus boy go, so they needed a swing (an understudy for every chorus member) who would also appear in several of the crowd scenes. The dance captain Larry Fuller, who was Michael Bennett's boyfriend as well as a friend of mine, asked me to join the show. I didn't even have to audition, which was a big plus in my book, but even better, I would now be in a hit show and wouldn't have to spend every day in the constant rehearsals required during tryouts.

I started watching the show and immediately realized two things: it wasn't a particularly good show, but at the same time it functioned very nicely as a vehicle for Barbra, who was giving a fascinating, quirky performance. I had two weeks rehearsal during which to learn all of the numbers, and those two weeks seemed like a lifetime compared to the pressure of two days of rehearsal on *Jennie*. I was to appear as a chorus boy in the pregnant bride number, "His Love Makes Me Beautiful"; as a porter in the railway station for "Don't Rain On My Parade"; and was to deliver one immortal line in Fanny Brice's dressing room: "You were great, Fanny." (The musical numbers had been staged by the talented Carol Haney, who committed suicide two months after the show opened. Her death was a tremendous blow to the company. She was so loved by everyone, but she battled many demons, including alcoholism, depression, and diabetes.)

Everything ran smoothly on the night of my first performance, and Barbra didn't see me at all except when I uttered my one line. As the weeks went on, I had to learn every dancer's "track"—meaning their complete show—number by number. The toughest part of the show for me was the big Act Two production number, "Rat-a-Tat-Tat." This Ziegfeld Follies number was an all-out military tap—and I don't tap. The choreography involved singing, tapping, spinning guns, and a very steep set of stairs. The real problem lay in the fact that rehearsal all took place without any scenery so I had to pretend I was climbing and dancing on stairs. I knew that would present a very big problem if I ever had to go on in that particular number. But, reassured by my good friend Bud Fleming that I should learn his track last because he was never out, I began learning the other chorus members' tracks.

And who was the very first person I had to replace in "Rat-a-Tat-Tat"? Bud, of course, who caught the flu. I not only had to replace him but also wear his costumes, and that's where I ran into big problems. Bud was a skinny little guy and while I was in good shape from dancing, there was no way I could wear his clothes comfortably. When the overture began I felt like I was being shot out of a cannon, but I got off to a smooth start and soon found myself in the midst of the big Act One "Henry Street" number, where the neighborhood celebrates Fanny's success in the Ziegfeld Follies. One by one, each of the boys took Barbra in their arms for a simple waltz. My turn came, I gathered Barbra in my arms, and she did a double take: "Oy—who are you?" "I'm the new boy" came my quick reply. She was clearly amused, and I was immediately smitten.

It came time for the military tap and, boy oh boy, did that lack of rehearsal with the scenery come back to haunt me. To get into place at the top of the stairs, I had to climb up the back of the stairs, but in Bud's tight costume that proved downright impossible. I was trying to haul myself up the back of the stairs while carrying my gun, not split Bud's extra-slim pants, and figure out how to tap my way through the whole number. I made it through, but that performance is a complete blank in my mind. Total self-protection. I eventually went on a great deal in that number and solved the problem of not being able to tap by unscrewing the taps so that I wouldn't make any sound.

I now had a steady paycheck in a big Broadway hit. I did a good job in the show, but being a swing is very hard work; swings are the unsung heroes and heroines of musicals. Those dancers have to be able to perform up to fifteen different people's shows, which is a monumental task. Fortunately, I liked the variety—every night I seemed to be on for somebody new, and in the process, all of us in the chorus became great friends; guys in the show would ask me to perform their second-act tracks so that they could leave early, and I was happy to oblige.

It was fascinating to be on the stage with Barbra, or even just to watch her from the wings. She was not warm and cuddly, but the company adored her and was protective of her. Those who had been with the show during the tumultuous tryouts in Boston, Washington, and Philadelphia had seen how she handled all of the new material thrown at her—how she actually thrived on the constant changes. She treated the chorus with great respect and invited everyone to the concert she gave at the Forest Hills tennis stadium during the run of *Funny Girl.* I can only shake my head in admiration at her drive during those days; she was giving eight performances per week on Broadway, making albums, filming television specials, and still giving concerts. Her commitment to the show and her fierce work ethic were very impressive.

I think that in the nearly two years she played the role on Broadway she missed exactly two performances. Barbra's understudy was Lainie Kazan who, month after month, was chomping at the bit to go on, but felt she'd never get the chance. Finally, the big day arrived—word circulated that Barbra was feeling ill and Lainie would have her big opportunity. Lainie made sure the tabloids knew, and had members of the press in the theatre, only to have Barbra come in and perform. Barbra did miss the following night and Lainie got to go on, but the press had moved on and the hoopla was diminished.

Knowing that with Barbra he had a chance for real chart success, composer Jule Styne happily gave her the works: the showstopping "Don't Rain On My Parade," the torchy "The Music That Makes Me Dance," and, of course, the ballad that quickly became her signature song, "People." I'd watch her on a nightly basis, and it was evident to me that even a Broadway stage couldn't contain her. We all knew she'd be headed to movie stardom in Hollywood, "kooky" looks and all. (It was no accident that Barbra herself had said: "To me being a star means being a movie star.")

Four years later, in the fall of 1968, I saw the *Funny Girl* movie when Michael and I were out of town with *Promises, Promises*; our show hadn't yet solidified, but we had an afternoon off, and went to see the movie, which was marketed as a "roadshow" attraction—complete with reserved seats and high prices (I think the tickets might have been a then staggering $4 per ticket . . .) There she was on screen—looking great, lit to a fare thee well by Harry Stradling, wearing the Irene Sharaff costumes beautifully, and singing with that amazing voice of hers. She made the transition to film incredibly well, which is something I didn't necessarily expect. Through sheer force of talent and will, she had made herself into not only the biggest new star in Hollywood, but also into the symbol of a new kind of beauty; unusual profile and all, she was starring not only on movie screens but also on the covers of fashion magazines.

I really liked those early films of hers like *The Owl and the Pussycat* and *What's Up, Doc?*; there was a looseness about her that seemed to fade as she solidified her "greatest star" status, but she was still capable of surprise, and I was caught off guard by how beautifully she directed *Yentl*.

During the run of *Funny Girl* she kept us on our toes; we never knew if she would sing "Who Are You Now?" in its entirety, just a part of it, or cut the song entirely. She was young, gaining experience, and carried the entire show on her shoulders.

Barbra had become not just a star on Broadway, but also the newest and hottest recording artist in the country, and the crowds by the Winter Garden stage door—on Seventh Avenue between Fiftieth and Fifty-first— were so huge that you couldn't get out of the theatre after the show. Every celebrity in the world came to see the show: Elizabeth Taylor, Richard Burton, even Greta Garbo. Sophia Loren came one day and supposedly said to Barbra: "I'd give anything if I could sing like you." Barbra's quick retort: "If I looked like you I wouldn't open my mouth." Witty both on- and off-stage.

To keep up her interest in the long run, she started changing costumes; her dresser would make her new gowns and one night she showed up in a completely different outfit during the "Sadie, Sadie, Married Lady" number. We were all startled, thinking, "What the hell is she wearing?" She kept switching costumes until producer Ray Stark came back to check on the show and told Barbra, "Back to the Irene Sharaff clothes."

As I said, Barbra was courteous to the company, but she came into great conflict with Sydney Chaplin, whom the company also liked. There were rumors that they had been personally involved during the out-of-town tryouts, but whatever had actually happened, it was clear that by now something had gone very wrong. Every night when they came offstage after the "You Are Woman, I Am Man" duet, he would start screaming at her in the most incredibly obscene language. They would exit stage right, where Barbra had a quick change going into "Don't Rain On My Parade," and Sydney would go into his nasty tirade for so long that the rest of us simply began to tune it out—it was like aural wallpaper. Barbra never said a word.

I was wowed by her singing, particularly on "The Music That Makes Me Dance." The scene began with Barbra wearing a trench coat. The coat had been rigged with special snaps in the inside pockets that she could undo because the spotlight was only on her face. As the drop came in behind her, the trench coat would fall to the floor while the light expanded to reveal Barbra in a beaded gown singing that great torch song. The audience was dazzled by the quick change happening right in front of their eyes; Michael Bennett and I used the same device twenty years later in *Dreamgirls* while Jennifer Holliday was singing "I Am Changing."

All in all, *Funny Girl* was a terrific experience. I had a steady paycheck, learned a lot, and got to watch Barbra in perpetual close up. I'm not sure she ever really learned my name, but for one full year, there I was, telling her: "You were great, Fanny!"

I left *Funny Girl* in 1965, because I was set on becoming a part of *Hello, Dolly!* The two shows had opened at nearly the same time, and I loved *Dolly.* It was a joyous show, and so beautifully directed and staged by Gower Champion that I was determined to be a part of that experience. It was a much better show than *Funny Girl*—it was like having a dream in an ice cream parlor—because the design, score, and performances all meshed into a seamless show that satisfied on multiple levels. Gower was one of my idols, and when I heard they were casting the international tour of *Dolly,* I figured my previous work for him on *Carnival!* would help land me the job. On one level, it made no sense to leave Broadway for a tour, but that's how much I loved *Dolly,* and furthermore the tour would star Mary Martin, who had signed on for a twenty-week cross-country tour, to be followed by runs in Tokyo and Moscow. No Broadway show had ever played Moscow, so it sounded like a great adventure to me.

I knew I was not really Gower's type of dancer, because I was short and dark, not tall and blonde, but when he offered me the job I decided that the opportunity was worth leaving Broadway—that is, if the *Dolly* team would also make me dance captain for the tour. I was given the job and gave notice at *Funny Girl*, fortunate to leap right from one hit show to another.

The tour was staged by Gower's associates, with Gower himself occasionally appearing to fine-tune the production. This was the first national tour of *Dolly*, but we were not playing the biggest cities; Carol Channing's contract called for her to play Los Angeles and San Francisco, so we played Portland, Seattle, and New Orleans.

Mary didn't quite remember me—how could she, given how quickly *Jennie* had closed. But, when the stage managers on the tour kept leaving, I got into the habit of coming in early to check in with Mary, asking if she was okay or if she needed anything. She loved that time together and we quickly became a team. Mary was all about the show and her attention to detail was extraordinary: "Bob, I noticed that Ernestina's hem was a little ragged—could you make sure that is taken care of?" Mary would give me notes about the book scenes and although it's a tricky business for anyone other than the director to give notes, I'd pass on the comments in a subtle way.

Her trust in me having grown, Mary now turned to me when a performance crisis erupted. Her dresser's husband was in the show and had developed a real drinking problem. Mary felt his behavior was upsetting the show, and she was also genuinely concerned about his well-being. Mary pulled me aside, as did the dresser, and said: "Please—you have to talk to him." I didn't know what to say, which is exactly what I said to him: "Mary and your wife have told me that they are very concerned about your drinking. The truth is that I don't know what to say to you, but I wanted to pass along their concern." He was very apologetic and actually stopped drinking—or at least stopped drinking before the show.

It was a big lesson learned because I found out that I knew how to handle people smoothly: treat them with respect and like family, not as a superior. The Ron Field/Jerome Robbins approach of belittling dancers would never work for me. I'm too low-key by nature, and I don't think it's the best way to deal with people. Both Jerry and Ron were truly gifted, but a quiet talk definitely proved to be more my style.

When the company landed in Tokyo there was press everywhere. We were all showered with presents, and even the chorus boys and girls were asked for autographs. We were the first Broadway musical to play in Tokyo, and we had to get used to the fact that the show was being translated as we performed it, which meant that we heard the normal laughs a full thirty seconds after the joke. The Japanese proved to be quiet and subdued audiences, saving their ovation for the very end of the show. They were respectful but not effusive, a marked change after the standing ovations we had grown used to while touring America. Those standing ovations were rare back in the 1960s, a far cry from the pro forma standing ovations which conclude every performance seen on Broadway today, hit and flop alike.

We had been receiving injections for tetanus and other assorted possible illnesses because of our international travel, the preventative care aimed most specifically at our upcoming trip to Moscow. The State Department also gave us lectures on how to behave in Moscow, warning us that we would be under scrutiny at all times. We would be held under a microscope and could expect to be bugged and followed, so all of our mail would be handled via the State Department. It was like something out of a Graham Greene novel, and as a twenty-five year old, I had one reaction: what an adventure!

An earthquake occurred while we were staying at the Frank Lloyd Wright-designed Imperial Hotel in Tokyo, but the bigger news was that our trip to Moscow was abruptly canceled due to "cultural harassment"; it was the height of the Cold War and relations between the US and the Soviet Union were subject to these unexpected reversals. Where to go? The answer proved to be very unexpected: Vietnam.

The request for a company trip to Vietnam had come directly from President Johnson himself. We were asked to travel to South Korea, Okinawa, and Vietnam; with the war in Vietnam raging, we would no longer be dealing with the State Department, but instead with the Defense Department. A number of the company did not want to go to Vietnam; conditions would be tough, and even though we were assured we'd be protected, many cast members simply didn't want to take the risk. A company meeting was held to discuss the issue, and Mary came to the meeting, hoping to persuade us to go. Mary promised all of us: "I'll be in the foxhole right next to you," a statement which instantly landed her the nickname "Foxhole Mary." Mary didn't know about the name, nor did she know the song we made up about it, to the tune of South Pacific's "Bloody Mary is the girl we love": "Foxhole Mary is the girl we love . . ."

There certainly wouldn't be any orchestra traveling with us to Vietnam, so we prerecorded all the tracks before we closed in Tokyo, and brought along only our key musicians: piano, drums, trumpet, conductor. We were loaded onto military transport planes and flew directly from Tokyo to Saigon. We knew we were really in for it when we started our descent into Vietnam and were told we'd be heading in on a penetration landing—a steep descent undertaken in order to avoid artillery. Nothing was going to be business as usual about this leg of the tour.

We landed, the airplane doors were opened, and whew! It was like standing in front of a furnace—100 degrees, with 90 percent humidity. We were definitely in the jungle, and what felt like a million miles away from Broadway.

Our hotel was in downtown Saigon, and was surrounded by barbed wire and fox holes, patrolled by soldiers brandishing machine guns. There was no air conditioning, the water in the sinks and showers was brown—and where was Foxhole Mary? In her air-conditioned, renovated, deluxe hotel suite.

Since President Johnson had requested this tour, the amount of press we received was extraordinary—we were international news. Our producer, David Merrick, even flew over at the same time NBC started to film a documentary about our visit, but the truth is that the soldiers who had to protect us really hated us. We all had long hair, sideburns, and access to the mess hall whenever we wanted. Of course, the top brass hated us even more—they were definitely not happy about an ensemble of gay chorus boys with special privileges.

We started rehearsals, but given how limited the playing area was—we were performing on flatbed trucks pushed together in airplane hangars—the only way we could exit was by jumping off the trucks. The solution was that GIs had to be stationed in front of the trucks to catch us when we danced offstage. What a great image!

We kept rehearsing but soon realized that the prerecorded orchestra tracks could never be used; electricity was far from a sure thing in Vietnam and the music often started out strong, before slowing down so much that it sounded like it was being piped in from underwater. We cut all the prerecorded tracks, and just had the key musicians playing live, in a quartet led by the old upright piano that was impossible to keep tuned in all the humidity.

When the time came for our first show, we flew out of Saigon to an air base for a 9 a.m. performance. We looked out at the audience and realized it was filled with 2,000 injured soldiers. That brought the war home to us in a hurry, and we were moved and grateful to be there. We somehow got through the show but we didn't know if it was working. The boys applauded but were fairly unenthusiastic; their favorite part was certainly when a chorus girl in tights paraded across the truck holding a card saying "intermission."

Mary was dying from the heat, but she possessed a true old-school work ethic where nothing stopped her from going onstage. (In her autobiography, she relayed a very funny story about being on this tour in the Pacific when a huge storm hit. She happened to have on the radio at the time, and the song playing was Ethel Merman belting out "Blow, Gabriel, Blow"; said Mary—"Ethel was louder than the typhoon!")

Traveling between air bases couldn't have been more different from the way we toured in the US. Instead of airfare and first-class hotels, we traveled by beat-up buses, and were always followed by a spare bus since the equipment constantly collapsed. When the first broken-down bus couldn't travel any further, we'd pull over to the side of the road and run to the cover bus, with a helicopter providing protection from potential artillery attacks.

We had one performance that wasn't on the back of flatbed trucks because we performed in a small movie theatre in downtown Saigon for the benefit of the top brass. Talk about dangerous. An entire square mile around the theatre was completely cleared out because General William Westmoreland was inside and that meant top security. There we were in a war zone playing in a theatre with literally no wing space: we had to line up in the alley outside the theatre in order to dance our way onstage for the "Put On Your Sunday Clothes" number. As a result, I had to restage each number to fit the space—or, more accurately, the lack thereof.

Once a performance was over our time was our own, but we were told not to go out of our hotel without military escort. We snuck out anyway because when you're twenty-five you think you're invincible, even in the middle of a war. Drinks were ten cents—that's right, ten cents—and we wanted to see the sights, but by the time we left Vietnam, I was nothing so much as relieved. It was trying, uncomfortable, and dangerous. We were all kids and oh-so naïve. That's what got us through.

We flew out of Vietnam to South Korea, which was cooler but still dangerous. We were now in Seoul, not Saigon, but the powers that be still did not want us to walk around town. True to form, we ignored the warnings and at night would sneak around between the two hotels where everyone was staying.

We had an actual orchestra in Seoul, not just an out-of-tune upright piano, and the Army Orchestra did their best with the Jerry Herman score, but I think it's safe to say Jerry didn't envision Dolly Levi gliding down the stairs of the Harmonia Gardens restaurant in Korea and Vietnam when he first wrote the show.

Relieved once again to be leaving, we flew from South Korea to Okinawa. When we stepped off the plane, it was like arriving in heaven. We were right on the China Sea and swam, waterskied, and stopped looking over our shoulders for danger whenever we walked around town. It had been quite an overseas tour, exciting but also frightening, and our company was now scattering; Mary and the principals were leaving to play the show in London, at the Drury Lane Theatre. The rest of us were flying back home to play a few cities before heading to Las Vegas with our new Dolly: Betty Grable.

After Vietnam and Seoul, it was great to be back in the United States, and it finally felt like we were performing a real show again. I would continue to perform and serve as dance captain, as well as help put the new principals into the show. I was excited to be performing with Betty, who had starred in many of those movie musicals I had loved as a young boy.

Betty was very welcoming to everyone in Las Vegas, and although she had recently divorced bandleader Harry James, she was still keeping Vegas as her home base. She threw a nice party at her house and treated everyone in the company to a show on the Strip. I was wowed by her status as one of the golden age Hollywood immortals. Mary was theatre royalty—Betty was Hollywood royalty.

Far from being egocentric, Betty was constantly putting herself down: "I'm only a star because lonely GIs in the war liked my pinup pictures." In truth, Betty was a solid dancer, always sang on key, and had a genuine star presence. She seemed to have a good time with the show, especially once they ditched the red wig and gave her a great blonde wig which was how everyone wanted to see her—as the luscious blonde from all those lavish Twentieth Century Fox musicals. Betty enjoyed the warm reception she received from audiences, and Dolly also brought her personal happiness; Bob Remick who was in the chorus of the show, fell hard for Betty, and they became a couple. He was in his mid-twenties and Betty was fifty-two, but they stayed together until the day she died.

Dolly had brought me back to Vegas, and I found myself working just as hard as I had on the "tits and feathers" show from several years earlier. We played at the Riviera Hotel, performing a stripped-down version of *Dolly* that clocked in at exactly ninety minutes; it was all designed to get the gamblers back to the tables as quickly as possible. All of the ballads were cut, and so was the intermission. Two shows a night, seven nights per week, we just raced from production number to production number, sweating so heavily that everyone in the cast had two complete sets of costumes. When I wasn't performing, I was rehearsing; as dance captain, I ended up putting no fewer than twenty-two replacements into the show. I look back on it now and wonder: "How the hell did I have the energy for all that?" The answer? I was twenty-nine years old.

The regular musicians played six nights a week and a swing band played the seventh night. Betty hated that situation because it meant the tempos changed constantly; she grew increasingly upset until one night I finally told the conductor: "Just watch my arms in the 'Hello, Dolly!' number and that will set the tempo." That solution helped, but Betty often still missed the second show on a swing band night.

Today, Actors Equity would never allow a schedule of two shows per night, seven nights a week, but at the time that was actually permitted. Everything about the Vegas production was tougher, shorter, and faster, and as a result a lot of the kids would call in sick; one night so many people were out that I had to dance a trio number all by myself. I was constantly rehearsing replacements, which meant that my day would start at noon with rehearsals, followed by two shows in the evening. I wouldn't get home until at least 2 a.m., at which point I'd grab something to eat and get a few hours rest. The alarm would go off all too quickly and I'd stagger out of bed, get some food, and head to the theatre for another endless day of rehearsals.

When we first met, Betty wasn't fully up to speed with the show, but she was better than I expected her to be. Her performance continued to improve and while the crowds liked seeing Betty in person and always gave her a nice ovation, it wasn't the same standing ovation as had been the norm with Mary. Betty continued to grow in the part and she eventually came up with a smart bit in the title song; she'd sing "Wow-wow-wow fellas—look at the old girl now fellas" and lift her red dress enough to show her still gorgeous legs and strike her famous head-over-the shoulder pinup pose. The crowd loved that bit of self-reference and would spontaneously applaud in the middle of the number. Betty was actually even more musical than I imagined she would be; she possessed great pitch, a more than serviceable voice, was very sensitive to the orchestra, and could still move very well. The difference between her approach and Mary's was that Mary was always a lady—warm and cuddly—while Betty brought a certain hard-edged pragmatism to the role. She wasn't soft and fuzzy in her approach, and given that difference in personality, she wasn't as touching in the speeches Dolly makes to her dead husband Ephraim. Betty was surprisingly effective, however, and when all was said and done, I admired her different take on Dolly.

I had now been with *Dolly* for well over a year, and since like many dancers I thrived on change, I started to look around for a new job. When I heard that Gower Champion was going to direct a new David Merrick-produced musical, *I Do! I Do!*, with Mary Martin and Robert Preston, I wrote to both Mary and the production stage manager Lucia Victor to express my interest in becoming the assistant stage manager.

I had danced in a lot of shows by now, and realized that I didn't want to ever be in the running for the title of "World's Oldest Chorus Boy." I was looking to change and better myself, and even though I hadn't stage-managed before, I had no problem presenting myself as the right person to stage-manage a two-person musical starring Mary Martin and Robert Preston. Gower had been hearing about me via the *Dolly* grapevine, as well as from Mary, so I figured I had a decent shot at the job. Whatever I said finally worked because I was hired. I would be handling things stage right, and more to the point, would be charged with taking care of anything and everything Mary wanted.

For the first time in my career, I would have to learn how to call all the scenic, light, and sound cues the way any stage manager does. As it turned out, I only had to call the show once or twice, which is just as well; in those pre-computer days, you had to personally count the length of all the light cues, a job now completely taken over by computers.

We began rehearsals, and with only two people in the cast, it quickly became the quietest rehearsal studio in Broadway history: no singers, no dancers—just two Broadway legends in Mary and Bob Preston. Usually rehearsal rooms are a hum of activity with principals, chorus, writers, designers, and managers constantly coming in and out. Here the only people ever in the room were Bob, Mary, Gower, the composer/lyricist team of Harvey Schmidt and Tom Jones, and the three stage managers. That's it.

Gower always worked in a very quiet way, and I was so nervous about upsetting his routine that I would find myself literally walking into walls. He asked me to come in early each day to work with him on numbers, a request that definitely excited me. I'd come in early, but he'd just sit in a chair looking at the script—he wouldn't talk and nothing would happen. This silent routine would go on for a solid hour, day after day, and I'd find myself thinking, "Does he not like me?"

Mary and Bob, who were both in their fifties, liked to start rehearsal later in the day, beginning at 1 p.m. We developed a routine where I would pick up Mary at her apartment in the River House on East Fifty-second Street mid-morning. We'd get into her Rolls-Royce and would be driven around the city, primarily through Central Park, and I would rehearse the dialogue with her. We'd do this for several hours and then head over for the 1 p.m. start of rehearsals.

It's a system that worked well for the most part, until the morning Mary wanted to rehearse the "Flaming Agnes" number in her apartment. This was a funny song in which Mary's character, Agnes, vents all of her frustrations with husband Michael, while belting out a burlesque-style ditty. Mary started to run the number and she added a piece of business that I thought was just great so I said, "That's terrific!" When we got to rehearsal that day, Mary got to that section of the number and said to Gower: "Bob just loved this." When we broke for dinner, Gower pulled me aside and said, "Don't you *ever* suggest anything to Mary again!" Gower was so intimidating that I didn't even try to defend myself, and simply replied, "Yes sir." He didn't scream as loudly as Jerry Robbins, but he sure was very powerful in his own way.

We tried out the show in Boston and I quickly came to realize that my backstage cues with Mary were complicated; she had a number of fast changes involving wigs and dresses, and during those quick changes she had to keep speaking from offstage even while in the midst of changing costumes. The dialogue was written on big cue cards that we posted in the quick change booth, and at the appropriate moment, while Mary was still being zipped up, I'd tap her shoulder and point to a line. She'd deliver the lines and be ready to sail back onstage without missing a beat. It was all rather tricky, but even while out of town, we fell totally into synch.

The show was selling well, and audiences were responding, but everyone wanted to continue making improvements, so we traveled to Cincinnati for an additional tryout. After we arrived, Mary hurt her foot so a performance had to be canceled; instead of just leaving the theatre, Gower said: "There may not be an audience, but let's do a dress rehearsal with the understudies and we'll really be able to gauge the effectiveness of the material itself." We ran the entire show, at which point the understudies found themselves on a plane back to New York. A decision had been made; the show would be played by Bob and Mary or no one at all. No new understudies were ever hired.

We spent Thanksgiving in Cincinnati while Gower, Tom, and Harvey kept working on the show. Gower and his wife Marge hosted Thanksgiving dinner for everyone and I was placed at their table along with their two sons. Finally, the realization dawned on me: "I guess he really doesn't hate me." A much-needed relief.

The show opened to very good reviews on December 5, 1966, at the Forty-sixth Street Theatre and turned into a solid hit. Given the fact that Bob and Mary were forty-eight and fifty-three, respectively, and had to carry the entire show themselves, the decision was made to play only six performances per week instead of the traditional eight.

Mary's dedication to the show was total. She really only existed, at that point in her life, to perform, and although her husband Richard was around a great deal, and her children Heller Halliday and Larry Hagman would stop by for occasional visits, the show consumed her. She'd come in hours ahead of curtain looking every last one of her fifty-three years—bent over with fatigue as she shuffled through the stage door. She'd go into her dressing room to prepare and when places were called she would emerge in the wedding dress she wore in the first scene, exuding enormous energy, and the girlish quality exactly right for Agnes, the young bride-to-be. It was an amazing transformation.

Mary was a good actress. I never saw her struggle with her character, and she remained wonderfully musical. Every one of her many hit shows tapped into the youthful persona that lay at the heart of her personality. She really was Peter Pan.

My job was to take care of Mary, so I didn't get to know Robert Preston all that well. He could be quite prickly, and although I tried to assist him as well, we never formed a bond. He liked a belt or two of alcohol, but he was always in good shape by show time, and he knew just how to handle Mary. He was thoroughly professional, and spectacular in the show, winning a Tony Award as Best Actor in a Musical.

Mary was nominated for a Tony, too, but lost to Barbara Harris in *The Apple Tree.* Those Tony Awards on March 26, 1967, were the first televised awards produced by Alex Cohen, and Bob and Mary were to host the show as well as perform a number. I was charged with taking care of them for the entire broadcast, and when we went to rehearsal I realized that I was a one-man band, overseeing all of the props, costumes, and tech elements. All of a sudden, it dawned on me that I could screw up the entire show and had one of those "how the hell did this happen to me" moments.

Mary and Barbara Harris may have been vying for the same award, but they were also sharing a dressing room for the show. Barbara was dating Warren Beatty at the time, so he was hanging around the whole day. Barbara was in the midst of emotional upheaval and much personal drama. Mary would glance at me in the mirror and roll her eyes. All in all, it proved to be a very memorable Tony broadcast, and I was relieved that my first TV stage-management job went pretty much snag free.

I was having a good time on *I Do! I Do!,* but on such a small show being a stage manager can quickly become boring. Very boring. The fun part lay in dealing with all the celebrities who came to the show, a true who's who of Hollywood and Broadway: Joan Crawford, Gloria Swanson, Merle Oberon—you name the famous actress and she came. Mary only wanted to learn who the visitors were after the show ended, so when the curtain came down I'd tell her who was on the list for the night. I'd then make the visitor a drink while Mary got ready to receive them. One night I told her, "Miss Martin—Jean Arthur is here," and Mary blanched—there's no other word for it. There had always been rumors that Mary and Jean had been involved, and that night, after everyone else visited with Mary, Jean came in and spent an hour alone with her. Jean was very quiet and shy—by now, she hadn't made a film since *Shane* back in 1953—but she came back the next night to watch the show from backstage. She came back a third night, but after that, we never saw her again.

Shortly before Mary and Bob were replaced by Carol Lawrence and Gordon MacRae (the show eventually had a very healthy eighteen-month run), I handed in my notice. It was time to move on because Michael Bennett had approached me about helping him on his new show *Henry, Sweet*

Henry. Michael had just choreographed his first show, *A Joyful Noise*, which had garnered him a Tony Award nomination even though it had only run for one week. Michael said to me: "I'd love you to be in *Henry, Sweet Henry*, serve as the dance captain, and work as my assistant choreographer along with Charlene Painter."

I was so bored at *I Do! I Do!* that I leapt at the opportunity. I told Lucia Victor, the production stage manager, and she said, "Talk to Gower." I told Gower, who said, "I think you should do it." Mary was sad but understanding, and gave me a terrific going-away present; it was a hobo stick like what you see tramps carrying in cartoons—a pole with a bundle of clothes tied up on the end. But this time, instead of clothes, the bundle held a beautiful gold cigarette case. Mary's face was engraved on a medallion attached to the case, and the present was completed by a beautiful inscription of gratitude. It sits in an honored spot in my Connecticut home.

I only had one further encounter with Mary, and that occurred many years later. After Michael and I signed a four-picture deal with Universal Studios, one of the projects we were considering was a movie based on a Tom Tryon story called "Crowned Heads." There was a part in it for an older star and Michael suggested, "Let's have lunch with Mary at Sardi's." It was all very pleasant, and Mary was still very girlish, but she had clearly aged and nothing ever came of the film, with or without Mary.

I was leaving the quiet atmosphere of *I Do! I Do!* to leap into a big splashy musical extravaganza. More to the point, I was about to begin my creative association with Michael Bennett. My life was about to change. Dramatically.

CHAPTER FIVE

HENRY, SWEET HENRY AND PROMISES, PROMISES

HENRY, SWEET HENRY WAS BASED ON THE MOVIE *THE WORLD OF HENRY Orient*, which centered around two lovestruck teenagers who stalk a composer and philanderer who was to be played by the movie matinee idol Don Ameche. Nunnally Johnson, who wrote the movie, would write the book for the musical, just as George Roy Hill, who had directed the movie, was going to direct the musical. The score would be written by Bob Merrill, who had already written *Carnival!*, *New Girl in Town*, and the lyrics for *Funny Girl*. With Michael providing the choreography, I went into the show with very high hopes.

This was to be my first experience being a part of the creative team from pre-production on. My first and biggest surprise came when Bob composed a new song, because he didn't play the piano, relying instead on a musical assistant. He'd say, "Give me a backbeat," and start snapping his fingers and humming a tune that would be transcribed by the musical assistant sitting at the piano. Definitely not the way Richard Rodgers composed.

Charlene learned Michael's steps instantly, but I didn't—I was simply a slower study. What I did learn, however, was that I made a good editor. It's a realization that crept in slowly, but as Michael constructed the numbers I found that I could turn to him and say, "I don't understand what this number is about" or "This is too long." Michael would really listen. I never felt like I was a hired hand. Our dance styles meshed very well because Michael's strengths were tap and jazz, while mine was ballet. Together we possessed an extensive dance vocabulary. In addition, we were the best of friends and even after spending the day together in the rehearsal room, we would talk on the phone every night. In these early days, we laughed together all the time—sometimes hysterically. It was only as the success and attendant pressures grew over the decades that the laughs diminished. Regardless of whatever happened through the years, we shared the unbreakable bond of having grown up in the business like brothers.

I also quickly realized that I hated being in the show while assisting Michael. I found it tough to be by his side during rehearsal and then jump up to be in the number. I was functioning as assistant choreographer until the thirty minutes before curtain, when I had to put on another hat and focus exclusively on performing the show. You lose your objectivity. I was playing a variety of roles, doubling as both one of the adults and, in certain scenes, as one of the sixteen-year-old schoolboys. Among those playing the girls were Pia Zadora, Baayork Lee, with whom I was to form a lifelong friendship, and Alice Playten, a small young woman with a very big voice who stopped the show at every performance with "Poor Little Person."

Once tech rehearsals and previews began, I was spending most of my time performing and it was Charlene who was always by Michael's side. We tried out in Detroit, where the response was okay but not great; my biggest recollection of Detroit is that I tried pot for the first time and thought, "Hmm, this sure is a lot of fun. And creative."

We came back to New York and opened on October 23, 1967. Audiences seemed to like the show—in his book about a year on Broadway, *The Season*, William Goldman even writes that audiences liked the show just as much as they did *Mame*. While I'm not so sure about that assessment, the show did have its supporters; the problem was that the big critics were not among them.

Clive Barnes, then the all-powerful *New York Times* drama critic, killed us in his review and we closed after sixty performances. The show hadn't been a lot of fun for me; I'd try to visit the dressing rooms to say hi and give notes, but the doors would be locked—the kids were being naughty with reefer, and the girls were worse than the boys. I was, truth be told, glad when the show closed. To be a dance captain is a hard and unrewarding job. You have to watch every dancer, make sure that every single replacement knows what they're doing, and in this case I didn't love the show itself, a fact which made the work all the more difficult.

Even though this was to be the last show I danced in, I didn't think so at the time. I just knew I didn't want to be dance captain, assistant to the choreographer, and performer all at the same time. What was next? More shows with Michael? I wasn't sure, but I figured there would always be more opportunities awaiting me down the road. My philosophy about my career was simply to go through any door that opened up. If there's an opportunity lying in front of you, take it. Don't be scared of change. You never know where it will lead.

Michael had received good reviews and a second Tony nomination for his work on the show. He was two for two: two shows and two nominations. It was confirmation of what I had felt all along: Michael had a singular gift. Such was his talent that even when he taught dance class he quickly amassed a following. That huge talent was also matched by his overwhelming ambition because Michael was incredibly driven. He had been on the move ever since, at age sixteen, he dropped out of high school and joined the European tour of *West Side Story*. Ironically, I think Michael had low self-esteem in some ways; I know he was uncomfortable with his own looks, and it seemed that he channeled those feelings into an all-consuming professional ambition.

In addition to choreographing for Broadway, Michael was also continually working on television shows, ranging from *The Ed Sullivan Show* and the *Kraft Music Hall* to a production of *Pinocchio* for Hallmark Entertainment. By now, he was in demand, and either I'd assist him or dance in the show. Our favorite of all the television shows we worked on was a Steve Lawrence and Eydie Gorme special. The concept was simple and clean: Steve and Eydie singing with a big orchestra on a set consisting of risers, platforms, and runways. We liked Steve and Eydie enormously, and we had a terrific time during rehearsal; while Steve and Eydie would sit in the studio to observe, Michael would be Steve and I'd be Eydie. They'd watch us perfect the moves and then they'd execute the steps themselves. We all had a ball.

I also "played" Carol Lawrence when we choreographed a big production number for her on *The Ed Sullivan Show*. It was a very complicated number with Carol conducting an all-female orchestra while simultaneously performing a huge tap number. She was present for the first two days of rehearsal but then had to go away until right before the show, so for the purposes of camera rehearsal, I was Carol. When the Sullivan people saw me working hard on this number and realized what I could do, they started hiring me to choreograph numbers on my own. I was now working steadily on TV, both on my own and with Michael.

The Sullivan show also featured in one of the wackiest and most entertaining episodes of my career when Michael and I were hired to choreograph a musical number for movie sex siren Gina Lollobrigida to be performed at the brand-new Circus Circus casino in Las Vegas.

CBS flew us over to Rome to meet with Gina, set the music, and discuss the choreography. It was our first trip to Italy, and we arrived on New Year's Day, a holiday which shut down the entire city, including the Vatican. We wandered around that extraordinary Eternal City until we met with Gina the next day. It seemed to take just as long to drive up Gina's endlessly winding driveway as it did to drive from the hotel to her villa, but after clearing security at her walled estate, we were buzzed into a beautiful home filled with Etruscan art.

My first impression of Gina was simple: she was gorgeous. Always pleasant, she was also nervous about *The Ed Sullivan Show*. Michael and I didn't know what we were going to stage for her—we hadn't even picked the music—but Gina had only one concern: what should she wear? She took us up to her bedroom, which was lined with huge walk-in closets. Gina flung open the doors and it was quite a sight: one closet was filled only with beaded gowns, another only with cocktail dresses. A third held hundreds of high heels. It all provided a fascinating close up view of how true golden age movie stars lived.

Realizing we needed to finalize the music, Michael and I went to a record store in Rome, where there were, understandably enough, very few English-language records. We certainly did not speak Italian, but we spied a copy of "Walking Happy" and decided that would be the right song for Gina's stroll through the casino. Circus Circus was going to feature trapeze artists flying over the heads of the gamblers, tigers walking through the casino—it was all up for grabs, and Gina was game for anything.

Michael was really in his element, scoping out all the possibilities to be found in this unusual casino/theatre/playground, and after studying the rigging, he decided to put Gina in a cage which would float over the casino. This would be followed by having Gina walk past the gaming tables with a leashed tiger by her side—it was all a long way from *Hello, Dolly!*, but what made it so much fun was Gina's fearless attitude. We asked her if she'd stand in a platform hung over the audience's heads and the answer came back: "No problema."

It was all very elaborate and glamorous. And, as a bonus, Michael's very Italian father flew out to have dinner with Gina. He was beside himself with excitement, and it gave Michael a kick to give his parents that special treat of a dinner.

Michael now automatically made me a part of all his shows; he'd say to me, "We're going to do this show," and that was that. There was never any discussion or hesitation about it, and one reason it worked so well was that I didn't want to be Michael and he didn't want to be me. I didn't know if I was a choreographer or not, but I was a great second banana. My ambition was strong, but it was much more muted than Michael's. Our working relationship really was a case of two heads being better than one, and we matched up well because we so trusted each other. I knew how talented Michael was and really pushed his star. It was also clear that temperamentally speaking, we were a great match. I was much more low-key than Michael, and could calm any waters that he stirred up.

At the time of this television work, producer David Merrick had called on Michael to help fix the problematic musical *How Now, Dow Jones*, and Michael had produced a showstopper in "Step to the Rear"; Merrick had been pleased and as a result hired Michael to choreograph *Promises, Promises*, the musical adaptation of the great Billy Wilder film *The Apartment*.

Promises had an all-star creative team from top to bottom: Neil Simon was writing the book, the score would be written by Burt Bacharach and Hal David, the team responsible for so many of Dionne Warwick's hits, and the director, Robert Moore, was fresh off his hit off-Broadway production of *The Boys in the Band*.

In order to familiarize himself with the syncopation, quirky rhythms, and off-beat counts that Burt liked to employ, Michael started listening to all the Bacharach music he could find. But, based on the script, he soon realized that the choreographic opportunities in *Promises* would be minimal, so he decided to maximize any and all possibilities by choreographing all of the scene transitions in order keep the show constantly moving forward.

There was to be a number called "Grapes of Roth," which took place in a crowded singles bar; Michael decided to choreograph it as an urban crush, the principals and ensemble members all packed together in a ten-foot square. Michael designed very specific moves for everyone in the packed bar, and it took a long time to plan out: each hip thrown left, or shoulder moved to the right, each swiveling body, or raised pair of hands—it was all aimed at highlighting the frantic New York singles scene that low-level corporate drone Chuck Baxter (Jerry Orbach) faced as he tried to maneuver his way through the crowd. The number had started as a throwaway moment, and Michael turned it into a telling commentary on the singles scene. When the show opened he received a lot of kudos for that number.

At the end of Act One, the script called for the secretaries to dance at the office Christmas party. The dance was designed to catalogue the frustrations of being stuck in an office all day, and although the number was proficient, the reaction at the end was "meh"—it was respectable but completely unexciting. On opening night in Boston, the creative team cut the number. In its place, we decided to use the same music but with a completely new orchestration, and on the next Sunday afternoon, we created "Turkey Lurkey Time."

"Turkey Lurkey" would feature Donna McKechnie, who had quickly become Michael's favorite dancer after they worked together on television shows like *Hullabaloo*. Donna would now be joined by Margo Sappington and Baayork Lee as a trio of secretaries performing at that office Christmas party. By the time we finished the number, all set to a driving rhythm culminating in two lines of dancers crisscrossing from upstage to down in the shape of an X, *Promises* had acquired a genuine showstopper. Michael had initially been afraid he'd be replaced as choreographer, and now he had created the show's musical highlight.

We also added another song on closing night in Boston, the lovely, melancholy "I'll Never Fall in Love Again." It went in without any orchestration since leading lady Jill O'Hara could play the guitar, and the audience responded instantaneously. A hit pop song was born.

We all kept fine-tuning the show, and it was extraordinary to watch Neil Simon at work. He was whip-smart, very clever, and could write a scene in five minutes. He was in the rehearsal room all the time, and if we hit a snag he'd say what all choreographers and directors dream of hearing: "Don't fuss with it. I'll just rewrite it." Nothing in his script was sacred; he always wanted to change, improve, and collaborate.

Burt and Hal were equally easy to work with. Hal was a completely charming man, but Burt, who was used to the recording studio environment so conducive to his perfectionist instinct, found himself very frustrated by the nightly variations of sound and tempo found in live theatre. He wanted the layers of sound that were possible in the recording studio, and it was actually Michael who suggested having girls in the orchestra pit sing background vocals in order to add to the aural texture of the show (we were to use that device again with the "Vocal Minority" female singers placed in the pit for *Company*). Perhaps because of that desire for perfection, in the end *Promises* turned out to be the only original score Burt wrote for the theatre. He was married to Angie Dickinson at the time and she was around the theatre a lot. Here was a movie star who was happy to go out and buy sandwiches, a terrific woman who was clearly the most beautiful "gofer" in the history of Broadway.

Our director Bob Moore was also a great guy. He was an actor-turned-director who had a terrific sense of humor, and was a joy to work with because of his sense of collaboration—he was open to suggestions wherever they came from. He went on to great success as the director of many television shows, as well as the Neil Simon films *Murder by Death* and *Chapter Two*; we lost him much too soon when he died in 1984 at age fifty-seven from AIDS-related pneumonia.

Jerry Orbach, who played the leading role of Chuck Baxter, was a constant delight who had already succeeded with *The Fantasticks* and *Carnival!* but we inadvertently caused him problems when the female swing we hired turned out to be someone with whom he had previously had an affair. We didn't know that when we hired her, but when Jerry's wife found out, she called me up, screaming about the girl being in the show. All I could think was: "Why is she calling the assistant choreographer to scream about this? Aren't there any higher-ups to yell at?" We didn't fire the swing, but we did keep her out of sight as much as possible.

It was a harmonious creative team, and we also had one thing very much in common: we were all scared of David Merrick, a state of affairs which suited David just fine. He kept us all off balance and we'd wonder, "What exactly does he mean by his barbed comments? Is he going to fire us?" He was determined to maintain total control, and could turn on anyone, no matter their position. Once "Turkey Lurkey" went into the show and proved to be a showstopper, however, Merrick left Michael and me alone.

After Boston, we moved on to Washington for more fine-tuning. The show was in good shape, but the process itself was proving stressful; this show represented a shot at the big time for Michael, and the pressure kept building. Opening night in New York fell on December 1, 1968, but even though the show was frozen, the drama was continuing. One of the chorus boys, a very talented dancer named Paul Charles, had a breakdown early on and couldn't perform in the show. Unfortunately, he showed up at opening night in New York, got on the stage before the curtain went up, and started dancing around while saying he was going to perform that night. He hadn't even been to any of the rehearsals! We were able to ease him off the stage, but these were the sorts of dramas that make working on Broadway shows very different than, say, punching the clock at an insurance company like the one depicted in *Promises, Promises*.

The show opened to rave reviews. Clive Barnes in the *Times* wrote: "[*Promises, Promises*] proved to be one of those shows that do not so much open as start to take root, the kind of show where you feel more in the mood to send it a congratulatory telegram than write a review." Michael's work was singled out for recognition, and almost every review mentioned "Turkey Lurkey Time." He had now vaulted to the top rank of sought-after Broadway choreographers. I remember that at capacity we could gross $105,000 per eight-performance week, which seemed like an extraordinary sum at the time. On *A Chorus Line*, seven years later in the same Shubert Theatre, the gross capacity was $150,000. Nowadays $150,000 represents a so-so box-office gross for a single performance.

Promises was nominated for a number of Tony Awards, including one for Michael as Best Choreographer. Jerry Orbach won as Best Actor in a Musical and Marian Mercer as Best Featured Actress in a Musical. When the show was revived in 2010 on Broadway, Katie Finneran won the Tony Award for the same role that Marian had played, that of barfly Marge Mac-Dougall. Both women were first-rate, but it also shows you how expertly Neil crafted the fifteen minutes in which the character of Marge appears.

In those years, we worked out of Michael's apartment at 145 West Fifty-fifth Street, a situation which did not immediately change, even though *Promises* gave us our first big multi-year financial hit. Michael was extremely generous and gave me 10 percent of his royalty, a practice he continued on every show until the day he died. I was tied in to Michael's contract on every show we did together; we had a private deal which was based on our friendship, not a legal document, which meant I didn't even need an agent. I never asked him for a deal, and with each new show Michael would simply say, "I'm going to give you this kind of cut." I'd say "great!" and always end up with a deal that was more generous than what I had expected.

Michael was loyal in all of these business dealings; he kept the same financial manager throughout his career, as well as the same agent, Jack Lenny. Jack had started with Michael when Michael was working in summer stock, and even though Jack no longer had to hunt for work because people now approached Michael directly, Michael continued to pay Jack an agent's commission. John Breglio handled all of Michael's legal affairs, and after Michael's death, I had John negotiate all of my contracts. With John handling the business matters, I felt no need for an agent or personal manager, and in the process of our work together, I formed a deep friendship with both John and his wife, the very talented writer Nan Knighton, which lasts until this day.

It's not that *Promises* completely changed my life in financial terms, but there's no question that it helped, assuring me of a steady weekly royalty check. That weekly check grew as the success of the show did; *Promises* mushroomed into such a big hit that a national touring company soon went out, and an additional production played London's west end. London was really the extent of a show's global reach in those days, but nowadays, in the aftermath of *Cats* and *The Phantom of the Opera*, a hit show becomes a global corporate entity, playing every continent except Antarctica. Asia, specifically Japan and Korea, now has a very big theatre fan base, as does northern Europe, most particularly Germany, Austria, and Scandinavia. The few exceptions to the popularity of musicals in Europe remain Spain, where they take a siesta at show time, Italy, where they go to the opera, and France, where, *West Side Story* excepted, they go to dinner.

With *Promises* open, we next worked on the most famous of all the industrial shows: the *Milliken Breakfast Show*. We did the show for two years, changing the format from a book show to a glamorous revue; we utilized ramps, platforms, and lights like the show was being staged for *Hollywood Palace*. The Milliken show used the biggest of stars: Ginger Rogers, Ann Miller, Juliet Prowse, Angela Lansbury—and proved to be such a success that it provided us with a brand-new calling card.

I was no longer thinking of myself as a performer. I self-identified as an assistant choreographer, and my calendar luckily filled up with one job after another. It wasn't a matter of just working on Broadway musicals, but on industrials and television shows as well. The one that really sticks out in my mind was an episode of the *Kraft Music Hall* show, set in Hawaii and starring Don Ho. You may not hear "oy vey" uttered in the same sentence as Don Ho very often, but in this case it proves to be an accurate summary of the experience.

There were going to be a lot of children in the show, and I'd have to pick all of them up at 7 a.m., beginning my day's work as "Uncle Bob," the child wrangler. While the endless camera preparations necessary for filming got underway, I'd play in the water with the kids, bury them in the sand, make sandcastles—it was all a long way from dancing for Jerome Robbins in *West Side Story*. Coincidentally, Carol Lawrence was to be the featured guest star, and Michael and I became her backup dancers by default. Michael had come up with the idea of Carol arriving on the beach in a rowboat, and when producer Dwight Hemion approved the idea, it quickly fell to Michael and me to haul the rowboat, with Carol in it, onto the beach. Pulling a rowboat onto the sand was exhausting, but just as we wanted to collapse we then had to dance the snappy full-on production number that immediately followed. Just writing about it makes me ready to drop all over again.

The time had arrived for the big leap forward. Michael followed the television work and *Promises, Promises* with *Coco*, and when people saw that, whatever the merits of the show, Michael had delivered sensational production numbers that showcased Katharine Hepburn beautifully, he became highly sought after. The phone rang—it was Hal Prince calling about a new musical entitled *Company*. In the hands of Hal and Stephen Sondheim, as well as Michael Bennett and Boris Aronson, the American musical was about to change forever.

CHAPTER SIX

COMPANY

WHEN GEORGE FURTH FIRST WROTE THE BASIC MATERIAL FOR *COMPANY*, he had structured it as five separate one-act plays about marriage; Hal Prince then had the idea to musicalize the plays into a two-act musical, knew that Steve Sondheim should write the score, and that he wanted Michael to choreograph the show. So determined was he to hire Michael that he said he'd hire Donna McKechnie for this show even though at the time it didn't call for any real dancing. We just needed to find a spot where Donna could work her magic.

As soon as we began pre-production meetings, I quickly realized that I had never been a part of anything like this. George, and particularly Hal and Steve, talked about the show in full-on intellectual and artistic mode. It was all very impressive. It wasn't my place to weigh in—I was the assistant choreographer—but Michael wouldn't go anywhere alone, so I was always in the room and had the best seat in the house from which to observe. Michael had to work with the big boys and say the right things, and he usually did. He was innately very smart and so gifted creatively that he could collaborate equally well with composers and book writers, set designers and orchestrators, actors and producers.

The initial talks centered on how to blend the five one-acts into a single cohesive musical show. Hal and Steve spoke in terms of very abstract ideas that were fascinating to hear. They began discussing the notion that the central character of confirmed bachelor Bobby could have five sets of married couple friends who would throw him a birthday party. Musing aloud, they next considered placing the birthday party at both the beginning and end of the show—it could be a hook to get to know each couple. Would Bobby even show up at his own party? Did the birthday party really take place or was it all in Bobby's mind?

I was in awe of the way they conceived a new nonlinear type of musical; they were building on the framing device found in *Cabaret*, but taking it to an entirely new level. Steve would play some of his songs, and the complexity of his music, the brilliant, tongue-twisting, and oh-so-smart lyrics reminded me that this was exactly why I wanted to be a part of the theatre. Hal was functioning as both producer and director, and proved to be first-rate in both roles. To be in the same room with these geniuses who were functioning at the peak of their powers was creative heaven.

Company was to be designed by the already legendary Boris Aronson, who had designed the original productions of *The Diary of Anne Frank*, *The Crucible*, *Fiddler on the Roof*, and *Cabaret*. Michael and Boris met and proceeded to fall in artistic love with each other. Their sensibilities clicked, and Michael was fascinated by envisioning all the different ways in which he could use Boris's set: Boris had developed an abstract, steel-and-glass New York cityscape that would give Michael multiple platforms on which to stage continuous movement. The entire set was anchored by two actual working elevators. *Anne Frank* and *Fiddler* couldn't have been further removed from this sleek modern look, but Boris's gifts were extraordinary and no style of design ever proved beyond his reach.

Michael would sit in front of Boris's set model for hours, planning out movement, music counts, and onstage traffic patterns that would utilize every inch of space. After Michael came up with his extraordinary ideas, I then functioned once more as editor, distilling them down to their essence: what worked, what didn't, what needed an extra twist. Michael's pre-production work was so detailed that the last thing we ever worked on were the actual dance steps. We needed the building blocks of the show: the look, content, message, and music came first. When working out the actual steps, our sensibilities dovetailed beautifully. We didn't dance like each other, which helped us to cover a wide variety of styles.

Hal emphasized acting and singing more than dancing when he cast the show, and I was thrilled when Beth Howland landed the role of Amy, the hysterically nervous bride-to-be. When Beth was in high school and I was in college, we had been in the same ballet school together in Boston. We both moved to New York and landed work on Broadway—I was in *West Side Story*, and Beth was cast in *Once Upon a Mattress*. We both had Sunday nights off and would hang out together; we'd go to the movies, gossip, laugh, and, most of all, talk about our hopes for the future. Beth was brilliant in *Company* and stopped the show at every performance with her 1,000 miles per hour rendition of "Not Getting Married Today." I was devastated when I learned that Beth had died from lung cancer in 2015, but I loved the fact that we shared *Company* together. The show not only provided her with one of her career highlights, but it's also where she met her future husband, fellow castmate Charles Kimbrough.

Teaching the cast the opening "Company" number—all those "Bobby's," "Bubbi's," and "Baby's" with which Bobby's married friends greet him—took a great deal of time. Stephen's score was so complex that initially it became downright confusing; on the first day of rehearsal, when we spent hour after hour teaching the lyrics and where each of the actors would stand and move, Elaine Stritch growled: "Imagine doing this in summer stock." Once the actors finally had the patterns imprinted in their brains, they were able to connect the jagged rhythms to the staging.

Very few of the cast members were trained dancers, a fact which stymied Michael until he hit upon the notion that he was going to approach the act two "Side by Side" number as if the characters were putting on a PTA show in the suburbs. Once he thought of the show in those dance terms, the movement started to flow organically, arising out of the actors' own strengths and weaknesses of movement, rather than out of steps forced upon them.

Those non-dancers worked hard but it was never a breeze. Barbara Barrie could be difficult, but she was also talented and game for anything. Her character of Sarah was called upon to execute several karate techniques during the song "The Little Things You Do Together." Michael read the script, turned to me and said, "You're going to have to go to karate class and learn some moves we can use in the show." I thought to myself, "Oh shit! Do I have to?" But off to karate class I went, where I picked up— badly—some chops and kicks we could use in the number. Rehearsals began and I started teaching Barbara the specific moves. Well, she was fantastic and in no time at all put me to shame. Good thing she was such a quick study: I wouldn't have wanted her executing moves like mine anywhere near an audience!

Whatever the problems with Barbara, compared to Elaine Stritch she was a dream. Elaine didn't want to do the same steps and movements as the other actors; she was only concerned with herself and how she would be presented. A genuine pain in the ass—but her talent was blazing, and watching her in a scene was like watching an ultra-Panavision movie in close-up. The rest of the cast was a joy to work with, and Charles Braswell, who played Elaine's husband and had been the leading man in Angela Lansbury's *Mame*, was particularly accommodating, a lovely man whose underplayed style meshed well with Elaine's overt theatricality.

The show changed shape continually. We never knew what was coming into rehearsal the next day or how it would all work out. Steve kept writing new songs—for the ending alone, he wrote and ditched "Happily Ever After," "Marry Me A Little," and "Multitudes of Amys" before finally arriving at "Being Alive." This was a blazingly original score, unlike anything previously heard in a Broadway theatre. It's no accident that Arthur Rubinstein came to see the show and commented afterwards: "A most brilliant score. I didn't catch all the words, but then of course I don't at the opera either."

Once rehearsals started, we were still trying to solve the problem of creating a genuine dance opportunity for Donna. She was playing one of the three girls in Bobby's life, and Steve had given the trio—Donna, Pamela Myers, and Susan Browning—the very funny Andrews Sisters pastiche "You Could Drive A Person Crazy," in which they sang about Bobby's refusal to commit. But where could Donna really dance? We finally realized that there could be a great opportunity for her during "Tick Tock," Bobby's voiceover-laden bedroom tryst with flight attendant April. Michael choreographed a sexy solo dance for Donna while Bobby and April's innermost thoughts were heard in touching and funny voiceover ("He really likes me!" . . . "If only I could remember her name"). Unfortunately, we were having trouble with the number musically. Michael realized that the dance arrangement wasn't working and that Wally Harper's arrangement would have to be cut. We brought in David Shire to provide a new arrangement, and when his work was coupled with Jonathan Tunick's brilliant orchestration, we had the number we wanted. Wally was a gentleman throughout; it couldn't have been easy to work so hard and have the arrangement cut entirely, but the new arrangement improved both the number and the show immeasurably.

The night arrived for the first preview in Boston, and Hal, associate producer Ruth Mitchell, Michael, and I took our seats in the fifth row; we wanted to sit where the audience sat and experience their reactions at the same time. There would be no pacing in the back of the house with a convenient escape to the men's room. Although the show worked in fits and starts, it certainly hadn't yet jelled, and nothing prepared us for what happened during Elaine's climactic "Ladies Who Lunch." Elaine began the song:

> Here's to the Ladies Who Lunch
> Everybody . . . Ahhh. Ahhh. Ahhh. Ahhh . . .

Elaine had completely forgotten the words, and was just making guttural sounds. We all started sliding down in our seats; Hal Hastings, who was conducting, kept throwing lyrics at her but she was now hopelessly lost. We looked up and Elaine literally had her hands in her mouth. She then began wiping her hands all over her face, an action which smeared her makeup and distorted her features. Mercifully, the song finally ended, and after the final curtain, Steve said to Elaine: "What were you doing with your hands in your mouth?" Elaine's answer: "I was trying to find the goddamn words."

We kept working on the show and it slowly came into focus. The final scene was reworked several times; at one point, and for one performance only, everybody onstage came back as a different character. It proved to be an intellectual conceit that didn't really add up; the audience was simply confused when Elaine Stritch showed up onstage as another person. "Who's that?" they asked. "Isn't that the woman who just spent two hours dispensing brittle asides and bon mots? Why, all of a sudden, is she nice?" That attempt may not have worked, but all of the ideas, even the unsuccessful ones, were interesting and creatively stimulating.

Steve's estimable agent Flora Roberts saw the show and made several valid suggestions, and the show took a quantum leap forward when Steve replaced "Happily Ever After" with the far more positive "Being Alive." I have a very clear memory of Steve starting to write "Being Alive" in the lounge of the Shubert Theatre in Boston. His ability to write under pressure is extraordinary; he wrote "I'm Still Here" for *Follies* during that show's tryout in Boston as well. He likes to see the show in front of him because experiencing the entire production inspires his unequalled gifts as a dramatist. He writes with extraordinary specificity and definition of character, which is what makes his songs so brilliantly theatrical.

Critical reception was mixed to highly favorable and our colleagues in the business loved the show. By the end of the tryout in Boston, this nontraditional, nonlinear musical now seemed to flow together smoothly;

the action seemed inevitable. Even when lots of people in Boston did not like the show, finding it dark, bitter, and anti-marriage, and even when there were quite a few walkouts, we just didn't care. We all loved the show.

It had been a real education watching Hal work. He was extraordinarily effective as both producer and director, and his wearing of those two hats simplified the process: what he said was the final word. There was no need to clear permissions with anyone else. He knew just how to get a musical working on the stage and was fearless in his approach. On *Company*, Hal and Steve were working at the peak of their powers, both intellectually and creatively. They were exposing us to a new form of musical theatre in terms of format, concept, and darkness of material—here was a musical for adults.

At the end of the Boston tryout, I remember driving back to New York with Hal and Michael, all of us feeling optimistic and satisfied with the show. Michael had turned in first-rate work, so smartly conceived that he managed to sum up the entire show in one eight-count break: during "Side by Side," each of the husbands would dance a simple step and the wife would answer with one of her own; in Michael's staging, when it was Bobby's turn to dance, he performed his step and was answered by—silence. For Bobby, there was no side by side. He had no partner, nobody to "hold him too close" or "force him to care." The entire show had been summed up in those four counts of silence.

Dean Jones, who played Bobby, was never really happy while in the show. He sang the role beautifully and was himself an uptight personality, which fit the character of Bobby perfectly. But he saw Elaine stop the show with "Ladies Who Lunch" and wasn't happy that he was being musically overshadowed, a problem solved when "Being Alive" was put into the show. Even then, however, he was bothered by the darkness of the piece. Questions about whether or not Bobby was gay were not Dean's cup of tea; he was a very religious man and also seemed to be having personal problems at the time. Shortly after the show opened, he asked Hal if he could leave, and was replaced by his understudy, Larry Kert, who brought a palpable warmth to the role.

The reviews in New York were great; critics seemed to recognize how groundbreaking the show was, but just as had happened in Boston, there were those who took a violent dislike to *Company*. Some audiences felt the show was anti-marriage, whereas in fact, as "Being Alive" made clear, it's a very pro-marriage show, ultimately saying that relationships and commitment are difficult, but the alternative is impossible. The show was ahead of its time and not to everyone's taste—many out-of-town tourists didn't respond to it at all—but I found it brilliant. Every time I listened to the music I found something new.

Company won the Tony Award as Best Musical, and Michael was nominated for the fourth time, a nomination that particularly pleased him, given the fact that while the show contained a great deal of musical staging, it was not, aside from "Tick Tock," a major dance show.

The show settled in for a solid run, which meant staying on top of brush-up rehearsals and cast replacements. When Michael ran a first clean-up rehearsal, he became so angry at one point that he picked up a chair to throw at either Elaine or Barbara—I can't remember which one. Instead, he threw the chair into the orchestra pit and said, "Bobby this is yours." Steve and Hal were used to seeing me at all of the meetings and trusted me, so the task of running those clean-up rehearsals fell to me. Because the dancing was deliberately kept on the level of parents performing at the New Rochelle PTA, precision dancing was not mandatory; as long as it was close to the proper style, it was OK.

All of the cast replacements brought their own different qualities and talents to the show. Vivian Blaine replaced Elaine in the role of the acerbic Joanne, and delivered a very solid performance, as did Julie Wilson. Best of all was Jane Russell, who had the requisite toughness and edge, but also a genuine warmth. I was really surprised by her—we all were. She truly was Joanne; she had been around the block a few times in her legendary Hollywood career, sang the role very well, and had a great presence. I was absolutely smitten with her.

A national tour was sent out and the show also proved a success in London. Through each and every production one constant remained: Elaine would blow it on opening night, forgetting lyrics or bits of musical staging. Opening night would pass and she would then deliver brilliantly. I wish I could say I eventually enjoyed working with her, but it was so difficult to navigate through all her sturm und drang; her need for attention was constant. If you doubt that assessment, watch D. A. Pennebaker's terrific documentary on the recording of the original cast album. Elaine can't nail "Ladies Who Lunch," and she goes through take after take, everyone's attention focused solely on her. By the time it passed midnight and she still couldn't deliver the proper take, it was decided that she would return the next day to record the song. It was now the Elaine Stritch Show, and when she returned the following day she delivered the song brilliantly.

Barbara Barrie was replaced in the role of Sarah by Marti Stevens, with whom I formed a lifelong friendship. She was and is a very talented actress/ singer, and she comes from Hollywood royalty. Her father Nick Schenck was the president of the Lowe's corporation, the parent company of MGM, and her Uncle Joe ran Twentieth Century Fox. It's amazing to think about these two immigrant boys from Russia working their way up to run two major studios during Hollywood's golden age. Marti's father didn't want her to work in show business but that didn't stop her: a beautiful woman with a wonderful singing voice, she found great success on the London stage.

As our friendship deepened, she would invite me to a casual dinner party on the porch of her California home and when I walked in, sitting at the picnic table would be Lillian Hellman, Billy Wilder and his wife Audrey, Jean Simmons and her husband Richard Brooks, and Vincent Price and Coral Browne. At one time, Marti had a walk-up apartment on the east side of Manhattan and she asked me over, telling me that she was just having a few friends over for cocktails and dinner. I walked into the apartment and it was just like California: there were Ingrid Bergman and Rachel Roberts, with Kay Thompson playing the piano. Marti scored a great success in the London production of *Company*, and on opening night, I found myself riding in a white Rolls-Royce with her. This was quite a journey from Amsterdam Avenue in Manhattan, but that was the glamorous world Marti inhabited, and we had become such good friends that she always wanted to include me in her life. Our friendship opened up a world I had never expected, and all these decades later, we are closer than ever.

Company was enjoying a very healthy run on Broadway, and the national tour also did well. Where we really ran into trouble, however, was with the bus-and-truck tour. It was a stripped down production, with what amounted to two-thirds of the original set and no elevators. I was sent to Evansville, Indiana, to clean up the show, but in the Evansville, Indiana, of 1971 the audience had no clue as to what they were watching—they only saw a show about marriage in the abstract and knew it was not to their liking. They weren't ready for Steve's meditations on ambivalence—where was the happy ending they wanted? Then, when the young woman in Donna's role came to do "Tick Tock," I was horrified to discover that she was dancing the number like a low-rent go-go girl—she just couldn't dance it, so

I cut the number. That was a somewhat ballsy move by me, but I knew Michael, Hal, and Steve would have felt the same way, and they approved.

That unfortunate incident aside, I remained incredibly proud of the show. It was eye-opening as well as door-opening—and our next show was to break even more new ground. We certainly had no idea that it would very quickly acquire the descriptive adjective "legendary," but that's precisely what *Follies* proved to be.

CHAPTER SEVEN

FOLLIES

COMPANY HAD PROVEN TO BE SUCH A TERRIFIC EXPERIENCE FOR EVE-
ryone involved that it seemed entirely natural for Hal and Michael to
quickly work together again, this time on a new musical called *The Girls
Upstairs*, a murder mystery written by James Goldman, with a score by
Steve Sondheim.

Hal talked to Michael about this new musical, and Michael agreed to
choreograph the show under one condition: he would co-direct with Hal.
Once Hal agreed, Michael gave me an early script to read, and the truth
is that it was incomprehensible. Jim Goldman was a very good writer, but
this was not a stellar script. Hal said: "Trust us— it's just the seed for the
show." Very slowly, through draft after draft, the show, now retitled *Follies*,
completely changed shape. Inspired by a photo of Gloria Swanson standing
in the rubble of the Roxy Theatre, the focus of the show transformed into
a reunion of showgirls at a soon-to-be torn-down theatre. The murder
mystery was completely excised, replaced instead by the story of two former showgirls, both unhappily married. Their story, set in the present day,
would be interwoven with vignettes of former Follies showgirls reliving
their glory days. The show would jump back and forth between past and
present, the former showgirls shadowed by ghosts of their younger selves.
This was one complicated, ambitious musical, and it's not an exaggeration
to call it Proustian in scope.

To begin research we went to a reunion of Ziegfeld girls at the Waldorf,
where we found a ballroom full of former glamour girls, all dolled up and
hanging onto the last clutch of their memories. Watching that reunion
really helped with our concept of performers haunted by the past. At this
point, Steve had only written half the score, but auditions began, and a

who's who of former stars showed up to sing and dance for us. Given the fluid nature of the show, it was decided that if we really liked a particular audition, we'd find a place for that person in the show.

First, Ethel Shutta knocked our socks off, so she was hired and Steve eventually came up with the showstopping "Broadway Baby" for her. She was a great old-time vaudeville broad. Fifi D'Orsay, with her over-the-top French accent, gave a solid audition and ended up with "Ah, Paris!" Once we heard Michael Bartlett's booming tenor voice he was hired to play Roscoe, the singing emcee from the Weisman Follies glory days, but he was almost seventy years old by this point (he had actually introduced the raccoon coat craze in the 1920s) and we were not sure if he'd cut it. Some of these performers had not been onstage in a long time and they were scared by both the physical challenge and by having to remember their lines. Dortha Duckworth had originally been hired to play Emily Whitman, half of the vaudeville pair singing "Rain on the Roof," but she was so scared—literally shaking backstage—that we had to replace her.

Yvonne De Carlo auditioned to play the patrician, icy Phyllis, but we all thought she'd make a better Carlotta, the faded Hollywood glamour girl. Jane Wyman and Virginia Mayo auditioned, as did Howard Duff, who would have made a terrific Ben if only he could have sung it. Dorothy Collins auditioned for the role of unhappy Phoenix housewife Sally with "Vanilla Ice Cream" from *She Loves Me,* and knocked it out of the park. We all immediately fell in love with her. Alexis Smith, tall and regal, came in to audition and although she wasn't quite there yet, we were all intrigued. I had done *Wonderful Town* with her in summer stock and when Michael asked me: "Can she dance?" I replied: "Enough."

Gene Nelson gave a terrific audition. He was a good-looking man with a salesman's smile and a winning personality—he actually was kind of like Buddy Plummer, the salesman who could never satisfy former showgirl Sally with married life in Phoenix. We looked at some of his film clips— the great routines found in his Warner Bros. musicals with Doris Day, and particularly his acrobatic number in *She's Working Her Way Through College.* He seemed exactly right to play Buddy, and Michael eventually choreographed a very athletic, swinging-around-the-set routine for him on "The Right Girl."

John McMartin was the last principal to be cast. Unlike Alexis, Dorothy, and Gene, he didn't carry film or television stardom with him, but he was a good actor, and a more than serviceable singer who had starred opposite Gwen Verdon in *Sweet Charity*. He was an all-around great guy who did a beautiful job as successful but empty businessman Ben Stone, and was particularly moving in Steve's extraordinary depiction of middle aged angst, "The Road You Didn't Take." It was a crime that he was not nominated for the Best Actor in a Musical Tony Award for his role.

Design meetings started quickly, because this was going to be a monumentally lavish show, and costume designer Florence Klotz faced a huge workload. She studied old-time photos for inspiration and would then create her own twist on the old styles. One look at her clothes for the cast and you knew just how much money these former showgirls now had, and how their clothes reflected their personal taste. Phyllis the sophisticated New Yorker had a glamourous, chic outfit, while Sally, the unhappy Phoenix housewife desperately trying to recapture the past, wore a girlish light-colored frock. With just a quick glance at Mary McCarty's dress—she led the "Who's That Woman?" mirror number—you knew everything about the difference between her situation in life and that of the now very wealthy Phyllis. Florence's work supplied great, detailed character information.

Boris Aronson had developed a stunning scenic concept—a poetic version of a broken-down theatre. He came up with the idea of a multilevel set, complete with moving units and platforms which could slide in and out of the dark, allowing performers and ghosts to materialize like visions out of a half-remembered dream. At the evening's climax, when the dramatic tensions had reached the point of no return, this crumbling façade would explode into a Valentine candy box Technicolor playland, suitable for the surreal Follies sequences with which the show would end. Michael spent hours and hours with Boris's model, figuring out how the twenty-two numbers were going to be staged. We had a huge cast, a towering score, and a gargantuan physical production—this was going to be one for the record books.

When Michael began talking about the six-foot-tall, larger-than-life showgirls whom he wanted to glide around the stage as ghostly apparitions, Boris's succinct comment was: "I don't want girls dressed as vegetables walking across the stage." We found those six-foot-tall showgirls in Las Vegas, and it was Michael's brilliant idea to have the girls stalk the stage in slow motion, pale ghosts in black and white costumes who shadowed the older performers.

Because we had so many older people in the cast and the set was tricky, everyone needed weeks of time in which to familiarize themselves with the physical layout. As a result, Hal and Michael decided that the show had to be rehearsed in Pete Feller's scenic shop, where the set was actually being built. So, every day a bus would take the entire company up to the studio in the Bronx and the show would be rehearsed in the midst of the enormous half-built set; it was an unusual set up to say the least, but then again, there was nothing usual about *Follies*.

The elderly cast presented real challenges. The song "Waiting for the Girls Upstairs" not only required the four principals to sing in tandem and counterpoint, but also to sing with their four younger ghosts; it was a very complicated song in terms of rhythm and syncopation, with Alexis, Dorothy, Gene, and John trying to keep Steve's cascading lyrics straight while they moved around a multilayered set, shadowed by their younger selves.

The secondary characters presented their own unique problems. Justine Johnston, playing Heidi Schiller, was slated to sing the operetta-like "One More Kiss." Originally the plan was to push her around the stage in a wheelchair, but on that raked set we realized that was a recipe for disaster, so we gave her a chauffeur to hang on to, as well as a cane. Fifi had a hard time learning Steve's tongue-twisting lyrics, and would get completely confused, especially when the decision was made to combine the pastiche numbers "Rain on the Roof," "Ah, Paris," and "Broadway Baby" all together at the end of the number. She would fall hopelessly behind and scurry around telling all of us: "Chicky Poo, don't worry—I'll get it!" Ethel Shutta definitely liked a pop or two of gin and could really only work effectively for an hour or two per day, but she knew exactly what worked best for her and how to sell a song in her own personal style. When Steve presented her with "Broadway Baby," I was told that she looked at him and said, "That's swell, sonny boy!"

Steve's score remained a work in progress but it was sublime, a beautiful blend of character-driven numbers for the modern-day couples, and pastiche numbers for the older performers reliving their glory days. I particularly loved the "Bolero d'Amour" number in which the characters Vincent and Vanessa (Jayne Turner and Victor Griffin) danced while shadowed by ghosts of their younger selves (Graciela Daniele and Michael Misita). All four dancers were sublime. Steve composed a beautiful swirling melody

(there was no lyric) and yet the number has never been included in subsequent major productions of the show. Such a loss.

"Who's That Woman," which came to be known as the mirror number,
became the turning point of the show, the moment where past and present converge; as the aged showgirls recreate their Follies number called
"Who's That Woman," the ghosts of their younger selves join the number,
unseen by the older women, but mimicking every last one of the gestures
in reverse, as if glimpsed in a mirror. It was a dazzling number, but it was
very tough for the older women to learn. Ethel Barrymore Colt and Yvonne
De Carlo both had difficulty, and while Alexis learned it pretty quickly,
for Dorothy it was a killer. Somehow the difficulty that the cast members
had in learning the number only added to the past/present theme of the
show, and further contributed to the drama. We ran the number for one
hour every single day of rehearsal. We couldn't run it any longer because
the number exhausted the older women, to the point where Helon Blount
(playing Dee Dee West) put a pedometer on her ankle to let us know how
many miles all of the ladies were clocking.

Steve's original concept for the number was that one woman had died so
there would be a hole in the lineup as the women recreated their routine.
It was a very interesting idea but when Michael, Graciela Daniele, and I
worked out the steps during pre-production (we knew that given the age
of the cast we had to have all of the steps clearly set ahead of time), we
realized that it would not play well on a big stage—the deliberately empty
space only made it look like we had made a mistake. We ditched the idea
of seeing a hole in the chorus line, and built the number in layers: in the
first section, the older Follies members would recreate their old routine
while facing the audience; halfway through the number, the young ghosts
would glide on stage but face upstage away from the audience, miming
the gestures in reverse. By the time of the song's last full chorus, the young
ghosts would blend in with the old-timers so that they were all dancing as
one. Talk about Broadway magic!

In those days, performers did not wear body mics, relying instead on
floor mics to carry the sound. It would have made a racket if the ladies
had actually been tapping on stage, especially because the degree of their
precision wavered on any given performance, so we placed chorus boys
on tap mats in the wings, with microphones nearby. (By the time of the

London production in 1987, the ladies could wear their taps during the number because of the use of body mics, as well as the positioning of those microphones.)

We never fully achieved the pure concept we originally wanted for the number, which was that since Sally and Phyllis danced the number when they were in the Follies together in the 1940s, we felt that the recreation should be danced only by the women who were in the Follies with them at that same time. They were the women who would know the number, not the women who had been showgirls decades before them in the 1920s and '30s. Necessity, however, dictated that we put the older women into the number as well. Mary McCarty as tough broad Stella Deems, the leader of the routine, really knew how to take center stage and work that number. When Dorothy finally mastered the steps to match Alexis and Mary, it all clicked into place. We didn't know exactly how the audience would react to the number, but at our first preview in Boston, when the number ended, the audience exploded like it was the end of the World Series. Michael and I looked at each other in surprise and delight. It ultimately didn't matter what age the former showgirls in "Who's That Woman?" were, because the number was an audience-pleaser par excellence.

The number has been recreated in all of the subsequent first-class productions of the show—London, Paper Mill Playhouse, and the Broadway revivals—and while it always stops the show, it has never elicited quite the same reaction; the chemistry and specificity of the casting in the original production—Yvonne, Alexis, Dorothy, and Mary McCarty—has simply never been equaled.

It was decided that the show would climax when the four principal characters and their younger ghosts would all converge in bitter argument, during which their overwhelming unhappiness would finally explode into the fantasy world of the Follies "Loveland," the mythical world where "Everybody Lives to Love." Of the Loveland numbers—a total of six songs for Phyllis, Ben, Buddy, Sally, and their younger selves—only one had been written by the time we went into rehearsal, so we couldn't even start staging the numbers. Only "Losing My Mind" was ready; this Gershwin-like song was originally planned for the character of Phyllis, but was ultimately given to Sally.

The past/present concept was not just carried out through dialogue and song, but also in every aspect of the physical production, right down to and including the makeup. The ghosts from the past would wear very pale makeup, while the present day characters would look bright: film noir vs. Technicolor. At first, the white makeup was too much—the concept was overpowering and made the ghosts look like Bette Davis in *Whatever Happened to Baby Jane*. We toned it down to a washed out pale look, and it added an entirely new dimension to the show. The showgirls, of course, not only had to change their clothes for the Loveland sequence but also had to wash off all of that white makeup and reapply a more brightly hued base. They spent a lot of time in the shower!

Yvonne was having a great deal of trouble with her big number, "Can That Boy Foxtrot!" It was a one-joke song, "foxtrot" definitely being a euphemism for the boy's principal talent. So, while we were trying out in Boston, Steve replaced it with the now iconic "I'm Still Here," composing it in large part in the downstairs lounge of the theatre. Yvonne had no problem learning that song and it landed with audiences the very first time she sang it. Yvonne was a good egg—she had a very sick husband at home, a former stunt man who was now a paraplegic, and she needed to work. She was not at all intellectual but she was very warm, had a surprisingly good voice, and brought an earthy movie star glamour to the role of the seen-it-all Carlotta.

Alexis's original Follies number, "Uptown, Downtown," was written to dramatize the inner conflict between her younger loose self and the older, repressed society matron she had become. That song was thrown out and Steve replaced it with "The Story of Lucy and Jessie," which told the same story in different musical terms. We tried to keep as much of the choreography as possible; both songs were taken at basically the same tempo and Alexis was very flexible about the changes. She was tall, stood up straight, had great legs, and could strut like hell! She was given all of Jim Goldman's best wisecracks: "We haven't had an honest talk since '41—think the Japs will win the war?" Audiences loved her.

When it came time to stage Dorothy's follies number, "Losing My Mind," Michael turned to me and said, "Bobby, take Dorothy into the studio and stage 'Losing My Mind.'" That's the number in which Sally sings of her unrequited love for Ben, a tearjerker par excellence. I had a real feel for that song because the number was all poses—straight from the old movies I loved so much. I'd say to Dorothy, "Turn your head on that beat," and she'd be able to do it right away. She understood it all. Our only conflict was when I said, "Close your eyes on this line," and she responded, "I've been told never to close my eyes while singing." I retorted with a smile: "Just try it." She did and it worked. Everyone flipped for the number when they first saw it, but one piece of business was cut: I had Dorothy gasp at one point, but when Hal's wife Judy didn't like that bit of business, we had to cut it. I still think that was a mistake, but the end result was the same: the beauty and pain Dorothy Collins brought to it have never been equaled.

When I look back on my staging of that number, it strikes me that I was being entrusted to stage a major musical number on my own, yet I still didn't think of myself as a choreographer. I was now being asked to do shows on my own, but would think: "I'm going to leave Michael Bennett, Hal Prince, and Stephen Sondheim, for some questionable show on my own? I don't think so."

Tech rehearsals in Boston gave lighting designer Tharon Musser her chance to shine, and her work proved dazzling. Showgirls would materialize out of the dark and then melt back into the shadows. Thanks to Tharon's ability to paint with light, we were able to pose the ghosts leaning against the proscenium or striking poses in flickering shadows. It all added immeasurably to the texture of the show.

The show opened in Boston and met with a mixed reception: those who liked it really loved it, but those who didn't, hated it. Some called it brilliant, others dark and dreary. There were walkouts from people who thought they were going to see an old-fashioned splashy musical and instead were faced with a musical about the failure of their lives. Much of the audience was expecting *No, No, Nanette*, and this sure wasn't that light frothy skip down memory lane.

The opening number, the prologue where the ghostly atmosphere is established through music, lights, and costumes, gave us weeks of trouble. We never could crack it until closing night of our tryout in Boston. Michael then completely restaged the number with Steve's new music, coming up with the idea that the first image seen in the show would be of one of the showgirls (Ursula Maschmeyer) lit by a bolt of lightning as the eerie almost dissonant music crescendoed; that one image told everyone that this was not going to be a typical happy-go-lucky musical. After that startling visual, Sally would now enter the empty theatre early, so eager to reclaim this part of her life that only the ghosts were present. Michael gave each of the stars an entrance, and as they walked across the stage in real time, they were shadowed by their ghosts moving in slow motion. Steve replaced his opening song of "Bring on the Girls" with a new song entitled "Beautiful Girls," and all of a sudden the show was off to the start we wanted.

We continued to work on the show and many audience members shouted their approval, but as time went on, Michael became strangely upset. His work was wonderful and we were very proud of what we had been able to accomplish, but the show wasn't fully working. Michael said to me: "I wish we could musicalize the entire show," thereby shortcutting our way through the downbeat book, but Hal wouldn't consider that. Hal and Michael had great respect for each other but it was tough to have two directors—the bloom was off the rose. They had two different visions for the show and that made the working relationship far more difficult than it had been on *Company*.

During previews in New York we were still fussing over the concept of an intermission, and we played the show both with and without a break; two-plus hours was a long time for audiences to sit, but there was no logical place to insert the intermission into the show. With or without the intermission, audience reaction continued to be all over the map. Some audience members stood in approval, others stood to walk out. There were no happy endings in this musical, and while those who loved it found it poetic, those who hated it didn't care one whit about the problems of well-to-do former performers who spent the evening regretting their empty, brittle lives.

Gene Nelson couldn't quite get the through-line of the "Right Girl" number, but Graciela Daniele, who was not only in the chorus but also one of our assistants, worked tirelessly with him on it day after day, and he performed it well. During previews in New York, however, he hurt himself and we had to cut the number for the opening-night performance. It was a tough time for Gene; one of his sons in California was in a very bad car accident and he was, understandably, highly distracted.

We opened on April 4, 1971, at the Winter Garden Theatre to very mixed reviews, garnering both raves and pans. Walter Kerr in the Sunday *New York Times* headlined his review "Yes, Yes, Alexis!—No, No Follies!" a reference to Alexis's universally acclaimed performance, his dislike of the show, and a poke at the fact that we had opened in the same season as the straightforward nostalgic revival of *No, No, Nanette*. In the end, audiences ultimately seemed more inclined to pursue *Nanette*'s rose-colored version of a worry-free America that, of course, never existed.

Follies had made Alexis a star all over again, and she landed on the cover of *Time* magazine. She had successfully reinvented herself as a glamorous Hollywood icon now enjoying a terrific second act in life. The funny thing is that when she began work on the show she had not looked at all like a glamour girl. But hair designer Joe Tubens gave her a great new hairstyle and said to her: "We're going to make you a star." She was more than game for it and their collaboration worked; he'd help prep her for photo shoots and suddenly she was the toast of the town, and the winner of a Tony Award as Best Actress in a Musical to boot.

Follies won seven Tony Awards, including two for Michael as choreographer and co-director, but the show struggled at the box office. If our potential gross was about $90,000, there were weeks when we were only taking in $35,000. Hal kept the show running, but our survival was hurt when we lost the Tony Award as Best Musical to *Two Gentlemen of Verona*. When we closed on July 1, 1972, the house was filled with the obsessive fans who had seen the show over and over—the ovations were so thunderous it was like being at a football game. I was sad that a musical so ambitious and so original just didn't fly commercially.

After we closed in New York, the show was scheduled to open the brand-new Shubert Theatre in Los Angeles. First, however, there was to be a stop at the MUNY Theatre in St. Louis. Hal's associate Ruthie Mitchell and I were deputized to get the show on its feet, which proved to be quite an undertaking. The MUNY is a 12,000-seat outdoor theatre with a tree growing in the middle of the stage and we soon discovered an even bigger problem: it's still light outside at 8 p.m. in the summertime, so the flash of lightning illuminating the ghostly showgirl at the start of the evening meant nothing. So much for dramatic atmosphere.

Just like the show itself, my recollections of *Follies* are both vivid and scattered. Flashes of rehearsals or performances come at me out of the corners of my memory. Somehow that seems fitting for a show that jumps back and forth in time—it's never really over. I knew even at the time of the original production that it was a bold show, although I had an even stronger sense of that with *Company*. So much was achieved on *Follies* because Hal and Steve were continuing to take giant leaps forward with the musical theatre: *Cabaret* had led to *Company*, and *Company* to *Follies*. Yet, with its dark subject matter, *Follies* was really about the failure of the American dream and would never be a show for everyone. Whatever its shortcomings, there is something haunting and undeniably brilliant about the show, and in all the revivals—at City Center Encores, in London, and twice on Broadway, people are still trying to find the missing pieces. I think Michael said it best: "80 percent of *Follies* is the best show ever."

CHAPTER EIGHT

STRAIGHT PLAYS

MICHAEL HAD RECEIVED A TONY AWARD AS CO-DIRECTOR OF *FOLLIES*, but he now wanted to prove himself as a solo director. His strategy was to first direct a straight play; without any production numbers or music, the focus would remain entirely upon the text and actors, and he'd have a chance to flex his directing muscles. He started looking for scripts and when George Furth, with whom we had gotten along so well on *Company*, showed Michael a play which consisted of four one-acts stitched together, Michael sparked to the material. George's four playlets centered around a mother and three daughters—the same actress would play all of those roles in the four scenes. George was a clever writer, and Michael related to the lower middle-class family George was writing about. It all reminded Michael of his own childhood in Buffalo, New York. Michael read and reread the play and finally told me: "I can do this."

Actually, Michael said the first order of business was to change the title of the play, which was *A Chorus Line*. Michael looked at George and said: "That's the wrong title for this play, but somewhere down the line I'd like you to give me that title for another show . . ." *A Chorus Line* would wait, but for now, George's play, retitled *Twigs*, would serve as Michael's solo directorial debut. Michael not only wanted to direct, but also wanted his production company, Plum Productions, to function as associate producer. He took the play to producer Freddie Brisson, with whom he had gotten along very well on *Coco*. I was surprised that Freddie agreed to produce this "common touch" play. He was a sophisticated, highfalutin European, and he and his wife, Roz Russell, moved in the highest echelons of Hollywood society. He tended toward more lush or esoteric fare. But Freddie believed in Michael, and when he agreed to produce, the billing was set as: "Frederick Brisson in association with Plum Productions present *Twigs* by George Furth."

The actress playing these four roles had to be versatile but also grounded; even though the evening would be a tour de force for that actress, there could be nothing showy about it. By this time, Michael had heard about the great Sada Thompson, although he had never worked with her. She was known in the industry if not to the general public, and we went to see her in a production of Eugene O'Neill's *Mourning Becomes Electra* in Stratford, Connecticut. She was terrific in the play, and Michael asked her to consider starring in *Twigs*. He was pleased when she said yes, and he quickly cast Simon Oakland, Conrad Bain, Nick Coster, and A. Larry Haines (with whom we had worked on *Promises*) in the supporting roles.

Michael also decided to bring in our friend Larry Cohen, who had been an observer on *Follies*, as a dramaturg on the play. We both respected Larry's opinions (he went on to write the movie and musical versions of Stephen King's *Carrie*, as well as the television version of *South Pacific*). The team was completed when Michael prevailed upon Steve Sondheim to compose incidental music for the show, music which helped the transitions between the four scenes.

The truth is that initially I was not overly enthusiastic about the material. You could have summed up my reaction in one word: "Why?" I wasn't sure why Michael wanted to lavish time and attention on this potentially entertaining but rather slim play; I read the play but it just wasn't my thing. All I could think of was "Where's the orchestra? When does the scenery move? Where's the dancing?" Rehearsals were too quiet for me, and I found myself missing the hubbub of big musicals. But, my job was to support Michael and that's what I did. I was to be billed in the program as "production assistant"—that's theatre talk for "gofer"—and it was fine with me.

I've always thought it important to step through any door that presents itself career-wise, and I realized that while working on *Twigs*, I learned more about acting by watching Sada than from any other experience in my career up to that point. I was in charge of helping her learn an extraordinary amount of text, and would run lines with her every day. She was so thorough, so painstaking in her analysis of character and motivation. She'd start running a scene and then say out loud: "I don't have the connective tissue I need to make the transition from this section to that—that's why I can't remember these lines." She was explaining the problem both to herself and to me, and I grew to understand exactly how it is that the best actors examine and flesh out their characterizations. Sada would explain, George would rewrite, and the play would improve. Sada's extraordinary preparation continued throughout the entire Broadway run; she kept the script on her dressing room table and would read it before every single performance, looking for new insights into the characters and motivations. It was like being a student in a master class. I gained so much from observing her.

Set designer Peter Larkin had created a technically complicated set, consisting of four different working kitchens (including running water for the sinks). As a result, the technical kinks took some time to work out. We tried out at the DuPont Theatre in Wilmington, Delaware, and received decent, if not stellar reviews; George, Michael, and Sada continued to make improvements, and when we undertook a second tryout at the Wilbur Theatre in Boston, both the reviews and the business improved.

At this point, the problem lay in the fact that the play ended too softly—it just kind of meandered towards a pleasant, somewhat forgettable conclusion. Audiences applauded politely, leaving with slight smiles on their faces as they talked about where to go for dinner. It was Larry Cohen who came up with the right ending; he focused on the fact that there was a line in the middle of the last scene that got the single biggest laugh of the evening. The joke was set up perfectly, and when Sada said "horseshit!" as the payoff, the audience exploded with laughter. Larry's suggestion was to end the play with that audience-pleasing punchline, and he was right—audiences now left the theatre grinning broadly.

We moved to New York and opened at the Broadhurst Theatre on November 14, 1971. We had absolutely no advance sales, and when I say "no advance," I really mean no advance; on opening night, I was walking up and down Forty-fourth and Forty-fifth streets stopping everyone I knew—and a few I didn't—asking, "How'd you like a pair of free tickets to the opening night of *Twigs*?"

The play received decent if mixed reviews but did have its fans; Walter Kerr in the *New York Times* called it "funny and touching and freshly conceived," and Sada received great personal reviews. This small, straight play may have been too quiet by half for my taste, but the compensation for me was being around Sada—she deserved every one of her great reviews. She had a no-nonsense personality, made everything moving even while still being stern, and she never tried to curry audience favor at the expense of her characterization. When all was said and done, I not only liked her, but also held the utmost respect for her extraordinary talent.

We ran for eight months, closing on July 23, 1972 (three weeks after *Follies* closed). Sada won the Tony Award as Best Actress in a Play, and for Michael it was a case of "mission accomplished." He had established himself as a solo director, and of a straight play to boot.

When *Twigs* went out on tour we changed the physical production, a decision which actually helped the show. We toured with a rather skeletal set; gone were the four different kitchens complete with running water. Instead of the lightning-quick costume and wig changes Sada had to undergo backstage in New York, she would now change her clothes and wigs right onstage in view of the audience. She was backlit and in shadow, but the audience ate it up. It all made the show better, quicker, leaner. It was reminiscent of the last scene in *I Do! I Do!*, where, instead of changing backstage between scenes as they had been doing throughout the evening, Bob Preston and Mary changed in full view of the audience. Two makeup tables would rise up through the floor of the stage, and Bob and Mary would sit, put on wigs and apply old-age makeup, and transform into older versions of Agnes and Michael right before the final scene. Audiences loved being in on the action and that inspired bit of Gower Champion direction actually added to the pathos of the ending.

I had a perfectly fine time on *Twigs*, but it hadn't contained enough action for me. I missed the music and the humming activity found in a big musical setting up shop. I was ready for that excitement again, and I was about to get it. Big time.

CHAPTER NINE

"IF HITLER'S ALIVE I HOPE HE'S OUT OF TOWN WITH A MUSICAL"

AT THE START OF 1972, MICHAEL WAS ACTUALLY OFFERED *PIPPIN* several times, but he didn't particularly respond to the material and turned it down repeatedly. We still weren't sure of what the next show would be when Michael received a call from the producers Joe Kipness and Larry Kasha; would he please go to Detroit to give his opinion on the musical *Seesaw*, which was struggling during its out-of-town tryout. Promising nothing, Michael and I flew to Detroit to check out the show.

Based on William Gibson's well-received play (and movie) *Two for the Seesaw*, *Seesaw* the musical told the story of the mismatched love affair between straight-laced Midwestern married lawyer Jerry Ryan and kooky single gal New York City dancer Gittel Mosca. What was an intimate, bittersweet two-character love story as a straight play had now been blown up into a big musical. It wasn't working, despite the talents of Cy Coleman, Dorothy Fields, Michael Stewart, Grover Dale, and director Ed Sherin.

In fact, saying that the show was in trouble was an understatement. There were flashes of inspiration but none of it fit together properly, starting with the casting of Lainie Kazan as Gittel. Lainie had been Barbra Streisand's understudy in *Funny Girl* and had a big voice, but she was a zaftig woman, and not believable as a dancer. Ken Howard, with whom we had worked happily on *Promises*, was in fairly solid shape in the role of Jerry Ryan, but none of the secondary characters invented by librettist Michael Stewart for the purposes of opening up the action really made sense in terms of the story.

As he had promised, Michael gave his notes on the show to Joe Kipness. Joe was a character straight out of Damon Runyon, a funny man who ran a very popular restaurant on West Fifty-second Street. Michael didn't want to take over direction of the show, but as we quickly learned, it was no accident that Joe was known in the business as "Crying Joe Kipness." When Michael turned him down, Joe literally started to cry, begging Michael to reconsider. Joe simply wore Michael down—he actually talked and cried Michael into taking over the show. Michael finally said yes, but with one proviso: "A lot—I mean really a lot—has to change." Through his tears, Joe agreed.

The first decision Michael made was to replace the talented but miscast Lainie Kazan with Michele Lee. We both simultaneously thought of Michele for the role and put out feelers to find out if she was available. She was pretty, a quick study, had a great voice, and was believable as a dancer. Michele flew out to Detroit to take a look at the show and when she said yes, Michael fired Lainie. Lainie was understandably devastated, at one point saying to Michael: "I'll cut off my left tit to keep this role." What made the situation even more difficult was that Lainie had to continue playing the role at night while Michele and the company were learning the ever-evolving new show during the day. Not an easy situation for anyone involved.

The next big change: Billy Star was playing the role of "David," Gittel's gay best friend, a dancer, and choreographer. Billy was a talented performer but we felt the role could be played to greater effect by Tommy Tune. We called Tommy, who agreed to fly out and take over. Billy, understandably enough, was distraught about being replaced, and left the business shortly after this bruising experience.

Lainie and Billy weren't the only ones who were let go. We replaced several members of the chorus, an action we could undertake back in the early 1970s because Actors Equity allowed cast members to be terminated at will. That situation changed several years later when director Martin Charnin went in to check on *Annie* and was so displeased with what he saw that he fired nearly half of the cast. The uproar that ensued caused Equity to change its rules; henceforth, in order to fire someone, "just cause" had to be shown, and a paper trail of three warning letters had to be produced as proof. When Michael got sick in the mid-1980s and I took over the upkeep of *A Chorus Line*, I hired actors on short-term contracts. That way, if I liked their performance, I could sign them to longer contracts. If they weren't right for the role, their short-term contract simply wasn't renewed.

Michael wanted to keep Grover Dale on as choreographer, but because Michael wanted to make so many wholesale changes to the show, everyone jumped in to help: Michael choreographed, I choreographed, and Tommy choreographed his own numbers at Michael's request. In fact, Michael's energies were most occupied with trying to fix the lackluster book, but Michael Stewart, who had also written the books for *Hello, Dolly!* and *Bye Bye Birdie*, was so upset by this that he quit the show. That left Michael restructuring the book with the help of his good friend Robert Pitcher. At the same time, I brought in Thommie Walsh and Baayork Lee to help with my numbers—the quiet environment of *Twigs* already felt like ancient history.

New songs were being written, numbers were being dropped and added, and all the while Michael kept slashing away at the script. He and Robert went back to the original Gibson material, using the general structure and even specific lines in order to try and make sense of the secondary characters. With Michael Stewart having quit the show, the question became one of who would receive credit for writing the book. The suggestion was made that Michael receive the credit, but he was leery—would he be slammed for a credit reading, "Written, directed and choreographed by Michael Bennett"? He might be, but no one else was going to claim credit, and in the end that's exactly how the credits read.

We already liked the score, but Cy Coleman and Dorothy Fields kept working on it, and it only got better. Music seemed to pour out of Cy, and he possessed the unique ability to walk the line between Broadway and pop music; a very gifted man, he composed great scores for *Sweet Charity* and *Little Me* but also wrote hit pop songs like "Witchcraft." (At the time of *Seesaw*, our relationship with Cy was very solid; it became noticeably strained in later years when, after *A Chorus Line* opened, he attempted to sue Michael, claiming that in putting together *A Chorus Line*, Michael had stolen the idea from a musical Cy had written with James Lipton about members in group therapy telling their stories.)

Dorothy Fields was a walking history of Broadway lore stretching back four decades, having worked with the likes of Jerome Kern and Jimmy McHugh in the 1930s while continuing her winning streak right into the 1970s. She had written the lyrics for dozens of standards, including "A Fine

Romance," "I Can't Give You Anything But Love," and "On the Sunny Side of the Street," and was a smart, tough, feisty woman whose work had to be done in the morning. After that, she liked her cocktails.

We were glad to be working once again with set designer Robin Wagner, with whom we had first collaborated on *Promises*. Robin's a gem of a guy and incredibly talented; as he continued to refine the *Seesaw* set, he gave us moving panels on which New York cityscapes could be projected, panels that moved fluidly around the stage and gave the entire show a pace and slickness which had been lacking. Academy Award-winner Ann Roth designed the costumes and multiple Tony Award-winner Jules Fisher the lighting; we had an all-star team—it was just the show that still felt minor league.

The addition of Michele Lee to the cast gave the show a big boost. She not only had that great voice, but also the ability to play both the comedy and the pathos. She was flexible, smart, and possessed a great sense of humor. She and Ken Howard got along beautifully, and with this show, Ken, who had been fresh off the bus when he won the role of the leading lady's brother in *Promises*, became a genuine leading man. He was a pleasure to work with, as was Tommy Tune. Tommy was smashing in the role of David, his six-foot, six-inch frame and inherent star personality making Gittel's confidante into a completely endearing character at a time when gay characters were rarely depicted in a sympathetic light.

So much was going on in every department—wholesale changes were being made to book, songs, costumes, lighting, sets, and orchestrations—that the experience still was overwhelming. I did some background choreography on "It's Not Where You Start," but Tommy really staged that number himself, working out the movements that best showcased his unique talents. He built the number expertly, contrasting his five-foot, eighteen-inch (as he called it) body with four-foot-ten Baayork Lee's, climbing six steps in one giant stride, and leaving audiences grinning with delight. This was the show that really put Tommy on the map, and there was a reason: he was full of talent as performer, choreographer, and director. In fact, my favorite moment in the show came with "Poor Everybody Else/Late Great State of New York," an upbeat contrapuntal number in which Gittel sings of her love for Jerry while David taps out the statutes that Jerry needs to learn for his bar exam. Thanks to Tommy, that giddy number with the soaring melody worked like gangbusters.

I helped out with the snappy Jerry/Gittel love song "In Tune," but I also got saddled with the worst song in the score, "Spanglish"—a number which made no sense in the context of the show. It was thrown into act one simply as another big production number, with the goal that it would help make sense of Gittel's friendships with her fellow dancers. It didn't. We were making great progress, but also, given the time constraints, making mistakes along the way. To help put over "Spanglish," we had Giancarlo Esposito (so great in television's *Breaking Bad*) carrying the number, and his voice alone helped us to get passable results. But I hated the number, and was happy when it was replaced on the post-Broadway national tour.

In the midst of all this insane activity (there's a reason why Larry Gelbart once said, "If Hitler's still alive I hope he's out of town with a musical"), there were still some hilarious moments. One night when we were all exhausted, a group of us—Michael, Robert Pitcher, Michele, and I—were hanging out in Michael's hotel room smoking pot. There was a knock at the door and a voice called out: "This is the police!" We all freaked out, and while Michele bolted into the bathroom to hide behind the shower curtain, we threw all the pot out the window. We opened up the door and there was Crying Joe Kipness! He came in and we gossiped for five or ten minutes, at which point he said, "See you tomorrow." Just as he was reaching the door, he turned his head and yelled out, "Good night Michele!" We didn't know whether to laugh at Michele behind the shower curtain, or cry because we had thrown all our pot out the window.

We came into New York with a mostly new show, but the truth is that the producers ran out of money, which meant that we ran out of the time required to completely fix the show. We opened at the Uris Theatre on March 18, 1973, with a show that had some great moments, but still fell short of exactly what we wanted. Reviews were mixed, although Walter Kerr in the Sunday *New York Times* called it "a love of a musical." Business was iffy, slowly increasing but not fast enough; we did, however, receive a big jolt of publicity when, in a one night, one-scene cameo, Mayor John Lindsay stood in for his lookalike, Ken Howard, during the "My City" number, in which the hookers of Times Square danced around the all-American Jerry Ryan. The photo of that moment ran not just in the New York newspapers, but in every paper across the country.

Michael had done yeoman's work—we all had—and people within the industry knew that we had fixed a tremendous amount of the show. It boosted Michael to yet another level within the theatrical community; people began joking that if you asked Michael to fix a show, he would change so much that he'd end up putting Act Two first! But—fixing shows is very hard work and not terribly rewarding, because the show can never really be yours. You are playing the cards someone else has already dealt: the design, the score, and the cast aren't of your choosing.

Musicals are such complex animals that if you change just one number, it changes everything: the book scene leading into and out of the song, the costumes, the orchestrations, the dance arrangements, the lighting, the scenery—and that's just for a single four-minute number. My advice: "Never fix anyone else's show!" One year later, we were asked to help fix *Irene* with Debbie Reynolds, which was then experiencing great difficulties during its out-of-town tryouts. It just seemed impossible; the basic material was drawn from a musical written in 1919, star Debbie Reynolds clearly wielded all of the power, and our reaction really was one of "Where would we even start?" Ultimately Gower Champion came in and fixed enough of the show for it to enjoy an eighteen-month run. When I was called in years later to help out on *The Scarlet Pimpernel*, it was the same thing all over again; you're a consultant, and how do you give your opinions without stepping on too many toes? How do you not go to war? On that show, for example, some of the cast were speaking with British accents, some with American accents, and Christine Andreas insisted on a French accent. It was an impossible situation.

Seesaw garnered sufficient audience and critical approval that we ran until the end of the year. Unfortunately, by the time we opened we had missed the Tony deadline for 1973, and when the nominations came out the following year, we had already closed. As it was, we were still nominated for multiple Tonys, including Best Musical, Best Book, Best Score, and Best Actress in a Musical. We lost Best Musical to *Raisin*, but did win two Tonys: Tommy as Best Supporting Actor in a Musical, and Michael for Best Choreography.

After we closed in New York, the producers wanted to send the show out on tour. Lucie Arnaz auditioned to play Gittel; Michael and I both thought she'd play the role well, as she certainly did, and John Gavin, who had replaced Ken Howard in New York, signed to repeat the role on tour. I had rehearsed John a lot in New York and he was stunning, a terrific guy—a real man's man. He had the manners of a true diplomat, which prepared him well for his subsequent job as the United States Ambassador to Mexico. Tommy Tune would repeat his Tony Award-winning role on tour, and best of all, we were able to finish working on the show: we cut "Spanglish," and replaced the final song of Act One, "Ride Out the Storm," with the last song Dorothy Fields ever wrote, "The Party's On Me." It was a much better song both musically and dramatically, gave the audience another big production number, and in its depiction of Gittel's drunken binge, added edgy momentum to the show.

We finally had the show we had wanted all along, and when the tour opened in Boston we received fantastic reviews. Business on the road was up and down, selling out in some cities but limping along in others. We did not arrive in towns as a smash Broadway hit, so business had to build as the word of mouth spread. Unfortunately, by the time the theatre-going public in a city had really heard about the show and the box office was building, it was time for the next city on the tour.

In the end, *Seesaw* ended up a genuine audience-pleaser and we were happy with our work. We just always wanted it to be that much better.

CHAPTER TEN

STRAIGHT PLAYS: THE SEQUEL

WITH *SEESAW* BEHIND US, WE MOVED ON TO TRY AND HELP FIX NEIL Simon's new play, *The Good Doctor*. Produced by Manny Azenberg, *The Good Doctor* was a play with music based on several Chekhov stories, and starred Christopher Plummer, Rene Auberjonois, Frances Sternhagen, Marsha Mason, and Barnard Hughes. The very talented Tony Walton was the designer, and the director was A. J. Antoon, who had recently scored a big hit with his turn of the century interpretation of *Much Ado About Nothing*.

We went in to help out as a favor to Neil, but A. J. didn't leave; Michael was really there to help out with the musical elements of the show, specifically the songs and transitions. It's tricky to have two directors around, especially because we liked A. J. In the end, he justifiably retained credit, but I also think we helped out a bit. Christopher Plummer responded well to Michael, and Michael and I were both taken with Marsha Mason. It was during *The Good Doctor* that Neil fell blissfully in love with Marsha; Neil's first wife, Joan, had died at a young age and he was a man who always wanted and needed a woman in his life.

We opened to so-so reviews on November 27, 1973, at the Eugene O'Neill Theatre. Neil was actually nominated for a Tony Award for Best Score because he had written lyrics to music by Peter Link! Tharon Musser was nominated for a Tony for her lighting, and Frances Sternhagen won the Tony as Best Featured Actress in a Play. But the episodic nature of the sketches never fully satisfied audiences, so we closed after six months. Nonetheless, Neil was grateful for our help, and as a result he offered Michael the opportunity to direct his next play, *God's Favorite*. First up, however, was Herb Garner's *Thieves*, which proved to be an unhappy experience for nearly everyone involved.

Given Herb's track record as the author of the very popular *A Thousand Clowns*, Michael said yes when he was offered *Thieves*. Michael was interested in directing another straight play—it had to be less exhausting than *Seesaw* and would further his stature within the industry. From the start, though, this was a show that never felt quite right.

Herb, who epitomized the look of a shaggy urban intellectual, had written a play about the residents of an apartment house on the Upper East Side of Manhattan. Michael cast Valerie Harper and Richard Mulligan in the leading roles of a married couple. Manny Azenberg would once again be producing, and Peter Larkin designed the big, and complicated, set. The problem for me was the fact that the play was just so slight. I took it as a very bad sign that I couldn't seem to stay awake in rehearsal. I loved Valerie, and liked the supporting players Dick van Patten and Ann Wedgeworth, but it soon became clear that no one was having a good time. Rehearsals were downright grueling.

Herb was upset with Valerie, neither Michael nor Manny were happy, and when we opened to mediocre reviews early in 1974 in Boston, Herb really began pushing to replace Valerie with his then girlfriend, Marlo Thomas. Herb was the real muscle on the show, and he fired Valerie and replaced her with Marlo. By this time, the rest of us just wanted to get out of Boston and leave *Thieves* behind us, and I retain an indelible memory of Manny, Michael, Valerie, and I riding the bus back to New York together, all of us miserable. We all took our names off the show, Charles Grodin and Richard Scanga took over as producers, and Grodin assumed the credit as director. The show opened on Broadway in April of 1974 and ultimately ran for nine months, but it's safe to say it was anything but a highpoint for Michael, Manny, Valerie, or me.

After all the unpleasantness on *Thieves*, Michael and I were very happy to return to the much more congenial territory of Neil Simon and *God's Favorite*. With Manny producing and Neil's track record as the hottest writer in the business, we figured the play would be a big hit; that didn't prove to be the case, but not for reasons any of us anticipated at the start.

God's Favorite was really the biblical story of Job set in modern-day Long Island. Neil instantly hit on the idea of casting Vincent Gardenia, that talented everyman of an actor, in the lead role of Joe Benjamin, the Job-like man who suffers one calamity after another. Once Vinnie was set, the key casting question became who would play Joe Benjamin's antagonist,

Sidney Lipton, who was really the devil in contemporary disguise. At this point, Michael and I were continually reading the play out loud to each other as a means of exploring the text, and in the midst of one such reading it hit me: Charles Nelson Reilly should play the devil! He's an easy man to imitate, and I began reading the script out loud as Charles; Michael's face lit up and he shouted, "Yes—that's it!" With Charles now set, the rest of the cast was easily assembled: Maria Karnilova and Rosetta LeNoire signed on, and on the technical side of things Bill Ritman would design the set, with Tharon Musser providing the lighting.

The first act of Neil's play was set in a Long Island mansion, while the second act showed that same mansion after it had burned to the ground. The burning of the house, the fact that Joe Benjamin's son would fall blind—it was all to be staged as a test of how much suffering one man can take and still go on. An eternal question, but in this case one to be filtered through Neil Simon's trademark humor.

Rehearsals began, and true to form, Michael would be absent for the first ninety minutes of each day. Neil was always at rehearsal, the better to rewrite as quickly as needed, and as Neil and I became increasingly friendly he would ask me, "Where's Michael? When's he going to show up?" I'd vamp for time and say, "He'll be here shortly. Meantime I'll review the blocking from yesterday and clean up some of the staging." If, in running those scenes, the action required a particular actor who was not called for rehearsal until later that day, I'd fill-in for them, a state of affairs which led to Neil wisecracking: "I hope when the actor shows up that he's as funny as you are!"

We were having a great time in rehearsal—everyone loved Vinnie, and Charles Nelson Reilly was great fun to be around. They fell into an easygoing camaraderie and for some reason began calling each other "Victor" and "Andre." ("How are you today, Victor?" "Very well, Andre. How is your day thus far?") It was a fun, loose atmosphere. Everything seemed to be falling into place, but it's always hard to tell in rehearsal. You don't have perspective because you can't; you're putting a show on its feet and everyone in the room is intimately involved with the proceedings.

So it was with a great sense of excitement that we began our tryout in New Haven. At the end of our first show, Neil raced backstage, cornered Michael and me, and bluntly told us: "The show doesn't work. We'll keep working on it and we'll fuss with it, improve all the bits—but it just doesn't work and it never will." We were devastated: here was Neil Simon telling us that his own play was never going to work. Why?

Neil was a very smart and savvy playwright, and he hit the nail on the head when he said, "It's all just too painful for the audience. It's too much for them to accept. The laughs can't make up for the despair they feel at Joe's situation." We never said this to the cast, but the writing was on the wall.

True to his word, Neil kept working on the play and tried to lighten it. We limped into New York, opening on December 11, 1974, but Neil was right. The reviews were mixed, and we closed three months later.

Michael and I had now worked on four nearly consecutive straight plays and here was the scorecard:

TWIGS: a moderate success that we managed to pull off.
THE GOOD DOCTOR: a so-so play and so-so experience.
THIEVES: we quit.
GOD'S FAVORITE: a good experience, but depressing and not a success.

So much for directing straight plays.

Michael did all of those plays for the sake of career credibility, which is precisely what he achieved. He was now thought of as a director of musicals and plays, not just a choreographer. He received some nice reviews, and when the notices were negative, it was generally the plays that were criticized, not Michael. He was never devastated by the play's lack of success. He had grown and this was all a far cry from *Coco* when, during the last weeks of previews, he couldn't even bring himself to show up at the theatre.

For me, the process with straight plays was just too tedious and unfulfilling. Make no mistake, I had learned a lot: about acting from Sada, about the construction of comedy from Neil, about producing from Manny—but I missed the action of musicals. I wanted the noise, the fun, the frenzied activity. And, most of all, I wanted the song and dance.

Which I was about to get in spades when Michael heard about a group of dancers gathering to talk about their lives and careers. In fact, he thought, why not tape-record the dancers in order to capture their stories. Who knew—maybe there could be a show in there.

CHAPTER ELEVEN

5-6-7-8: A CHORUS LINE

SHORTLY AFTER WE FINISHED WORK ON *GOD'S FAVORITE*, MICHAEL heard that Tony Stevens and Michon Peacock had invited a group of gypsies for a late-night session of dancing and schmoozing, with the idea of sharing experiences and camaraderie. Michael asked if he could attend, bring Donna with him, and tape-record the evening—a group of Broadway dancers talking about their work sounded interesting to Michael. He mentioned the evening to Baayork Lee and me, and we both had the same reaction: "No way!" That was the last thing we wanted to do. We wanted to go to our country houses and just chill.

The dancers gathered late one night after they had finished their shows and began by dancing; Michael later told me that the dancing became competitive among the men. After dancing for about an hour, everyone sat down and started talking, at which point Michael turned on the tape recorder. Everyone was to start with their name and where they grew up. Information was dutifully exchanged, but the flow was slow until Michael himself talked about his childhood and his sexuality. Suddenly the doors were open. Everyone in the circle took their turn talking not only about their background but also about their desires and dreams, and as the early morning hours headed towards daybreak, the dancers became more and more candid about their heartbreak and neuroses.

Michael now had ten or twelve hours of tapes, which he had transcribed. A second gathering of dancers was arranged, but this one was much smaller—maybe six dancers in all, including Baayork and me. By the end of that session, Michael had twenty hours of tape, and one overarching thought: he knew he wanted to turn the raw material into a musical called *A Chorus Line*.

Michael hired Nick Dante to take a first stab at transcribing the material into a script. Nick had danced in a number of Broadway musicals, and during the first session had delivered the most potent story of all: his real life experience dancing in drag at the Jewel Box Revue. It was a startlingly raw confession which eventually found its way into the script as Paul's monologue. Nick had always wanted to be a writer and was eager for the chance. Although not formally educated, he was a smart and loving young man and I grew very fond of him.

Together, Michael, Nick, and I started shaping the material. Michael suggested we structure the stories in individual chronological order: each character would begin with the story of childhood memories and on through adolescence, into adulthood. This would give us a road map—the building blocks for the piece. Once we nailed down that basic concept, we began naming the characters, a fun and amusing process; I named the petite Asian dancer, drawn from Baayork Lee's life story, "Connie Wong," after the television news anchor Connie Chung.

I kept telling Michael, "This should be set at an audition—we can somehow make the audition confrontational between the dancers and the director." Michael was hesitant about that device, even though Nick supported the idea; Michael knew that a real audition would never include these sorts of soul-baring confessionals. At the same time, he realized that the director, now called Zach, could be given lines explaining why he wanted to hear these personal stories. The device allowing the stories to spring forth was now in place.

At this point, we had a very rough draft of the script, and Michael decided he wanted to bring in James Kirkwood to help with the book. He was a fan of Jimmy's novels and although Jimmy had never previously worked on a musical, Michael felt that he had the right sensibility for the material. Nick Dante was very gracious about our bringing in Jim and accepted the idea right away. Fortunately, Nick and Jimmy got along very well right from the start, and ultimately they split the bookwriter's royalty.

In particular, Michael felt that the Cassie storyline needed to be fleshed out and that Jimmy was the right man to do it. We knew we wanted Cassie and Zach to have had a prior relationship but that's all we had—an idea. The assumption has been made that Cassie's story is synonymous with Donna's personal story, but that was not the case. Donna's own story was primarily that of Maggie, whose lyric runs: "My fantasy was that it was an

Indian Chief . . . And he'd say to me, 'Maggie do you wanna dance?' And I'd say, 'Daddy, I would love to dance.'" Cassie's story was actually based on a dancer we knew who had been plucked out of the chorus to go to Hollywood for work on a Warren Beatty film. Hollywood soon discovered that she couldn't really act—or, put another way, that her gift was just not strong enough. She was through in Hollywood and headed back to New York to once again begin auditioning for jobs in the chorus. She came in to be seen for one of the Milliken industrials we directed, but Michael didn't hire her: "How can I hire her for a job in the chorus and look at her sad eyes every day in rehearsals when I know she was out in Hollywood starring in a Warren Beatty film?" Was this life imitating art or art imitating life?

Jimmy went to work on strengthening the romance between Cassie and Zach, which gave us the emotional through-line we wanted for the piece. It wasn't, however, that only Jimmy worked on Cassie-Zach, or that Nick was the only one who worked on the characters of Mike and Sheila. Throughout the workshops, we all had a say in shaping the book, and the collaboration was almost entirely free of friction. We all loved the material, and all contributed ideas, with Michael as our leader.

By the end of the first workshop, we had a very rough script but no music, so Michael called up Marvin Hamlisch. Michael, Marvin, and I had remained friends after working together on *The Ed Sullivan Show*; Marvin had written a big arrangement for Liza Minnelli, we helped with the staging of her number, and we all just hit it off. At this time—late 1974 into spring of 1975—Marvin was at the peak of his success. He had just won multiple Academy Awards for *The Way We Were* and *The Sting*. But, when Michael called Marvin to come work on this amorphous project about a bunch of Broadway dancers, Marvin immediately said yes and hopped a plane to New York. Marvin's manager at the time, Allan Carr, said to him: "Are you crazy?! You can have any movie project you want and you're going to leave Hollywood to go make $100 a week on an off-Broadway show?!"

Who to write the lyrics? We remembered that Steve Sondheim's agent Flora Roberts had introduced us to Ed Kleban, who had written a musical called *Gallery*; it was an iffy show, but Ed's work was good and Michael approached him. Ed's response was like Marvin's: "Let's give it a try and see what happens."

We needed a backer and a place to rehearse, so Michael went to Joe Papp, the head of the New York Shakespeare Festival and a man willing to take chances. More to the point, Joe had previously said to Michael: "If you have an idea let me know—I'll give you the space." Michael explained his idea, Joe said yes, and we started rehearsals at the Jerry Robbins Rehearsal Lab on Nineteenth Street, with Joe footing the bill. We were each paid exactly $100 per week.

We were leaping into the unknown. Shows usually had a solid script in place before rehearsals began, but we didn't have much of a script, let alone any kind of a score. We wanted to explore the idea and toy with the concept, which is how we came up with the then brand-new idea of a workshop; we didn't know what we had or would end up with, so a bare-bones multi-week exploration of constantly changing material was exactly what we needed. Would the material warrant a full-scale musical? We didn't know, but the workshop format allowed us to investigate the material without facing the overwhelming pressure of looming public performances. Actors Equity said yes to our request for this new style of putting together a show, and our first workshop got underway.

We first assembled a group of actors (which included Barry Bostwick as Zach), but it was a rather fluid cast because several started work only to abruptly leave for jobs that paid more than $100 per week. As the cast members came and went over the course of a yearlong series of four separate workshops, both the roles and the very nature of the show started to change.

When the second workshop began, Marvin and Ed started tinkering with a few songs and we set a run-through to see what we had, which turned out to be something resembling a bad musical version of *Long Day's Journey Into Night*. It dragged on forever, all of the characters were crying or having breakdowns—it was, in a word, dreadful.

For the third workshop, we moved to the Shakespeare Festival, where Joe Papp gave us the Newman Theatre and an empty rehearsal hall. We assembled our design team, beginning with set designer Robin Wagner. One day, Robin was talking to Michael about possible ideas for the set, and Michael grabbed a piece of chalk, drew a line from one side of the stage to the other, and said: "That's the set." Robin loved it. Costumes would be designed by Theoni V. Aldredge, who was Joe's in-house costume designer and a smart, inventive woman. We asked Tharon to sign on as lighting designer—after *Follies* we knew we wanted to keep working with her—and slowly but surely, the design elements of the show started to take shape.

Marvin and Ed began writing a few more songs, trying them out on Michael, Nick, and me. When they played "At the Ballet" for us, Michael pounced: "That's the score. That's how particular it has to be." Marvin and Ed began writing more songs, the process taking some time but now landing with the specificity Michael sought. There was just one roadblock; Marvin and Ed repeatedly pleaded with Michael: "Please let us write a song that can have a life outside of the show. No one's going to record 'At the Ballet'—it's too specific." Michael didn't want to say yes, but he finally gave in to their desire. The result, of course, was "What I Did for Love."

We began staging the numbers and putting the show on its feet. There was now a lineup of dancers standing right behind the white line drawn across the stage, and we tried to personalize each dancer with a specific physical presentation: some stood boldly, others turned inward—characters would emerge in the dancers' very body language as they stood waiting their turn.

We knew that in order to establish the dancers' childhood wants and needs, we wanted the personal stories to begin with Mike singing "I Can Do That," but we soon realized that if we simply had one character after another step forward to tell their personal story, the audience would feel trapped by the sameness of it all. They'd tune out and begin counting how many more stories were left. It was actually our desire to avoid this potential trap that led to the montage "Hello Twelve, Hello Thirteen, Hello Love," which grew into a free-flowing exploration of exuberant adolescence featuring the entire cast.

In order to figure out the best and most expressive way to condense sixteen separate stories into this one number, Ed and Marvin worked at the piano with each one of the cast members. They lifted phrases and sentences directly from the dancer's humorous or sad tale of adolescent angst, and began writing a new song to fit within each actor's vocal range. Because they were utilizing fragments of the actors' stories, no attempt was made to rhyme the lyrics: "Dance for Grandma! Dance for Grandma!" would shortly be followed by the phrase "Bob Goulet out—Steve McQueen in," so the entire number was designed in stream-of-consciousness fashion. The montage was like assembling a puzzle: bits of one character's story bled into and under another's, dancing would begin and then stop as another character began speaking, and a chorus of "Shit, Richie" was added underneath Richie's confession that he once thought he was going to be a kindergarten teacher. The montage ended up running for twenty minutes and took almost an entire workshop to stage.

Songs were written only to be dropped abruptly: the original opening number was called "Picture-Resume" and found the characters singing about their credits. The lyrics ran along the lines of Connie Wong singing: "Played Ethel Merman's little girlie, did a year or two in *Purlie*." It took weeks to stage, and when it was completed, Michael ran it, looked at me, and said, "I hate it!" Out it went. We realized that we were missing the "I Want" song, that opening number in which the leading characters express their determination and goals. The key was turned when Marvin and Ed wrote "I Hope I Get It," in which all of the characters expressed their one overwhelming desire: to be cast in the show. In the course of a single song, motivation was now made crystal clear for every one of the characters.

During the fourth workshop, things really started falling into place, so we began running the show. We liked what we had but were still working and changing. There was now an emotional through-line in the relationship between Zach and his former girlfriend Cassie, a dancer with ambitions of stardom who was now humbling herself by auditioning for a job back in the chorus. Michael now choreographed a spectacular dance to Cassie's song "The Music and the Mirror"; we ran the number, liked it, but then cut the male backup dancers when we realized that it landed with much more power when Cassie sang and danced by herself.

It came time to stage the first version of "One," the song in which the gypsies learn the number designed to frame the star; Michael turned to me, said, "Stage the number, Bobby," and sent me into a studio with Baayork, Donna, and Wayne Cilento. We all contributed steps, and in literally one half-hour we had the number. We put it together and ran it for Michael, who said, "That's it. Done."

By now, we had decided that for dramatic purposes we wanted to have one of the dancers—Paul—get hurt, an event which allowed us to explore what anyone does when they are no longer able to follow their life's dream, whether it be dancing, singing, or playing a sport. Michael called this proposed plot twist "the symbolic death scene," and it's one found in a surprising number of musicals: Tony is shot and killed in *West Side Story*, and in *The King and I*, the King of Siam dies. Michael knew that staging the scene would be difficult, so he told three of us—Donna, stage manager Jeff Hamlin, and me—"I'm going to dance with the company and purposely take a fall. Bobby, you react by running for the phone. Jeff, you go to the doors." One minute after the number began, Michael fell to the ground—very believably. The company gasped, and in their responses to the accident, the dancers' basic personalities emerged: the strong ones ran over to Michael right away, the more passive dancers withdrew, and some stood rooted in shock. Many of the cast members began crying, at which point Michael stood and said: "Everyone stand up and remember exactly what you just did." The cast was understandably angered by his manipulation; Baayork in particular expressed fury between her tears. Michael understood why they were mad, but turned to me and said: "The scene is now staged."

We ran the show for the Public Theatre's technical staff, and by the end, they were all sobbing. We still weren't sure of what we had, and actually figured maybe they were moved simply because the show was so "inside"—this was home territory for those who worked in the theatre business. Whatever the reason, Joe Papp, who was now running the Vivian Beaumont Theatre at Lincoln Center, took note of the extraordinary response and told Michael that he wanted the show for the Beaumont. Michael said: "Absolutely not. This is the ultimate proscenium show. It's not made for a thrust stage like the Beaumont." Michael and Joe were at a standoff, so Michael brought Marvin and Ed up to the Shubert Organization headquarters to have them play the score for Gerry Schoenfeld and Bernie Jacobs, the Shubert chairman and president. Marvin sat down at the piano in the executive offices, struck a chord—and the piano collapsed. The Shuberts still said yes to the show, but Joe eventually acquiesced and gave us the Newman Theatre instead of the Beaumont.

We began tech rehearsals, and unexpectedly ushered in the era of computerized lighting. While still finalizing the lighting plot Tharon said to us: "This isn't a union house so we have more freedom in terms of work hours. I want to try a computer for the first time." Although the setup was modest compared to what computers can do in the twenty-first century, it still proved revolutionary, paving the way for the extraordinary effects possible today.

We had been working on the show for one year, were beginning performances, and still had no finale. The top-hatted, gold tuxedo outfits Theoni designed for this version of "One" were a riff on the red tuxedos used in the final two "Loveland" numbers in *Follies*, and our first idea was to give every cast member their own brief star turn while taking their bow. Very quickly, however, we realized that with eighteen dancers each performing a specialty, the number would soon become endless. We knew how we wanted to stage the last chorus of the song, the moment when the cast collectively sings "One" while precisely tilting their heads in unison. The problem was that we didn't have the five minutes that led up to that moment.

We figured we'd begin the number with Paul taking the first gold tuxedoed bow; he was already offstage as the show ended because he was the character injured during rehearsal, so he would have the most time to change into his costume. We'd follow with the assistant choreographer Larry because he had also left the stage early in order to look after Paul. We then gave an entrance to each of the men and each of the women—they could doff their top hats and have their fleeting moment of recognition. The number started to come together, but what about the actual steps? The ideas flowed quickly: we'd use a strut step we had employed in one of the Milliken industrial shows. We resurrected formations we had used in previous shows. Wanting to emphasize the fact that for these dancers, all the classes and skills and dedication usually led at best to a lifetime spent backing up the Dolly or Mame who was holding forth center stage, we kept the second half of the number unison in nature, with the dancers ending the show by high-kicking their way into darkness, into infinity, forming a never-ending chorus line.

At our first preview, we were still starting the show without Cassie taking part in the opening number; in this early version, she arrived late for the audition, telling Zach, "I'm so sorry I'm late . . . I'm not really sure why I'm here." None of it felt right because it didn't ring true. Even more strikingly, at the end of the show, she didn't get the job in the chorus. We knew this was what would happen in real life, but when Neil Simon and Marsha Mason came to see the show at our invitation, Marsha expressed deep disappointment that Cassie didn't get the job. Marsha felt that Cassie's failure left the audience bereft of hope, both for Cassie and for any thoughts of starting over that they held themselves. As a result, she felt there was no real growth shown for either Zach or Cassie. We listened and restaged: Cassie was now in the first number and at the end of the show landed a job in the chorus. Thank you, Marsha.

Numbers were changed, dropped, and reinstated: at one point we cut "I Can Do That" and replaced it with the song "JoAnn," in which Mike sang about his sister; after one performance, we went back to "I Can Do That," and JoAnn was relegated to: "All thanks to sis—now married and fat."

There was already a big buzz about the show and the entire run at the Newman had sold out in one day. The 299 seats were so coveted that celebrities started showing up right away: Katharine Hepburn, Richard Rodgers—you name the celebrity and they came down to the Public Theatre. Seats were so impossible to find that a very pregnant Diana Ross ended up watching the show while sitting on the steps.

Such was the talk that before we even opened, several movie studios expressed interest in buying the rights. Bids of $1 million came in. The same Allan Carr who had advised Marvin against taking the job even put in a bid, but no matter the offer, Michael held out, saying: "We can get more." He was right, and while we were still playing at the Newman, the movie sale to Universal was finalized for $5 million.

Everyone knew the show was going to move to Broadway, and the Shuberts wanted it in their flagship theatre, the Shubert. The theatre we really wanted was the Forty-sixth Street Theatre; the orchestra seats rise towards the back, which would have allowed audiences a terrific vantage point, as well as the ability to take in all of Tharon's lighting patterns on the floor of the stage. We liked the Majestic Theatre (later the home of *The Phantom of the Opera*) for the same sloping orchestra-level seating, but in the end we went with the Shubert, second balcony and all.

Off-Broadway, the score had been orchestrated for an eighteen-piece orchestra, which was placed in the wings. Every top-notch orchestrator in town worked on the show: Ralph Burns, Hershy Kay, Phil Lang, Billy Byers, Harold Wheeler, Jonathan Tunick—the best of the best were working on the show as favors to Michael, Joe Papp, and Marvin.

Unfortunately, on Broadway the minimum number of musicians required by the union for the Shubert Theatre was twenty-five, so for the fifteen years that *A Chorus Line* ran, we paid seven "walkers"—musicians who were paid for not showing up—a full weekly salary. In the end, that bill ran to $5 million, plus benefits. Nowadays, theatres set lower minimums for the number of required musicians, so the issue is no longer contentious.

We began performances at the Shubert in July of 1975, and although scheduled to open in September, we were actually delayed a month due to a musicians' strike.

The response at the Newman had been sensational—audiences laughed and sobbed—and when we officially opened at the Shubert in October, the uptown response and reviews proved to be just as overwhelmingly positive. We had a huge opening-night party at the Public Theatre downtown, and the reviews were so positive that it remains the only show I've ever worked on where the reviews were actually read aloud. We were thrilled out of our minds at the response and I realized that my life was going to change; it was clear that there were going to be multiple road companies of the show, which meant my financial life would change. Now I could buy that pricey oven I wanted for the house in Connecticut . . .

The show was never hotter or better than when it first opened at the Shubert. It was all so new and fresh, and with the original cast, audiences were watching very skilled performers play a beautifully crafted version of themselves. The fit could not have been better.

A Chorus Line landed on the cover of all the major magazines, with features running in *Newsweek, Vanity Fair*, and *Vogue*. The demand for tickets was so intense that in those pre-computer, all-cash business days, I think there were several treasurers, who, thanks to *A Chorus Line*, were able to retire to Florida . . .

We cleaned up at the Tony Awards, even when faced with strong competition from Bob Fosse's *Chicago*. *A Chorus Line* won nine Tony Awards, including Best Musical, Donna as Best Actress, and Michael for choreography and direction. I won my first Tony Award as co-choreographer with Michael. I was absolutely thrilled to win, especially since it was in tandem with my best friend of so many years.

Everyone wanted to be involved with *A Chorus Line*, and Michael White and Robert Fox quickly expressed interest in producing the show in London at the Drury Lane Theatre. Michael and Joe Papp agreed, and the prospective London company, cast with American actors, was booked to first play Toronto before moving to London for a six-month run, after which they would be replaced by an all-English cast. At the same time, the Shuberts booked another company of the show into their theatre in Los Angeles, but although the plan called for the original cast to open the show in Los Angeles, Kelly Bishop, Thommie Walsh, and Wayne Cilento wanted to stay in New York, a fact which caused some consternation and disappointment.

In addition to the Los Angeles production, there was also talk of mounting a second road company, and while the prospects were exciting, the realization of just how much work would be involved in directing three separate companies proved overwhelming. One solution occurred to me, and I finally said to Michael: "With all those companies happening, let's rehearse them all at the same time. We might as well teach everyone the show at once." Michael agreed, and along with a great support staff, we went on a national tour in order to audition dancers. We flew to Los Angeles, Las Vegas, and Chicago, and along the way ran into some unexpected problems: it turned out to be particularly hard to find Cassies and Sheilas (the tough, seasoned dancer, originally played by Kelly Bishop, who's "thrilled" about turning thirty). In the end, we saw 5,000 people before picking the casts for each production.

I was the one demonstrating all the steps at every audition, and with all of that work, I became skinnier than I had been since the days of dancing two shows of *Hello, Dolly!* every night in Vegas. During all of those *A Chorus Line* auditions, I would teach the combinations over and over, but when it came time for the photographers to snap photos of the auditions, I would leave the stage and Michael would pose as if he were teaching the steps. I actually was fine with that—I was the co-choreographer, but this was Michael's show.

We brought all three companies to New York for rehearsal at City Center on West Fifty-fifth Street, turning the basement of City Center into the *Chorus Line* factory: in the morning, we would rehearse the replacement cast for New York, and in the afternoon, we would rehearse the Toronto/London company. During those afternoon rehearsals, dancers from all of the companies would be incorporated into the musical staging rehearsals. None of us had previously been involved with an enterprise of such mammoth proportions, which was not surprising because no show in history had rehearsed so many companies at the same time. It was daunting but exciting, with the most memorable day of all occurring when we combined all of the companies into one huge ensemble, culminating in ninety people performing the "One" finale in unison. It was thrilling.

As it turned out, the three companies opened on three consecutive Monday nights in the summer of 1976. The first was the opening of the new New York company; we immediately saw quite a few mistakes and scheduled a clean-up rehearsal. The Los Angeles company opened exactly one week later, and while the handful of new cast members fit in quite well, we were still left with the need for further rehearsal. The company that was in the best shape of all was the Toronto company, and after their successful opening and sold-out run, we flew to London in order to get them off to the best possible start overseas. *A Chorus Line* was now a global phenomenon, and one thing remained constant: the audience response was tremendous wherever we went.

The show opened to terrific reviews in London, filling the very large Drury Lane Theatre to capacity. Casting quickly began for the new all-British company set to take over after six months, which is when all of our troubles started.

The London producers had thought it was a sensational idea to cast Elizabeth Seal, best known for the musical *Irma La Douce*, as Cassie; she had been out of the business for quite a while and her "comeback" story seemed to reflect that of Cassie in the show. Michael agreed, and Baayork and musical associate Fran Liebergall did a wonderful job rehearsing the British cast. But, when Michael and I flew over for the last week of London rehearsals, we quickly realized that Elizabeth Seal was not up to playing Cassie. She didn't have the requisite energy and couldn't dance "Music and the Mirror"; she looked like she was marking the number because she simply couldn't summon the energy. I said to Michael, "She's not cutting it—we have to let her go." We fired her and the British tabloids went crazy; they all took on the tone of: "How can these awful Americans fire our beloved Elizabeth Seal." There were reporters camping out at our hotel, headlines in the tabloids, political cartoons depicting Michael as Fidel Castro, and all because poor Elizabeth no longer had the dance chops.

Just to complicate the picture, Michael, who was bisexual and through the years had girlfriends as well as boyfriends, had by now married Donna. It was a case of life imitating art: the story of Cassie and Zach. Michael and Donna flew off to Paris to get married, where they became very friendly with the French actor Jean-Pierre Cassel and his wife, Sabine. In fact, Michael cast Jean-Pierre as Zach in the London replacement cast of *A Chorus Line*, which proved to be an extremely odd choice: the role of this quintessentially American director and choreographer was now being played in London by a French actor who talked about "zee Chorus Line" . . . Jean-Pierre and Sabine had two sons, but Sabine proceeded to fall head over heels for Michael. When Michael and Donna eventually broke up, Sabine left her husband and sons in France, pursued Michael and came to America where she and Michael had a long, torrid affair. She had a vibrant personality—people were always drawn to Sabine—and she set her sights on Michael and a life in America.

At the time of the London *A Chorus Line*, however, Michael and Donna were still officially married, and Michael flew Donna over in hopes that she could take over the role for four weeks while a British actress was cast and rehearsed. British Actors Equity said no. It wasn't just Equity causing problems; the idea of Donna taking over only exacerbated Michael's continuing bad press. With Donna unable to play Cassie, we had to choose between the two current Cassie understudies, both British. The problem was that we weren't sure which one to choose: one danced well but was a tenuous singer, while the other, even though competent in all areas, was less than thrilling. By now, of course, there was tension backstage, with two members of the company competing for the same job. Everywhere we turned, problems, and the press, loomed.

Finally, Michael settled on Petra Siniawski to play Cassie, and in the process decided to make her over: Cassie would now wear a blue dress, not the already iconic red dress Donna wore, and since Petra was better as dancer than singer, we decided to have an off stage choir add backup vocals during the "Play Me the Music" section of "Music and the Mirror." We implemented these changes right before the British cast opened to the press, and then left town as quickly as possible in order to escape the press.

The British cast was fine, but that quintessential American sense of driving energy had been lost. Aside from a show like *Billy Elliot*, British blockbusters like *The Phantom of the Opera* and *Les Miserables* are not high-energy, dance-driven shows in the way shows like *A Chorus Line* and *Dancin'* are; they are through-sung spectacles, effective and audience-pleasing, but cut from a different cloth.

Maintaining all of the *Chorus Line* companies was proving to be a monumental task, because in addition to the national tours and London, a company was now set to open in Australia. The only way we could keep track of it all was to hire an extensive staff of assistants. We had great dance captains for all of the companies and had them come to New York at the same time so that everyone learned the exact same staging. We wanted audiences all over the world to experience the same *Chorus Line* that was

playing on Broadway: sets, costumes, lights, and choreography would du-
plicate everything found on the stage of the Shubert Theatre in New York.

As the need arose, cast members were switched from one company to
another. Oftentimes the road companies ended up receiving more press
attention than did the Broadway cast, because every city on the tour required a new opening and hence new reviews and attention from the press.
People became possessive about the casts and had their favorites; Martin
Gottfried, who was, at the time, reviewing theatre for the *New York Post*,
was furious that the original cast was no longer intact in New York, and
wrote a biting review to that effect in the paper. I still don't know what it
was he expected.

With involvement in all of these companies, my life changed, starting
with how and where I lived. Right after *Follies* opened in 1971, I had bought
a very small house in Connecticut. *Follies*, however, had run for only one
year, and none of the straight plays that followed were major hits, so in the
pre-*Chorus Line* days, a new stove represented a major cash outlay. After
that first tiny house, I had bought and renovated a second house, but with
royalties now coming in from multiple companies of *A Chorus Line*, I
sold that second house and bought a ramshackle structure in Kent, Connecticut, one which had functioned as a hunting lodge. An all-consuming
and never-ending job of renovations began.

I was also in the midst of a serious relationship with Wayne De Ramme-
laere, with whom I had first connected during *Company*. He was a dancer
who had appeared in *Do I Hear A Waltz?*, and I fell in love with . . . his
neck. He was a big, strapping guy and a very talented handyman. When we
started renovations on the lodge, he was able to fix, hammer, and reconfig-
ure the structure in numerous ways, making my life better and much easier.
Wayne wanted horses for the lodge, so we bought horses; as the renovations
went on, we added a tack room and lived in an apartment over the stalls.

Our problem lay in the fact that my success with *A Chorus Line* was
now proving difficult for Wayne—his dancing career had stalled and he
was faced with my unexpectedly big success. It might have been easier if
he was more of an intellectual, able to process the turn of events and figure
out a new path for himself, but that was not the case. He felt left out of the
Chorus Line phenomenon, a problem which only grew bigger, given my
nonstop involvement with all of the companies. Adding to this problem
was the fact that Michael was always on the scene and in my life. Michael

and I were never involved romantically, but we were creative partners and the best of friends. It wasn't an easy situation for Wayne.

We stayed together for seven years, but the pressures we faced constantly increased, and Wayne suffered a heart attack when he was only thirty-seven. He survived the heart attack, but our eventual breakup while I was rehearsing *Ballroom* proved difficult; acrimonious words along the lines of "Get out—I don't want to see you again" were hurled back and forth, and sadly, Wayne died a few years after our breakup, during the early days of the AIDS epidemic.

After we split up, I continued work on the house. When I put a deck on the back of the house, I was so happy with the results that, with each company of *A Chorus Line*, I'd add another feature to the house. After *Ballroom* failed, I pulled back on the renovations, but with the success of *Dreamgirls*, I added a pool. There was an ebb and flow to the size and shape of the house just like that of my career: hits were intermingled with flops, additions were added or never got off the architect's drawing board, and I continue working on the house to this day.

While my relationship with Wayne was no longer, my relationship with my parents was terrific. They were thrilled by the success of *A Chorus Line*, and my mother, who had always questioned my decision to make my living as a dancer because she feared the uncertainty, was now over the moon: "You stay with that Michael—he has been good to you and helped you succeed." She saw that I was now secure and that my life was growing in unexpected and interesting directions. My parents were uneducated immigrants, and the truth is that they didn't understand the artistic aspects of the shows I worked on, but they were incredibly proud of my work.

At the same time, I remained very close to my sister Laura. It was Laura who had taken me to shows and movies when I was younger, and we always got along extremely well. To this day, we talk on the phone every single week, and after she and her husband settled in Boston, if one of my shows was trying out there, I would have her attend the rehearsals and orchestra readings. She loved being a part of the show business scene, and to this day talks about the afternoon she spent at the Shubert Theatre in Boston during tech rehearsals of *Company*. After she arrived, I brought her to a seat a few rows behind Hal Prince and Michael, a prime spot from which to listen in when Dean Jones came onstage to ask Hal about problems with a particular costume. Dean walked out from the wings, fussing with his jacket and saying, "Hal, I'm just not comfortable with this—can we change it here and modify it there, and maybe reconstruct this panel?" Hal smilingly replied, "Sure, Dean, no problem." Dean walked offstage, satisfied, at which point Hal turned around with a smile and said, "Aw fuck it. Leave it like it is." Laura loved seeing and hearing that kind of inside exchange. Laura also grew to know Michael over the years, and they liked and respected each other. Even now, after reading some of the books written about Michael, she will ask me: "Was he really like that? That's not the Michael I knew through all those years." He was, in fact, extremely generous, a fact that is often overlooked or downplayed.

With the worldwide financial success of *A Chorus Line*, business problems now arose over the show's use of the original cast's life stories. Michael gave a percentage to the original-session participants as well as to the original cast, but even this grew complicated when we realized that we had to divide the participants into three groups: those whose stories had been recorded on the original tapes, those in the original cast of the show but not on the tapes, and those who were both in the show and on the tapes.

Through all the success, Michael and I remained as close as ever. When we moved our base of operations from Michael's apartment to the building at 890 Broadway that he had bought and turned into rehearsal studios, we worked the way we always had—at a partners' desk, facing each other head on. Although Michael was now one of the giants of Broadway, he was still my loving kid brother.

Pleased as I was with the show, the truth is that the global success of *A Chorus Line* was difficult to manage. It was exhausting being on planes all the time, and we found ourselves in constant rehearsals and casting sessions. Just as happens with every big show, there were cast problems to be dealt with, but the entire scene was magnified to the near breaking point when the AIDS crisis hit in the early 1980s, and so many bright, talented, handsome dancers and singers succumbed to the plague. It grew overwhelming, and at times it seemed as if those years were all about funerals. In my circle of ten close friends, eight died from AIDS.

I had the closest seat possible from which to watch Michael try to deal with his incredible success. His lack of education did not bother him (although he remained a terrible speller throughout his life), and he actually became a voracious reader who particularly loved complicated spy novels, books which he felt helped him in analyzing the structure of his own work.

He always carried a book with him, and in fact, after *A Chorus Line*, his high school in Buffalo, New York, awarded him his high school diploma.

As to that tremendous success, however, he sometimes handled it well but at other times succumbed to drugs, alcohol, and the bouts of paranoia that affected all of us. He was looking to escape the pressures and have fun, and I plead guilty to some of the same charges; Michael, however, flew particularly high and too close to the sun.

We were now a part of a very big business and in many ways, the triumph of *A Chorus Line* was more difficult to deal with than the disappointment we faced at the lackluster reception accorded *Ballroom* three years later. Don't get me wrong—I loved *A Chorus Line*, appreciated the rewards, and was very proud of our work. But the pressures were growing and the laughs diminishing—it was all a long way from *Henry, Sweet Henry*. I missed the days of climbing the mountain, when the journey itself was the reward, and the prospects and horizons seemed limitless.

CHAPTER TWELVE

HOORAY FOR HOLLYWOOD

THE SONG "HOORAY FOR HOLLYWOOD" IS USUALLY SUNG AS A RAH-RAH anthem to the movie business, but if you listen closely to the song you realize that the Johnny Mercer lyric is not just funny but also filled with irony—irony that perfectly describes the year Michael and I spent at Universal Studios preparing to direct the movie version of *A Chorus Line*.

When the deal granting the rights to Universal was signed, the contract stipulated that the movie could not be made for at least five years. With that caveat in mind, in 1977, two years after the Broadway opening, Michael and I headed out to Hollywood in order to learn the movie business. Michael was going to direct the movie and to that end we were given an office at Universal, part of a suite we shared with both Steven Spielberg (who was actually at Columbia making *Close Encounters of the Third Kind*) and Universal vice president Verna Fields, who had recently won an Oscar for editing *Jaws*. Verna was slated to be our teacher about the film business. The office space was nice, but they kept asking us, "How do you want your office decorated?" We kept answering, "It's fine just the way it is," because what we really wanted were our own parking spaces at the studio—which proved to be a near impossibility. Not a good omen, but as it turned out, a prophetic one.

Our time at Universal seemed surreal right from the start; our windows overlooked the streets where tourist trams went by with loudspeakers blaring: "This is Lucille Ball's dressing room" or some other nonsense. Hovering over everything, just like the Dr. T. J. Eckleburg billboard in *The Great Gatsby*, was a gigantic billboard proclaiming: "Coming soon—*A Chorus Line.*"

Before tackling such a big-budget, highly publicized musical, Michael and I were to cut our teeth with a smaller film, and hit on the idea of filming Tom Tryon's "Bobbitt," one of the novellas making up his book *Crowned Heads* (another of the stories was "Fedora," which Billy Wilder eventually directed as a film of the same title). We knew and liked Tom Tryon, but after we had spent quite a bit of time developing the property, we realized that there were so many holes in the story that it would never make sense. Michael grew disenchanted, so we dropped the property. Tom never spoke to us again.

As part of our education, we'd watch the dailies with Verna, and I still remember the films we saw: *MacArthur* with Gregory Peck, *The Car* with James Brolin, and *Smokey and the Bandit* with Burt Reynolds and Sally Field. Watching the dailies of *Smokey*, you could actually see Burt and Sally falling in love, because the camera kept rolling even after the director yelled "Cut," and you'd see them in unguarded moments. The film I remember best from that time was *Airport '77* with Jack Lemmon, Lee Grant, and Olivia de Havilland, not because it's a classic of the cinema (it sure isn't) but because one day we saw Olivia standing right outside the soundstage. She not only looked beautiful but also very happy to be back in a studio in Hollywood. Olivia de Havilland sightings aside, we would find ourselves spending days watching endless retakes of the plane being flooded in *Airport '77* and think: "Why are we here? Is this what we want to do—spend a day watching them flood a cutaway section of a fake plane?"

Having dropped "Bobbitt," our next idea came to us from the writer Jerome Kass. Jerry brought us a script about a country-western singer, and although we had reservations about the script, we took to Jerry immediately: he was a mellow, fun, smart, man. Together with Jerry, we ultimately decided not to make the country-western script, but instead, to turn *Seesaw* into a movie.

We reconceived the material as the story of a bus-and-truck tour of *Seesaw*, with Gittel and Jerry played by Bette Midler and Robert Redford. Bette would be shown auditioning to take over the role of Gittel on an already existing tour, and we'd open up the story by showing her having a very hard time even finding the tour; she would be caught in a snowstorm, cars would break down, and at one point we had her scooped up by a snow plow and dumped in a drift, her wedgie shoes dangling in the air as she lay buried under the snow. Then, when she finally caught up with the production, we would show life on the tour bus as everyone tried to teach her the show; those rehearsals on the bus would be juxtaposed with both the actual musical numbers seen during a performance of *Seesaw* and the developing friendships among the cast members. The title was not *Seesaw*, but *Roadshow*.

As we began to prepare the material, Stanley Newman, the head of publishing at Universal, became our technical guide, explaining how to deal with contracts, above-the-line costs, and shooting schedules. We held numerous conferences with the music department, and Michael attended a series of meetings with the heads of the studio, Ned Tannen and Sid Sheinberg. He went to those meetings alone and upon his return would say to me: "I think I make them very nervous." George Roy Hill, a well-known figure in the film community and a friend since the days of *Henry, Sweet Henry*, reflected on our relative lack of knowledge about the film world by telling us: "You're like two kids walking through a minefield." Michael may have been the King of Broadway, but in Hollywood he still couldn't get a parking space . . .

We were both excited about *Roadshow*. It would be a great first picture because we felt very safe with the material: we knew the story, the characters, the staging—we could make this movie and do it well. With all our ducks in a row, we hit a big roadblock: the studio said no to Bette Midler. Bette was a well-known recording and concert performer by 1977, but she had yet to make *The Rose*, so there were many questions about her viability as a film actress. The studio wanted Barbra Streisand, who was, after *The Way We Were* and *A Star is Born*, the biggest female movie star in Hollywood, not to mention a hugely successful recording artist. Michael said no to Streisand. He did not want to make the movie with Barbra because he knew he would have to play second fiddle—it would be Barbra who yielded the power on the set.

It was an incredibly frustrating turn of events; we had spent a long time developing *Roadshow*, were ready to go, and now the studio flatly said no to the star around whom the film had been shaped. (We did work with Bette for exactly one day a couple of years later when she said she wanted help with one of her concert tours. What quickly became apparent was that Bette actually wanted Michael's help in staging routines for her backup singers, the Harlettes. What she didn't want, however, was a director—she wanted the Harlettes' routines solidified and then she would bounce off their routines in whichever manner felt right to her. Bette was her own director and a great one, too.) We had now been in Hollywood for a full year and what did we have to show for it? We had dropped "Bobbit," and *Roadshow* with Bette as the star had been nixed by the studio. We were right back where we had started. Hooray for Hollywood.

What added to the sense of frustration was the fact that Michael and I both hated the reality of Hollywood. We disliked the studio politics, the drives to the studio, the traffic, the living in homes that weren't our own—it all felt wrong. Finally, Michael turned to me one day, said, "Let's go back to New York"—and we did. We wrote a sign reading "Gone Fishing," left it on our desks, and walked out the door. We expected massive repercussions and a trail of lawsuits. What we got was—nothing. We never heard from the studio again. I think Michael, in fact, scared the big boys.

Obviously, we were now never going to make the film version of *A Chorus Line*, and the property was put on hold until Universal could figure out what to do with it. Mike Nichols was attached to the property for a bit and called Michael many times with a number of questions, but he eventually dropped the property. The same thing happened with Sidney Lumet, and then in 1985, it was picked up by the Broadway producers Feuer and Martin, who developed it for Embassy Pictures, with Richard Attenborough directing. Seriously. Richard Attenborough, the director of *Gandhi*, who had never directed a musical. What's wrong with this picture? Well, almost everything.

The film was released in 1985 and flopped; I didn't rush out to see it but a month after it was released I went by myself to a Monday night showing at a small theatre in New Milford, Connecticut. It was winter—$1 per ticket—and there were about five people in the theatre. It started out OK, but after the opening number it was just all wrong. Everything was watered-down and Hollywoodized, including the happily-ever-after romance shoehorned into the Cassie-Zach relationship. The entire movie was humorless. Richard Attenborough certainly didn't feel this material in his bones. I know that Michael saw the movie at some point, but he literally never said a word about it to me; that silence constituted his review in and of itself. When all was said and done, Michael's idea for the movie remained the best: the dancers in the film would be auditioning for the film version of *A Chorus Line*. It was a great idea—and it never saw the light of day.

CHAPTER THIRTEEN

HOW DO YOU FOLLOW UP
A CHORUS LINE?

WHEN WE LEFT UNIVERSAL TO "GO FISHING," WE FELT GUILT OVER ONE thing: leaving Jerome Kass in the lurch. He was a great guy, and our walking away from *Roadshow* meant that he had lost a big opportunity. But we remembered that Jerry had also written a highly acclaimed 1975 television movie called *Queen of the Stardust Ballroom*, based on the life of his own mother. The film starred Maureen Stapleton as a widow who finds a new life dancing at the Stardust Ballroom, a dance palace where she meets and falls in love with a married man. The television movie had a few songs scattered throughout, so we decided to explore the material with an eye to developing it as a Broadway musical. This never would have happened if Michael, Jerry, and I hadn't survived the Hollywood wars together, but as it was, we felt we owed Jerry.

We were like the three musketeers at this point, and began working on the script while scheduling a series of meetings with composer Billy Goldenberg and lyricists Alan and Marilyn Bergman, who had written the score for the television movie. Alan and Marilyn had recently won an Oscar for *The Way We Were*, and were at that time the king and queen of Hollywood songwriters, while we had known Billy since he wrote the dance arrangements for *Henry, Sweet Henry*. We'd meet at the Bergmans home, where we discussed the script and suggested both song titles and the placement of the numbers throughout the script. Because the workshop process had proved to be so helpful on *A Chorus Line*, the decision was made to utilize the same format on a series of workshops, which eventually took up nearly a full year.

Our initial dream cast would have featured Beverly Sills playing the widow and Dick van Dyke as her married boyfriend; we put out feelers, but neither one showed any interest. Instead, for the first workshop we cast the former MGM musical star Dolores Gray opposite Alan Oppenheimer, who was a friend of the Bergmans. By this time, Dolores had gained a bit of weight, and when she showed up for rehearsal in stiletto heels, long manicured fingernails, and too much makeup, we realized she was not a natural choice to play a lower middle-class widow who had led a somewhat sheltered life. Dolores had a great big singing voice, which is what had attracted us in the first place, but she also carried a certain toughness with her that didn't work for the character of Bea. Rehearsals were looming, however, so we decided to go with her.

After the first workshop, we let Dolores go and asked Dorothy Loudon to audition. This was shortly after Dorothy had won a Tony Award for her hilarious, iconic portrayal of the evil Miss Hannigan in *Annie*, and she auditioned by sitting at the piano and singing saloon songs. She was genuine and definitely more relatable than Dolores. She was also, however, a prickly woman, and we had to maneuver our way around her—if she had had a couple of drinks, you wanted to get out of her way. I was assigned to be her babysitter, particularly at the Stratford, Connecticut, hotel where we had adjoining rooms during our out-of-town tryout. Since we chose not to use Alan Oppenheimer for the second workshop, Michael asked our friend Vincent Gardenia to come in and help us find the role. Even though Michael didn't necessarily intend to cast Vinnie, he felt that Vinnie's down-to-earth everyman personality would help us flesh out the character of Al Rossi, the married postman who begins a love affair with the widowed Bea Asher, played by Dorothy.

Auditions were set for the lesser roles, and during that casting process, Shirley Rich brought in an unknown actor who had just arrived in town to read for the role of Bea's son. Accompanying himself on the guitar, Mandy Patinkin sang "Over the Rainbow" and got the part. As the role grew smaller and smaller, however, he left the show for the greener pastures he soon found in *Evita*.

The most interesting casting, however, lay with the chorus, because this was going to be a chorus with a difference: the regulars at the Stardust Ballroom were to be men and women ranging in age from their forties into their seventies, and we began auditioning dancers who hadn't appeared on

Broadway for decades. Joseph Nelson, who was maintaining and casting the *Chorus Line* companies along with Baayork Lee, gathered names of former dancers to come in and audition, and after seeing hundreds of former gypsies, we successfully cast the oldest chorus in Broadway history. At which point an amazing transformation occurred over the course of the workshops: these men and women began the process as senior citizens whose glory days lay behind them, out of shape and stiff of limb, and by opening night they all appeared to be in their twenties. They were all so elated to be in the rehearsal room and dancing again. They loved performing the show, and during the Stratford tryout, they would even hang out in the lobby together after the show, thrilled to once again be part of that backstage camaraderie.

The show developed in a very hit and miss fashion in the workshops. We would push book scenes and songs in and out and constantly revise dance numbers. This was a show with a lot of dancing, and Michael assigned me a lion's share of the work. I was fortunate to have great assistants in T. Michael Reed and Drusilla Davis, because we were all kept busy from early in the morning to the end of the rehearsal day. What made *Ballroom* such a bear of a show to choreograph was that only one number was danced in unison; the rest of the numbers featured individual couples getting a chance to strut their stuff in the ballroom, which meant choreographing separate routines for every single couple in each number—seven different versions of the lindy or the waltz. It all proved to be exhausting and very time-consuming.

The script remained our biggest area of concern because we didn't know if the story was strong enough to support a big musical, but we also had problems with some of the numbers. We couldn't solve the difficulty of the opening—not many musicals began with the funeral of the leading lady's husband. An even bigger problem lay in the fundamental structure of the show: the principals did not sing many of the songs because the numbers took place inside the Stardust Ballroom, with the band singers handling most of the vocals. On the one hand, it made sense to have vocalists with the band in a ballroom setting, but on the other, they threw off the very balance of the show since the leading characters themselves were rarely given the chance to sing about their emotions.

As we started another workshop, Vincent Gardenia was still on the scene playing Al. It had not been our intention to cast Vinnie in the role, but he loved being a part of a musical and begged Michael to let him take over the role. Michael loved Vinnie and finally said yes. Because Vinnie had never done a musical before, in order to help make him feel more at home, at the end of the rehearsal day we would transform the rehearsal studio into a nightclub setting like the Stardust Ballroom itself. Out would come the tables and chairs, where Vinnie and the dancers would sit and chat just like the characters they were portraying.

By now, Michael was so preoccupied with the actual show that he couldn't focus on the myriad issues surrounding the nuts and bolts of producing the show. As a result, he wanted to bring in our lawyer John Breglio as a co-producer; John was thrilled with the idea and left his job at the esteemed law firm of Paul, Weiss to work on *Ballroom*. When Shubert Organization president Bernie Jacobs got wind of this, however, he went ballistic. Bernie and Michael had a very close relationship—Bernie was like a godfather to Michael—and Bernie felt John's role as co-producer was an unwarranted usurpation of his own position. With the head of the Shubert Organization against John's participation, and with the show set to play at the Shubert-owned Majestic Theatre, John was forced to quit. Fortunately, he was able to go back to his job at the law firm, and Bernie Gersten, who had been Joe Papp's first lieutenant at the Shakespeare Festival, came in to help us out. By the time the show opened in New York, the billing read: "Produced by Michael Bennett: Co-Producers Bob Avian, Bernard Gersten, and Susan MacNair." Sue was our associate—she held down the fort at Plum Productions and was a great combination of troubleshooter and problem-solver—while as producer, I continued to follow Michael's lead and support him in every manner possible.

After our final rehearsals in New York, we traveled out of town to Stratford, Connecticut, and the American Shakespeare Festival Theatre. That theatre had never before been used as a tryout house for a big musical, but we could rehearse in the theatre itself, the financial deal was a good one, and Stratford was close to New York City. We were working once again with our *Chorus Line* design team of Robin Wagner, Theoni V. Aldredge, and Tharon Musser, all of whom were doing their usual extraordinary job. I remember being blown away by the costume parade held during tech rehearsals in Stratford. It's not that the clothes were so opulent—this was no *Follies*—but instead, Theoni had designed clothes that were so rich in detail that they provided complete characterization all by themselves.

We opened in Stratford to mixed reviews, and the process grew bumpier. We all realized that there were problems with the book, and given that we were going to play the Shubert-owned Majestic Theatre in New York, it was no surprise that the Shuberts began advising us to bring in help. Near the end of the run in Stratford, we asked Larry Gelbart to come in and help out with the book. He began rewriting the show from start to finish, providing us with much-needed humor, but devastating Jerry Kass in the process.

We began butting heads big time with the Bergmans, and Michael became somewhat disengaged. This resulted in the splitting of the creative team into three factions: Michael and me, the Bergmans, and Jerome Kass. Relationships really broke down between Michael and the Bergmans, and although Jerry Kass retained credit for the book, it had now been half-written by Larry Gelbart. Everywhere you turned, constant tension abounded.

We had our hands full fixing the problems found onstage, and as the pressures grew, the cast, creative team, and Shuberts would come to me and ask: "How is Michael? Can we talk to him?" As happened throughout our working relationship, my job was to calm the waters that Michael had stirred up, and in this case, we had financial as well as creative turmoil. This was a big show in every way: the cast, crew, orchestra, and budget of $3.5 million were all outsized, and Michael's Plum Productions had bankrolled the entire show.

After Stratford, we went back into rehearsal in New York, and while the show still had problems, we all felt that real progress was being made. The Bergmans wrote a new opening song; gone was the downer of the funeral, and in its place Bea sang about her determination to forge a new life for herself in the upbeat "There's a Terrific Band." Everything was better, but was it enough?

We opened in New York on December 14, 1978, to very mixed reviews. Everyone seemed to like the dancing, but the very negative review in the *New York Times* really killed us. Word of the *Times* review came while we were at Windows on the World for the opening-night party, and Michael grew increasingly despondent. We were further hampered by a newspaper strike at the time when our ad campaign should have been moving into high gear, and in those pre-internet days, the lack of a print presence hurt us enormously. As it was I was also never thrilled with the logo: the colors seemed much too somber for a big splashy musical. Nothing about the show worked the way it should have.

We ran for three months, but one day as Michael and I were walking in midtown, he turned to me and said he didn't know what to do about continuing the run of the show. When he told me that the show had lost money for three consecutive weeks, I advised him to close it. It was the middle of winter, and business was not going to improve in the bad weather. There was not going to be any miraculous turnaround at the box office, and right after our conversation, the closing notice was posted backstage.

The worst part of closing the show was telling the cast, who were devastated that their dream was being cut short. The entire creative team could all go on to a next project, but for most of these onstage veterans there would be no next job, no other show on Broadway for older dancers. For all of their slightly jaded attitude—old gypsies have truly seen it all—they had all been thrilled with their unexpected return to the spotlight, and the premature closing proved devastating to them. I was equally saddened that our relationship with Jerry Kass had been permanently ruptured in the process of putting together the show, and even though we talked when we ran into each other in later years, our relationship was never the same.

In retrospect, I wish that we had cast two different leads. Dorothy and Vinnie possessed great strengths, but she was very quirky and moody, and Vinnie couldn't handle the musical portions of the show, so the balance was off. We also never solved the structural problems and consequently ended up with two shows going on at the same time: one was a play and one was a musical, with dramatic scenes in Bea's apartment plopped next to splashy production numbers taking place inside the Stardust Ballroom. These two different shows lay uneasily side by side, never fully blending together.

Three months after *Ballroom* closed, we received eight Tony nominations, including one for Best Musical. Michael and I won the Tony Award for Best Choreography, which provided us with a nice consolation prize; we had worked very hard on the show for a long time, and it was great to be recognized. But the truth is that in the best tradition of schadenfreude, Michael felt people in the industry wanted us to fail, that we had to pay for the extraordinary success of *A Chorus Line*. That certainly may have been so, and it's also true that whatever jealousy existed had been exacerbated by Michael's behavior; there was nothing subtle about his arrogance in the aftermath of the global success of *A Chorus Line*. Now, however, having bankrolled *Ballroom* entirely by himself, he was poorer to the tune of $3.5 million.

Through the years, there have been attempts to resurrect *Ballroom*: Dorothy Collins played the role in a summer stock tour, Tyne Daly starred in a workshop production, and at one point there was talk of an all-Hispanic version starring Chita Rivera. But the split structure of the piece has defeated any attempts at successfully reinventing the show, and in the almost forty years since we closed on Broadway, there has never been a major revival. *Follies* never completely worked, but that brilliant show has been revived repeatedly. *Ballroom* lives on only in memory.

And a bittersweet memory at that.

CHAPTER FOURTEEN

DREAMGIRLS

AFTER THE FAILURE OF *BALLROOM*, MICHAEL AND I WANTED TO TAKE extra care in choosing our next show, and it took about two years before we plunged into *Dreamgirls*. In the meantime, we worked on a number of interesting if never fully realized productions.

In 1980, Marvin Hamlisch approached us about his proposed musical based upon the life of the movie star Jean Seberg. After *A Chorus Line*, Marvin had scored another big success with the semi-autobiographical *They're Playing Our Song*, but that was a small, light, and frothy musical, one driven as much by Neil Simon's book as by Marvin and Carole Bayer Sager's score. Marvin wanted to work on a serious, full-scale musical again, and although we had turned him down about any involvement in the show *Smile*, since we didn't like the show's subtle slam against American values, the idea of a musical about Jean Seberg intrigued both of us.

The book was to be written by Julian Barry, a first-rate playwright who had scored a big success with the play *Lenny*. Julian was planning to make Warren Beatty a major character in *Jean* and also wanted to focus on J. Edgar Hoover, who had relentlessly pursued Seberg because of his belief that she was a genuine subversive. Any musical with those two polar opposite men among the characters was definitely going to be ambitious and full of interesting ideas.

Michael was attracted to the basic idea of the show, but I was more leery; to me the entire show had an even more overtly anti-American tone than *Smile*. The idea was to focus on how Jean Seberg had been transformed from a small-town Iowa girl into a seventeen-year-old movie star by the Otto Preminger film, *Saint Joan*, before becoming the darling of the French New Wave because of the film *Breathless*. An ardent supporter of the Black

Panthers, she was purposefully discredited by the FBI, and was found dead in a car in Paris in 1979. She had been dead for ten days without being missed.

This was all fascinating stuff, but the material did not strike me as particularly commercial. Because of Marvin's involvement, however, Michael decided to work on the show, guiding Julian Barry and lyricist Chris Adler as best he could. What became clear, however, was that even with some ingenious sections the show simply didn't hang together as a satisfying emotional experience. We had the highest regard for Marvin, but we knew this was not a show we wanted to spend years of our lives on, and we withdrew, feeling that it had a better shot in a non-profit theatre than in the overtly commercial atmosphere of Broadway. *Jean* ultimately received a major production at the National Theatre in England in December 1983, where it flopped and never came to Broadway.

Just as we hoped to work again with Marvin, we also wanted to work once more with the *Chorus Line* lyricist Ed Kleban. Ed was also interested in a second collaboration, and brought along Treva Silverman, a key writer from the hugely successful Mary Tyler Moore television show. Treva was extremely talented and a lot of fun, and we began tossing around ideas, eventually finding the beginnings of what became *Scandal*, the almost-seen-on Broadway Michael Bennett musical. Treva proved to be a wonderful collaborator, but Ed was in a dour mood at the time, and the discussions weren't coalescing into a single "that's it!" idea. We put the project on hold.

Later that year, I was walking down Broadway one day and ran into the playwright Tom Eyen. He seemed to think I was Michael because he instantly blurted out, "I have to meet with you. I have an idea for a show and you'd be perfect for it." He explained that this new musical was to center around three young African American women trying to make it big in the music business. I instantly loved the idea—the music, the glamour, it all sounded fantastic to me.

I rushed back to the office and told Michael about the idea and he coolly replied, "I was just offered the whole Motown catalogue to build a show around, so I don't know about this." I instantly replied, "This is more specific!" That was enough for Michael to set up a meeting with Tom and the show's composer, Henry Krieger, who auditioned the material for us, using Sheryl Lee Ralph, Loretta Devine, and Ramona Brooks to play the three girls. Tom began explaining the story; the show would focus on the

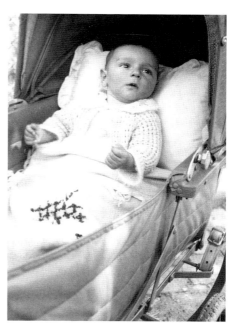

Mom and Dad—newly arrived in America. *Photograph courtesy of Laura Nabedian.*

Bobby baby. Bobby bubi. Washington Heights, New York City, six months old. *Photograph courtesy of the author.*

Starting Boston University, 1955. *Photograph courtesy of the author.*

My headshot while dancing in *West Side Story*, 1960. *Photograph courtesy of the author.*

Barbra Streisand clowning in *Funny Girl*. As an ensemble member, I had one immortal line: "You were great tonight, Fanny!" 1964. *Photograph courtesy of Photofest, Inc.*

Hello, Dolly! in Vietnam with Mary Martin. I'm fourth from the right. Soldiers had to guard the stage. *Photograph courtesy of Photofest, Inc.*

Rehearsing the "Grapes of Roth" number from *Promises, Promises*, 1968. I'm in the center, standing in for Jerry Orbach. *Photograph by Friedman-Abeles © The New York Public Library for the Performing Arts.*

Coco, 1969. Katharine Hepburn's one and only musical. Not a singer and definitely not a dancer—but an actress and star presence of the highest order. *Photograph courtesy of Photofest, Inc.*

With Michael Bennett and Hal Prince during Boston rehearsals for the groundbreaking *Company*, 1970. *Photograph courtesy of the author.*

Company's show-stopping Act Two opener, "Side by Side." *Photograph courtesy of Photofest, Inc.*

The famous "Who's That Woman" mirror number in *Follies*, 1971. *Photograph courtesy of Photofest, Inc.*

Rehearsing "One" from *A Chorus Line*, 1975. *Photo by Martha Swope © The New York Public Library for the Performing Arts.*

Michael giving notes to the original *A Chorus Line* company at the Public Theatre. *Photo by Martha Swope © The New York Public Library for the Performing Arts.*

A Chorus Line Tony winners celebrating at Sardi's. Left to right: me, James Kirkwood, Joe Papp, Donna McKechnie, Marvin Hamlisch, and Michael Bennett. *Photograph by Bob Deutsch.*

Dorothy Loudon and Vincent Gardenia in *Ballroom*, 1978. It was hard to follow the success of *A Chorus Line*. *Photo by Martha Swope © The New York Public Library for the Performing Arts.*

My favorite photo with Michael. I was thrilled to win another Tony, this time for *Ballroom*. *Photograph by Bob Deutsch.*

Having fun rehearsing *Dreamgirls* alongside Michael Bennett and Michael Peters, 1981. *Photo by Martha Swope © The New York Public Library for the Performing Arts.*

A great trip to Spain with Peter Pileski early in our relationship. *Photograph courtesy of the author.*

The fabulous Dreams in Theoni V. Aldredge's gorgeous costumes. Deborah Burrell, Sheryl Lee Ralph, and Loretta Devine. *Photo by Martha Swope © The New York Public Library for the Performing Arts.*

Dreamgirls. The confrontation leading into Tony-winning Jennifer Holliday's searing "And I Am Telling You I'm Not Going." *Photo by Martha Swope © The New York Public Library for the Performing Arts.*

Follies in London, 1987. My first show as solo choreographer. *Photograph by Michael Le Poer Trench © Cameron Mackintosh Ltd.*

With producer Cameron Mackintosh before we started work on *Miss Saigon*. *Photograph courtesy of the author.*

"The American Dream" in *Miss Saigon*, 1989. The idea for this number came to me while I was watching American television in London. *Photograph by Michael Le Poer Trench © Cameron Mackintosh Ltd.*

With friends on New Year's Eve in Connecticut, 1993. Left to right: John Weidman with Laura Weidman and Jonathan Weidman, me, Lila Coleburn, Marc Shaiman, Scott Wittman, Mia Farrow, Steve Clar, Peter Wooster, Steve Sondheim, Peter Pileski, and Jim Sacksteder. *Photograph by Patti LuPone.*

Patti LuPone in *Sunset Boulevard*, London, 1993. Nobody ever sang it better. *Photograph by Donald Cooper / © The Really Useful Group.*

With the sensational Julie Andrews, 1993. Steve Sondheim's *Putting It Together* marked her return to the New York stage. *Photograph courtesy of the author.*

Six years later, *Putting It Together* came to Broadway, this time starring Carol Burnett. *Photograph courtesy of Photofest, Inc.*

A favorite photo with Peter, taken by our close friend, the photographer Stephen G. Jennings. *Photograph courtesy of Barbara A. Callahan.*

The exciting but challenging *Martin Guerre* gave me another chance to work with Cameron Mackintosh in London. *Photograph by Michael Le Poer Trench © Cameron Mackintosh Ltd.*

Right after New York State passed marriage equality, Peter and I headed for City Hall, 2011. *Photograph by Stanley Steinberg.*

The Witches of Eastwick, 2000. I never thought I'd be choreographing a John Updike novel. *Photograph by Michael Le Poer Trench © Cameron Mackintosh Ltd.*

With my pal Baayork Lee. Friends and colleagues for over fifty years. *Photograph by Paul Kolnik.*

One of the great thrills of my life was when Peter and I met President Barack Obama. *Photograph from Democracyphoto.*

Back on Broadway with the revival of *A Chorus Line*, my directorial debut in 2006. *Photograph by Paul Kolnik.*

Contentment. *Photograph by Paul Kolnik.*

struggles the girl groups of the 1960s faced at the time of the pop music "British Invasion," as well as the problems encountered by black artists trying to cross over into the white market. The three women sang several of the songs which Henry and Tom had completed, and at the end of the audition, Michael said, "We'll produce a workshop of the material. Tom will direct and write, and we'll see how the material plays out."

Tom already had several cast members in place, specifically the three girls and Cleavant Derricks, who was playing James Thunder Early, a James Brown-type of performer. He also told us that for the purposes of the workshop he very much wanted to use a young girl named Jennifer Holliday to play the role of Effie, the soulful lead singer of the group who is pushed out in pursuit of a smoother, more pop sound. The role of Effie had actually been written with Nell Carter in mind, but after her Tony Award-winning turn in *Ain't Misbehavin'* her career was in full swing, and she wasn't available for the workshop. Jennifer was available but was very inexperienced, a kid of no more than twenty at the time. In true *A Star is Born* fashion, she had been discovered by the singer/dancer Jamie Patterson, who had heard her sing in a Texas church; one listen to Jennifer, and Jamie had contacted his friend, director/playwright Vinnette Carroll, to say, "You have to bring this girl to New York and put her into the cast of *Your Arms Too Short To Box With God*," Vinnette's gospel musical then playing on Broadway.

An offer for the workshop was extended to Jennifer, but when she first walked in, we were, to say the least, startled. She was very young, heavy, and definitely did not fit the glamorous image of a leading lady. She did, however, possess a voice that was a gift from heaven. We were interested.

Michael decided to bring in the up-and-coming choreographer Michael Peters to stage musical numbers for the workshop; Peters had recently choreographed the Broadway musical *Comin' Uptown*, a black version of Charles Dickens's *A Christmas Carol*, and although the show only lasted a month on Broadway, his work had proved stylish and provocative.

We began the workshop with Tom directing, and most of his work was quite good. It all was slow going, however, because Tom was writing as well as directing, and he was not one to sit at home, write a scene, and come in with the new material the next day. Instead, he let the actors improvise from a basic situation, feeding off their energy and attitudes as a means of inspiring him to write another scene.

Scenes were now coming and going at a fast pace as we tried to get a firm handle on the story; at this point, Ramona Brooks was playing Michelle, Effie's replacement in the Dreams, and her introductory number was "I'm the New Girl." Michael had one listen to the song, saw where the number was slotted in the first act, and said: "You can't have her come onstage singing 'I'm the New Girl—and *you're* going to be replaced' right before Effie's big number. The audience will hate her." The song was cut, leading Ramona to quit.

Jennifer was proving to be temperamental and at the end of the first workshop, when decisions were being made as to whether or not there would be another workshop, she decided to leave the show. This caused us a big problem because Jennifer's character of Effie was the most interesting one in the entire piece, and we were all in love with Jennifer's singing; she was so young yet held so much pain and emotion in her face and voice that she lifted the piece to an entirely different level when she stood front and center.

We began the second workshop with the show still known by several different titles: "Big Dreams" or "Project Number 9." Jennifer and Ramona had both quit, and Cheryl Barnes was now playing the role of Effie. She was good, and a real pro, but she didn't possess the inherent pain and soul required for Effie. Work was proceeding very slowly, and at the end of the second workshop, we realized that we hadn't progressed the way we wanted, so Michael announced, "I'm going to take over the show as director and co-choreographer." This move was actually okay with Tom Eyen because he knew how good Michael was, and realized he could now concentrate on his duties as book writer and lyricist. I was not going to choreograph the show with Michael—that job was Michael Peters's. Instead, Michael made me an above-the-title producer.

For our third workshop, Jenifer Lewis came on board to play Effie and did a very solid job. She was and remains a big talent with a tremendous sense of humor, but she could not channel Effie's pain in the same way as Jennifer Holliday. We were also still refining the book, which at that point had Effie leaving the Dreams and becoming a nurse; Estelle Getty was playing one of Effie's patients, an elderly woman given to statements like "It's not the race I don't like—it's the radios." We had a long way to go.

When it was decided that we'd hold a fourth workshop, Michael dictated that the entire workshop would concentrate only on the script; we would gather at the 890 Broadway rehearsal studios, sit around a horseshoe table, and get the script and score onto the written page. There would be absolutely no staging of scenes. It turned out to be the best decision we ever could have made.

We knew that Effie was the lynchpin of the entire show, and that we needed the stubborn, temperamental, but immensely gifted Jennifer back on the scene; Michael cajoled and flattered Jennifer, explaining how she could help make the show while at the same time the show could help make her career. Finally, she said yes.

We sat around the table, and as we developed the storyline we decided to create an entire audio track to help tell the story and propel the plot forward: voiceovers would announce the clubs the Dreams were playing, the co-opting of the black sound by white artists, and the Dreams' rise to top-of-the-charts Vegas headliners; these recordings could overlap in montage-like fashion, furthering the story with an ever increasing sense of momentum.

The show was falling into place, and at the end of the workshop, we decided to present the show to the prospective financial backers: Bernie Jacobs and Gerry Schoenfeld, the heads of the Shubert Organization, John Kluge, the head of Metromedia, and David Geffen. After the bruising experience of losing over $3 million backing *Ballroom*, Michael was leery of funding the show himself.

Another major obstacle loomed. Shortly before the end of the fourth workshop, Jennifer quit the show yet again. Unhappy with the material and with her perceived treatment, she pronounced herself through with the show. We had exactly one week to find a new Effie and prepare the show for presentation before the potential producers. We called up Alaina Reed, whom we knew could act and had a solid singing voice—and, yes, she was available. In one week, she learned the entire role for what we called our "radio" version of the show: all of the actors would be seated at a table with microphones in front of them, reading and singing the entire show as it then existed. There was to be no musical staging. It all came down to a question of "will they or won't they give us the money for the show"—and the answer came back that they would. Great news, although Michael and I did laughingly realize that we could now either quit or be fired because we were no longer in absolute control.

There was just one thing still missing: Jennifer Holliday.

No one else could sing the score like Jennifer, because no one else had that searing combination of power and pain. Michael once again pursued Jennifer and convinced her to come back to the show; when she did she was in a much better mood and proved cooperative, providing key input regarding the arrangements of her songs.

It was right around this time that I began keeping a detailed diary of the entire show, and in looking back on the daily entries I am reminded of what a tumultuous journey it was:

May 1, 1981—Michael announces he wants to be co-producer of record, but the whole deal is off because Bernie Jacobs walks out in a huff. Their father-son type of relationship was complicated.

Ultimately, as always happened, their disagreement was worked out, but there were definitely bumps along the way.

Further diary entries:

May 22, 1981—The cast has begun demanding more money.

June 17, 1981—Michael has contracted hepatitis.

June 30 1981—Squabbles have begun with David Geffen's lawyers as well as Tom Eyen's and Henry Krieger's agents about music publishing rights.

With so many powerful men and enormous egos on this show, at times it all resembled a row of dominoes: Bernie Jacobs would yell at general manager Marvin Krauss, Marvin would yell at me for getting in the middle of negotiations with hair and wardrobe—people with whom I had a personal history—and sometimes I would yell at Michael. Even after all the years I had worked with Michael, I realized that I still had to learn exactly when to approach him about problems; there couldn't be a single hint of panic when it came down to issues about money. For Michael to feel stifled over artistic decisions because of money concerns drove him crazy. Yet, even with all the stress inherent in creating a new show, Michael and I never exploded at each other. Did we get mad? Yes. But it never developed into a verbal fight, because we understood the dynamics of the show, all of the outside influences at play, and never lost sight of our decades-long friendship.

By mid-May, Michael had decided that the title of the show would be *Dreamgirls*, a one-word title that painted a complete picture in and of itself. There was much discussion, of course, about how closely the story of the Dreams resembled that of the most famous girl group of all, the Supremes. Would Motown sue? Would Diana Ross? There were similarities between the stories of the Dreams and those of the Supremes, but there were major differences as well. This show was not going to be a carbon copy of the Supremes, and in creating the show, we also deliberately drew upon elements from movies like *Love Me or Leave Me*, *A Star is Born*, and *Sparkle,* as well as from the stories of groups like the Marvelettes and Martha and the Vandellas. Our inspirations were numerous and diverse. In the end, for all the talk of similarities with the Supremes, it was really the "imagery"—the glamour and the crossover success—that provided the closest links.

Chorus casting was completed while our *Chorus Line* team of designers, Robin Wagner, Tharon Musser, and Theoni V. Aldredge, began meeting about the design scheme. Michael did not like the idea of traditional musical comedy scenery; he wanted architecture on the stage, fluid set pieces which could be quickly moved in order to suggest multiple locations. The brilliant Robin Wagner came up with the idea of six skeletal towers. Michael immediately loved the idea; he would sit in front of the tower models for hours on end, planning the show from start to finish. He wanted *Dreamgirls* to move at such a quick pace that the audience would feel like they were watching a movie, complete with wipes and dissolves. At Michael's request, Robin began designing towers with the capability of turning, a refinement which increased both the fluidity and the number of possible locations.

Theoni began designing the hundreds of decade-spanning costumes such a glamorous show would require, charting the change from home-made costumes to fashion icons. It was a tall order but she was, as usual, organized, and dramatic, endlessly receptive to collaboration. Tharon developed a lighting plot which allowed for the switch between dozens of locales in the blink of an eye. It was in fact Tharon who came up with the idea of putting lights inside of the towers, a terrific idea which in the end served as additional eye-catching glitz. Those lights inside the towers got the audience's attention and added to the visual delights, but they ultimately proved simply decorative; the constant movement of the towers meant that each time they switched positions, the lights within would lose focus, so they were never functioning lighting instruments. It didn't matter, because Tharon's dazzling design pinpointed time and space instantaneously, ultimately netting her a third Tony Award.

By now, I had fallen in love with every aspect of the show: the design, the cast, the story, and the music. A diary entry from July 1 laid it on the line: "The disappointment if the show is a failure could kill me, I believe in it so much." The only other time I had felt this strongly about a show was *A Chorus Line*.

At the start of August, Michael began working closely with Jennifer on her acting. She possessed the raw talent, but very little experience, so Michael not only explained various approaches to the role that would help—"acting is just pretending, so pretend as best you can"—but also took Jennifer to see performers like Lena Horne in her dazzling one-woman show *The Lady and Her Music*. They even worked together on "Don't Rain on My Parade" as an acting exercise.

In the midst of this frantic activity, I noted in my diary that Michael had flown over to London to take a look at *Cats* at the request of Bernie Jacobs; Bernie wanted to produce *Cats* on Broadway, but hadn't yet obtained the rights. Even in previews, *Cats* was a very hot property, and Cameron Mackintosh, who was producing the show in London along with Andrew Lloyd Webber's Really Useful Group, subsequently told me that David Merrick offered him the London rights to *42nd Street* if he would let Merrick produce *Cats* on Broadway. Bernie had seen *Cats* in previews and said: "It is terrific—it is a work of genius—but the choreography stinks." When Cameron pointed out to Bernie that the show was 95 percent choreography, Bernie's reply was "a genius show requires a genius choreographer" and asked if Cameron would meet Michael when he came to London. Michael saw the show and told Cameron, "Sure, I could do better steps but that wouldn't make it a better show. It works great as it is and making changes to it is pointless." That was the end of Michael's involvement with *Cats*.

Back on *Dreamgirls*, we began interviewing possible musical directors and immediately took to Yolanda Segovia. She had impressive credentials, having worked on *Dancin'* with Fosse, and also carried strong recommendations from both Marvin Hamlisch and music director Paul Gemignani. Michael responded well to her, and when in the course of the interview he basically built in the possibility that she could be fired if the chemistry didn't prove to be right, she took that possibility in stride. After Henry Krieger worked with her and had a positive reaction, we hired Yolanda as the show's musical director. In a position traditionally held by white males, we were very proud to have a woman conducting our show.

Through David Geffen's connections, Warner Bros. became involved in submitting various renderings for the show's possible art work. Most just didn't capture the proper tone, but by August, we found one in particular that we really liked: the legs of three women, exposed within glamorous slit dresses, with microphones held in hand. It gave us the entire glamorous show business setting in one fell swoop.

When we officially begin full company rehearsals on August 24, 1981, Michael was fully prepared and greeted everyone, making all of the appropriate introductions. He proved funny, charming, and managed to relax everyone—he was the true captain of the ship.

As the full company rehearsals began in earnest, Michael began working in a new way; he rough-blocked musical numbers while concentrating on pulling out the essence of the book within those numbers. As a result, right from the start the book beats were very strong in the numbers. You could already tell that, high glitz and all, this show possessed the potential to be a musical of substance. One of the most impressive aspects of the rehearsal period was the camaraderie in the room. It was not about race but about the talent. There was mutual respect all around.

Jennifer was always on the verge of being difficult; it seemed to be a form of self-protection for her, and I was constantly building her up, hoping to encourage her. Her talent was so deep and so extraordinary that I felt this show could make her a true star. She was vulnerable, tough, ambitious, smart, and touched by the gods musically. She was untrained technically and felt her lack of acting experience keenly, telling me that she was merely parroting what Michael told her to do. I explained that it was okay—that it didn't matter how she got there, as long as she made it in the end. There was something endearing about her insecurity, but at the same time she was very career-oriented; well aware of all the talented people who had screwed up their careers with dumb decisions, she was determined not to join their ranks.

Even though I was not choreographing the show with Michael, I helped build many of the numbers with the two Michaels, and the three of us would play the Dreams while creating the staging. Michael Peters was incredibly talented and loads of fun to be with; when Michael Bennett would become tense and short tempered, Michael Peters and I could joke and laugh with each other in order to ease the tension. He knew the 1960s and '70s style of choreography inside out, the steps welling out of his memory bank with great ease. He would give the cast steps for the numbers and Michael Bennett would then give the numbers an epic feel, guiding Michael Peters and enhancing his work.

This show was growing bigger and bigger by the day, and I remember Jeff Hamlin, our terrific production stage manager, informing me that between cast, orchestra and crew, there would be 105 people backstage!

At the beginning of October, we began run-throughs for the wardrobe, music, and hair departments, as well as for Bernie and Betty Jacobs, Gerry Schoenfeld, and David Geffen. We felt nervous—would the "money" like the show enough so that they stayed off our backs? As it turned out, they loved the show and seemed more than happy—excited even—but we were not all that ecstatic; the emotional beats were right but the "thrills" and excitement were missing. The play itself worked, but we what we needed now were concrete improvements in the craft. By this time, I was so emotionally invested in the show—after all those months; those years!—that as we headed to Boston for our tryout, I was downright scared. Reality had set in because the public would soon pass judgment.

When we first saw the set onstage at the Shubert Theatre, we all had the same reaction: gorgeous. It's always a huge and exciting leap from the bare-bones rehearsal studio to a multi-million dollar set onstage, and we were all thrilled. This beautiful but complicated set caused the technical rehearsals to proceed very slowly, and with such an intricate set filled with constantly moving pieces, Tharon had to work at a glacial pace. The biggest problem, however, lay with the sound department. Otts Munderloh, our designer, was very good, but the orchestra was playing so loudly that we were missing all the dynamics in Harold Wheeler's terrific orchestrations, and the actors were ending up in competition with the orchestra.

As the tech rehearsals continued into a second week, we got to see the full range of Theoni's clothes, which were staggering. She had really outdone herself with gowns that defined character all on their own. The show was looking great, but as we headed towards the start of previews, disaster struck: Jennifer lost her voice. Michael turned to me and said, "Go backstage and take care of her." I walked through the pass door, and found a very distraught Jennifer, head in hands, plaintively saying, "If I don't have my voice I have nothing." I tried to console her, saying, "You'll get it back. Just rest. We'll put the cover on until you're back at full strength." (In the end the understudy, Sheila Ellis, played the dress rehearsal and we canceled the first two previews, by which point, fortunately, Jennifer was ready to return.)

We knew that people in the business, including Cameron Mackintosh, wanted a first look at the new Michael Bennett musical, and there is nothing more frightening than preparing for a first preview: after all the years of preparation, you are in effect about to send your child out into the world. The curtain went up and it felt like "Gone With the Dreams"—three hours of beaded gowns. But, in spite of the show lasting forever, the audience at the end stood to scream their approval. At the time, standing ovations were only just becoming a pro forma means by which people stand in order to assure themselves that the money they've spent was worthwhile. This standing ovation, however, really meant something, because in the fall of 1981, Boston was still a very white separatist theatregoing town: if the show worked in Boston, we felt very confident about its chances in New York.

As previews continued, our big problem became one of where to cut. In its totality, the show worked, but many of the individual pieces were proving less than stellar when evaluated on their own merits. We began by fixing the problematic second act and cleaning out the dead weight.

Working with Harold Wheeler, we put in numerous small musical fixes that helped us condense the material. Elongated intros and transitions were cut back—a minute here, a minute there—and it all started to add up to a cleaner, more emotionally satisfying evening. Audiences now loved the show even more, and it was clear that Jennifer was becoming a "star." October 24, 1981, opening-night diary entry: "The two big Boston reviews from Kevin Kelly and Elliot Norton are raves."

We were all riding high and I remember not getting to bed until 6 a.m. We awoke to additional great reviews, but the show quickly assumed secondary status when I found out that same morning that my father had died. He was eighty-four years old and had simply said to my mother: "I'm tired. I'm going to bed early." He never woke up. I left Boston for three days to go home for the funeral. I was, of course, most concerned about my mother, but she seemed to be coping as well as could be expected. My parents were good people, immigrants who spoke accented English for their entire lives and who didn't know what Broadway theatre really meant. In fact, the only time they went to the theatre was when I was involved with a show, but they were very proud of what I had been able to accomplish. I knew I would miss my father, a good and quiet man who fortunately had lived long enough to witness his son's success.

There was a lot going on during our tryout; while we were putting the show on its feet the tour of *A Chorus Line* came to town and fortunately received rave reviews, but it was *Dreamgirls* that proved to be the talk of the town. By the end of our run in Boston, we were selling out every performance, breaking the house record with a gross of $326,000. As the word drifted back to New York, our advance began growing, but we continued to make refinements in the script, cutting extraneous dialogue, and adding connective music between scenes. Julian Barry, with whom we had been working on *Jean*, came to see the show; his critique proved helpful, most substantially when he noted that the girls needed to be the focus of the through-line in act one, not Curtis, their manager/Svengali.

By the time we finished our arduous technical rehearsals at the Imperial, we felt cautiously optimistic. More to the point, however, we now felt that we had finally fixed the ending of the show: originally the character of Effie had not been a part of the final scene, but everyone kept telling us that Effie had to be there, that her presence would bring the show full circle and give the audience a sense of closure. Our solution was to have all four of the Dreams—Effie, Deena, Lorrell, and Michelle—sing the song "Dreamgirls" in close harmony, with Effie dressed in black and the Dreams all in white. That fix had been right in front of us the whole time, but it took us a while to arrive there. Of course, that ending may not have represented how it all would have played out in real life, but it was right for the show. The new ending helped cement Jen as the star of the piece, and while it didn't help smooth relations between Jen and Sheryl, the necessity of that reconciliation lay right there in the structure of the piece: Effie is the character around whom all the others pivot.

Our first preview in New York came on December 9, 1981, and all the "professional bitches," as Sondheim calls them, were out in force as they often are at first previews. I was scared to death. This wasn't the same as *A Chorus Line*, where it seemed that from the first preview on we could do no wrong; here there was an element of uncertainty as to how the show would be received. We hoped we had presented black music and culture in the 1960s with both realism and love, but how was the tough New York audience going to respond?

They loved it. Oh, the relief. Word of mouth on the street was great, and the lines at the box office grew daily. The show was frozen on December 15, and when Tom Eyen handed in two pages of book and lyric fixes the next day, it was simply too late. Critics were about to begin attending performances.

On December 19, the day before opening, we received a rave review from John Heilpern of the *London Times*: "Thrusts the American musical theatre into a new age"; "genius." This was obviously a very welcome reception, and the show played really well on opening night. The performance was followed by a glamorous black-tie party fit for a smash hit, but when we headed to the ad agency to listen to the television reviews, our spirits plummeted. Both of the television critics disliked the show, and when we went back to the party we received word that Clive Barnes in the *New York Post* and Douglas Watt in the *Daily News* were dismissive in their assessments.

Michael and I both felt very despondent, until we received word that Frank Rich in the *New York Times* had written a love letter to the show. The first sentence told us we were safe: "When Broadway history is being made, you can feel it." Filled with praise for Michael's work, the critic laid it on the line in the most glowing possible terms: "Mr. Bennett has long been Mr. Robbins's Broadway heir apparent, as he has demonstrated in two previous Gypsy-like backstage musicals, 'Follies' (which he staged with Harold Prince) and 'A Chorus Line.' But last night the torch was passed, firmly, unquestionably, once and for all." When Rich's review was combined with the rave we had received from John Heilpern in the *London Times*, as well as the positive notices in a number of out-of-town papers, it more than made up for the number of secondary reviews that seemed to dismiss the material with little reference to Michael's dazzling production. There were lines at the box office throughout the next day, and Jennifer was now the newest star on Broadway. New Yorkers may try to affect a blasé attitude about established stars, but they love to anoint a new star, and Jennifer was the dreamgirl of the moment.

But it wasn't just about Jennifer—the entire cast was extraordinary, thanks in large part to librettist Tom Eyen and composer Henry Krieger, who were responsible for bringing in many of the leads. Sheryl Lee Ralph, who has brains, beauty, and talent to match, was our other leading lady. Although she and Michael never became friends, she knew how to handle him, and their occasional conflicts provided a show in themselves. It was a shame that she and Jennifer were never pals, but it was in the nature of the show that these two women would be in conflict.

Sheryl turned in a sleek, stunning performance as Deena Jones and richly deserved her Tony nomination as Best Actress in a Musical. Loretta Devine, who played Lorrell, is a unique talent who never failed to surprise us with her spot-on choices as an actress and singer. She soon went to Hollywood and has worked constantly in the movie and television industries ever since, proving herself to be a dynamic, varied performer.

Ben Harney, who played the Dreams' hard-driving business manager Curtis, was an earnestly religious man with one of the most beautiful voices I've ever heard. Something I never understood was Michael's habit of giving him a really hard time regarding his performance. But Ben remained stoic and centered and a soothing presence to all of us. He won the Tony for Best Leading Actor in a Musical and is now minister of his own church, having left show business. Cleavant Derricks was a blazing performer with an energy and acting technique that jumped off the stage and made you sit up in your seat. And what a voice! He so deservedly won the Best Featured Actor in a Musical Tony Award, and always spread such a life-affirming energy in the theatre. He was a great presence backstage, as were Deborah Burrell, Vondie Curtis-Hall, and the rest of the company, all of whom made us feel truly blessed to be a part of the newest hit show in town.

Though we were the new hit, there were pain and disappointment mixed in because the negative reviews took so little note of Michael's incredible work. But the bottom line was that Michael has delivered another smash hit and confirmed his status as a true auteur of the American musical theatre, the leading director/choreographer of his generation.

After opening, the next big step lay in recording the cast album, which would, of course, be released on Geffen Records. But, instead of the usual process, in which the entire score is recorded in one feverish day right after opening, David wanted to make a true pop album, a painstakingly compiled track-by-track recording produced over the course of eight weeks. The orchestra would be recorded first, and then over the next eight weeks, the artists would come in and record the vocal tracks. To make the deal even sweeter, David recruited David Foster, the multi-Grammy Award-winning, top-of-the-line producer, to oversee the recording.

Because of the multilayered approach, only forty-four minutes of the score would be recorded, but those forty-four minutes would have the polish of a full-scale pop recording. In those pre-compact disc days, this approach meant deleting several extended musical sequences like the recitative breakup of the Dreams ("It's All Over"), but David Geffen sensed that unlike most cast recordings, which appeal only to the niche audience of show tune lovers, this score had the potential to reach a pop music audience. He was right. The album shot into the top ten on the charts, won Jennifer a Grammy in the process, and years later, the cut sequences were restored for the twenty-fifth-anniversary CD rerelease of the recording.

As we settled into a sold-out run, during the spring of 1982 we began hearing a lot about Tommy Tune's new musical, *Nine*. How could we not hear? Tommy's show was in production at the Forty-sixth Street Theatre, and that theatre's stage door was positioned right next door to ours. Michael and I were still friendly with Tommy, but the press pounced on a "rivalry" between the shows, playing up a competition not only between the shows but also between Tommy and Michael, as well as the shows' respective theatre owners/ producers—the Shubert Organization versus the Nederlander Organization. Although a lot has been written about this supposed rivalry, in truth the competition was more between the casts than the creative teams.

I went to a see a preview of *Nine* and thought Tommy's work was extraordinary—smart, chic, elegant, and visually stunning. It was a beautiful, unique production with some fine music, but at the same time I wondered about the show's durability and its appeal to the mainstream tourist. I felt that New Yorkers would love it, but what about out-of-towners? In fact, *Nine* opened as the last show of the season, riding its momentum as the underdog favorite straight through to the Tony Awards: *Dreamgirls* actually won six Tonys to *Nine*'s five, and the two Michaels shared the Tony Award for Best Choreography, but Tommy was chosen as Best Director, and more to the point, *Nine* won the Tony for Best Musical over *Dreamgirls*. Americans love an underdog, and there was a feeling that a win for *Nine* would bring Michael down a peg or two.

I think that *Dreamgirls* succeeds because it tackles the big subjects of race, corruption, and the American dream, yet does so within the framework of a glamorous, all-stops-out Broadway musical. As a result, I remain convinced that *Dreamgirls* is a stronger show than *Nine*, and in fact it did run nearly twice as long on Broadway. In the end, the *Nine/Dreamgirls* controversy can really be boiled down to the fact that the press always needs a rivalry, especially between a big show and a smaller, more idiosyncratic one. That same rivalry was played out through the media in the years when *Avenue Q* faced off with *Wicked*, and *Fun Home* with *An American in Paris*. In all three cases, the quirky underdog won the Tony Award for Best Musical. As the refrain heard throughout *Dreamgirls* puts it: "Show biz. It's just show biz."

With the show settling in for an extended run on Broadway, we turned our attention to the road company, which would start in Los Angeles at the Shubert Theatre. Jennifer would be headlining the otherwise entirely new cast. We made changes for this production, most notably a new opening to Act Two featuring the Effie-less Dreams performing a slick, smooth medley of their hits in Las Vegas. The second act now got off to a much quicker start, and with a big production number to boot. The other substantial change we instituted for Los Angeles came at the end of Act Two, when we costumed cast members to look like part of the orchestra, placing them with instruments behind the upstage scrim; it really looked like there was now a full-scale orchestra onstage.

One real difficulty with instituting these changes was that Michael Peters was absent from many of the rehearsals; he was shooting and choreographing Michael Jackson's "Thriller" at the time, so was unavailable for any of the fine-tuning he would normally have provided. We were, however, very happy with the changes, and the opening night in Los Angeles proved to be a very big glamorous affair, complete with Michael Jackson himself. And it wasn't just Michael Jackson who showed up—the theatre was filled with movie stars and numerous high-profile friends of David Geffen.

The show received sensational reviews, the box office got off to a solid start—but then Jennifer started missing performances. A lot of performances. The audience heard about her absences, and uncertain as to whether they would actually get to see the new star they were hearing so much about, stopped buying tickets. As a result, the show closed much earlier in Los Angeles than it should have.

The tour moved to San Francisco, where Jennifer was replaced by Lillias White. This was actually a cast change which had been planned all along because Jennifer had signed on for Los Angeles but nothing further. Lillias did a wonderful job and could certainly sing the score, but because of the show's complicated technical elements, it was proving too costly to move the show from city to city; the next move from San Francisco to Chicago cost $1 million in 1982 money. The show received brilliant reviews in Chicago, but at the time people were very hesitant about venturing into downtown Chicago at night, and we closed after only six weeks. That tour shut down permanently, but the show did return in a bus-and-truck version, which cut costs drastically by having the actors push the non-motorized towers around the stage. We called these new non-motorized towers "the refrigerators": short but wide. Without the huge overhead, the bus-and-truck production did very well and enjoyed a lengthy national tour.

We put the Los Angeles changes into the still-running New York production, and the resulting improvement in the show was worth the effort; fans of the show returning for a second or third viewing were pleasantly surprised to see brand-new material, and word spread that *Dreamgirls* was more than worth another visit. The show eventually ran for nearly four full years, not closing until August of 1985.

There had been a great deal of talk throughout the years about filming *Dreamgirls,* but the movie did not become a reality until Bill Condon stated that if he could direct any movie at all it would be *Dreamgirls*; with that pronouncement the movie was greenlit, quickly went into production, and was afforded a major studio release in December of 2006. I was not involved with the film but did meet with Bill to discuss the show. It was clear that he knew and loved the material, and would lavish great time and attention on the property.

I waited a bit to see the film, but several weeks after it was released I did. The movie had received a number of highly favorable reviews and there was a good-sized crowd present, but I found myself responding in a very mixed fashion. The filmmakers had made the conscious decision to take out the recitative which had started the show and established the musical vocabulary of the piece. As a result, the first songs, which are all set onstage or backstage, registered as they should—these were singers performing in their natural milieu and the audience accepted the style. But, when it came time for "We Are Family," the number in which the principals reassure Effie after she has been demoted from her position as lead singer, the characters were suddenly singing directly to each other, and it felt false; the style of the film had shifted and we weren't ready for it.

I thought the cast was good: Beyonce did a solid job as Deena, Jennifer Hudson, who eventually won a Best Supporting Actress Oscar as Effie, sang very well, and Eddie Murphy was first-rate as James Thunder Early. But in the end, I felt the movie captured the show-biz pizazz without ever touching me emotionally. I did receive a nice credit on screen as an original producer of the show, but the movie wasn't mine. Or Michael's. It helped spread the material I loved around the world, but it's the original Broadway production that lives on in my heart.

CHAPTER FIFTEEN

RECORD-BREAKERS, MIGHT-HAVE-BEENS, AND A MARRIAGE

EARLY IN 1983, MICHAEL AND I BEGAN TALKING ABOUT THE FACT THAT in September of that year—September 29, to be exact—*A Chorus Line* would be setting a record as the longest-running show in Broadway history. Michael wanted to mark the occasion with a special performance, and when he spoke about his ideas to Joe Papp, Joe immediately responded: "Whatever you want to do is fine with me."

Michael's overriding thought: anyone who had ever performed in one of the first-class companies of *Chorus Line* could be in the show for the record-breaking performance. Word went out through the Broadway grapevine, and hundreds of dancers responded that they wanted to participate. Michael began laying plans, and I think this was the time when his genius was at its absolute peak. I'd never seen him so intense and so singularly focused as he was in the one week of rehearsal for that special performance. I knew it would be a thrilling night, but it entailed so much work in such a compressed period of time that just handling Michael's intensity was a full-time job in and of itself.

Michael decided that he wanted projections to run above the stage—the evening would start with the words "Current Broadway Cast" written in bold relief above the proscenium as the current cast performed the opening number of "I Hope I Get It." During the blackout at the end of the number, the casts would switch and the projection would now read: "Original Broadway Cast." This would be followed by numbers performed by "The First National Tour" and "The London Company."

These ideas were exciting on their own, but Michael deliberately picked up the pace with "Dance 10, Looks 3," which would be performed by no fewer than three women playing "Val." Building upon the multiple actor approach, Michael decided that Cassie's dance to "Music and the Mirror" would be performed by seven actresses, and Paul's monologue about performing in drag would start with one actor, who would be joined by another, and then another, until there would be ten different Pauls. The "What are you going to do when you can't dance anymore" scene would be performed by members of the international companies so that the material could be heard in Japanese, German, Dutch, and Spanish. The performance would build and build in this manner until the finale, when over 300 dancers would fill the stage, the aisles, the mezzanine, and the balcony, kicking in unison in their gold, top-hatted costumes—an image exciting, thrilling, and even a little bit scary at the same time. By the time of the final bows, every single dancer would be onstage, which meant that the stage of the Shubert Theatre had to be reinforced in order to bear the weight of 300 dancers.

These were truly exciting ideas, but we had only a one-week rehearsal at 890 Broadway in which to blend all of these performers into cohesive units, so the pressure was high from the very first moment of rehearsal. Some of the original cast members had a hard time sharing what they had come to think of as "their" material with other actors, and one dancer walked out, never to return, but most everyone else was thrilled to be part of this historic occasion.

When September 29 arrived, a tent was erected over Shubert Alley, with drinks and food served to the invited guests. NBC television wanted to shoot the finale live, and the coverage in print, radio, and television was extraordinary—*A Chorus Line* was saturating the airwaves just as it had when opening eight years earlier.

For me, the best part of the evening was the camaraderie which pervaded the entire undertaking, with the Booth Theatre (which is next door to the Shubert) functioning as a giant dressing room for the hundreds of dancers involved. We set up very long tables on the stage of the Booth, one table after another, where everyone sat and put on their makeup while changing into the costumes. A closed-circuit television screen showed what was going on next door at the Shubert, and all of the dancers cheered loudly after every bit of dialogue and dance. For that one special night, we really were one big family, and by the time of the high-kicking "One" finale, the cheers which filled the theatre were deafening—the noise and exhilaration seemed to last forever.

As of this writing, six shows have now broken the *Chorus Line* record as the longest-running show in history: *The Phantom of the Opera*, the revival of *Chicago*, *The Lion King*, *Cats*, *Les Miserables*, and *Wicked*—but that fact has not diminished one bit of the pleasure we experienced from that one-of-a-kind evening.

In that same year, Michael and I resumed work with Treva Silverman on the material we had first looked at a few years back. Ed Kleban had dropped out by this time, but Treva began writing a script and Michael asked Jimmy Webb to begin work on a score. Jimmy had made it big a decade earlier with "MacArthur Park" and "Wichita Lineman" and seemed the right guy for the show. After casting Swoosie Kurtz, Treat Williams, Fisher Stevens, and Victor Garber, we had the leads in a show we were now calling *Scandal*, a musical exploration of a woman's sexual experimentation. Michael scheduled a workshop where we began staging five big musical sequences. It was a major undertaking, so we were very fortunate to have Jerry Mitchell, Jodi Moccia, and Danny Herman assisting us.

We spent quite a bit of time choreographing the huge opening number, in which Swoosie's character finds out that her boyfriend, played by Treat, is cheating on her. It was an elaborate sequence, lasting between ten and fifteen minutes, and was so complicated that we actually had a turntable installed in the rehearsal studio.

Michael was doing extraordinary work, and the material proved to be really provocative; one scene was set in the Swiss Alps with the startling (for 1983) exploration of the lead's bisexuality, while a ballet featured Botticelli-like angels descending from the ceiling in nude leotards. He was continuing to stretch his talent, but we ran into problems when the collaboration between Treva and Jimmy failed to catch fire. Treva would write a terrific speech, Jimmy would say, "We can turn that into a great song," and Treva would balk; she felt those were her words, not fodder for musical numbers. We kept plugging away through multiple workshops, during which Michael and Treva developed a relationship I can best describe as love/hate: back and forth they went between admiration/respect and outright dislike/frustration.

We had progressed far enough that an advertising tagline was even developed: "A *Scandal* is coming to Broadway," and at the end of the fourth workshop we took stock. I thought we had some terrific dance sequences but that the score was not where it should be. Michael, then immersed in trying to buy the Mark Hellinger Theatre, where *Scandal* would have played, assessed the state of the script and score and announced: "We don't have a show. I can't proceed."

This was all unfolding in 1984, at the same time that we were working on another show with Jimmy Webb entitled *Children's Crusade*. Jimmy was actually better suited for that show, and he began composing a rock score which fit the material quite well. John Heilpern was writing the script, and the plan called for the show to be performed in arenas with an enormous cast and physical production. It was going to be an immense undertaking, featuring pirate ships and a sequence in which the children crossed the Alps. Jimmy composed some very good songs but the show ended up on the back-burner because the focus was falling more squarely on *Scandal*. It's a fascinating "what if" kind of show, but in today's political climate, it's impossible to even think of creating a show featuring children trying to convert Muslims to Christianity.

Another provocative "might-have-been" came in 1985 when Michael became very interested in turning the Doris Day/James Cagney musical *Love Me or Leave Me* into a stage musical starring Ann-Margret. Michael loved the movie, which featured a terrific and atypically tough performance by Doris Day, and he envisioned a rough-edged musical that would, like the movie, center around the compromises singer Ruth Etting makes in order to advance her career, most notably selling herself to gangster Marty "The Gimp" Snyder. Michael wanted Marvin Hamlisch to write original songs, which would function as a counter-score to the period standards like "You Made Me Love You" and "10 Cents a Dance." The biggest production number in the movie featured Irving Berlin's "Shaking the Blues Away," so it was a fun moment when Berlin himself called Michael to bark: "Hey, you're the guy that did that show *Chorus Girl*?" Michael dryly replied, "That's me," before continuing, "I'm considering doing *Love Me or Leave Me* as a stage musical and your songs . . ." Michael got no further before Berlin interrupted with a clipped: "Use what you want."

Michael's plan was to co-star Mandy Patinkin with Ann-Margret, but she had just completed the television movie version of *A Streetcar Named Desire*, in which she had given a first-rate performance as Blanche Du-Bois, and nice as she was, she kept talking about how tired she was. Her participation involved making her husband Roger Smith a co-producer, and for Roger, the entire show was about Ann-Margret. I pointed out to him that if he were a producer and the show proved to be successful, it would also be about all the other women who would star in tours and international production, but at this point they seemed to lose interest. Somehow all of these reasons added up to the show falling apart. Michael was preoccupied with *Scandal* and, to a lesser degree, *Children's Crusade,* and *Love Me or Leave Me* quietly faded away.

When none of these shows went into production, a certain amount of professional frustration ensued, but in 1985, I became very happily settled in my personal life with Peter Pileski. Peter and I had actually met years earlier at a cocktail party given by mutual pals while *Ballroom* was running. Peter had recently moved from Boston and was pursuing an acting career, having trained at Boston University and the Actor's Workshop of Boston. He soon realized, however, that the endless auditioning game was not for him, and while studying with the master teacher Herbert Berghof at HB Studio found that his calling was in directing. We had lots in common, and I found him to be whip-smart, talented, and with a wicked sense of humor. More importantly, we each shared a deep connection with our families and had the same, solid work ethic.

I asked him out and we began dating. The problem was that we were both "gun shy"; having come out of difficult relationships, we were each hesitant to seriously commit. We would date, then cool off, begin dating again and cool off again. Finally, in 1985, we both realized that something felt very right in this six-year "engagement" and decided to take the commitment plunge. Peter was also feeling a professional security as he segued from working in off-off-Broadway productions and showcases to producing and directing television. He'd go on to have a great career of more than twenty years at USA Network and the Sci-Fi Channel, yet still kept his foot in the theatre, often working with me. When marriage equality was passed in New York State in 2011, we didn't hesitate to take the legal plunge. We are so fortunate to be each other's best friend and constantly remind one another of that fact.

One amusing anecdote regarding our relationship and Michael Bennett: Peter knew Michael for about two years before Michael's untimely death in 1987, and they got along very well. Peter, who has great instincts, also knew when to defer to Michael. But when I announced to Michael that Peter and I were committing to each other, he gently said, "Peter's a terrific and smart guy. So he, of course, understands that I'm *really* your lover, right?" That was Michael all over.

Just before Peter and I officially became a couple, and while Michael and I were working on both *Scandal* and *Children's Crusade*, Michael's plan to buy the Mark Hellinger had put him at odds with Bernie Jacobs. Their relationship was very much one of father-son, and Bernie in fact had pictures of Michael throughout his home. I think Bernie saw Michael as an ambitious, important, high-achieving near-son, but both men were used to total control and it was inevitable that they would clash at times.

Bernie certainly held the highest respect for Michael, and along with producer Judy Craymer, lyricist Tim Rice, and the ABBA composers Benny Andersson and Bjorn Ulvaeus, asked Michael to direct and choreograph a musical based upon *Chess*, a concept album that the ABBA boys had developed with Tim Rice. The album was about a high-stakes international chess match and love triangle—it was all reminiscent of Bobby Fischer and Boris Spassky, with the chess competition as metaphor for Cold War hostilities. Michael thought the material was strong enough to warrant a full-scale production, and that taking on the show would be a good way to patch up his frayed relationship with Bernie.

Michael really saw the story as a variation on the plot of *Casablanca*: here, the two men (one is Russian and one American) are in love with the same woman, who manages one of the players but falls in love with the other. The problem lay in the fact that the creative team did not fully share his vision. Tim Rice looked at the show in different terms than Michael, and Bjorn sided with Tim. Benny Andersson, on the other hand, held an outlook similar to Michael's. The collaboration went forward, with meetings held in both New York and London, but it proceeded in fits and starts and proved to be a frustrating experience; Benny, a man of great talent, was very collegial and collaborative with me, while Tim and Bjorn treated me as if I were invisible.

Michael asked Robin Wagner to design the show, explaining that he envisioned the show taking place on a giant chessboard that could revolve and tilt at different angles. In those pre-CGI days, he talked of utilizing a great deal of video footage, with real onstage cameras broadcasting the videos onto giant screens. We held auditions in London, and a detailed production schedule was set up.

But when Michael and I flew home on Christmas break, Michael found a lesion on his foot and realized that he had Kaposi's sarcoma—a cancer associated with AIDS. He told me, and we both broke down in tears. Faced with this devastating news, he quickly pulled out of the show. In those early days of the AIDS epidemic, ignorance was rampant, and there was such a social stigma that Michael chose to keep the news private. He did share the news with John Breglio and Bernie Jacobs, and it was decided to say that Michael was withdrawing from *Chess* because of heart problems.

Trevor Nunn was asked to take over the show and although he said yes, he did not want to utilize Michael's design concept. The problem was that the show was already underway—those gargantuan musicals take on a life and speed of their own—and when the show opened in 1986, Trevor ended up with a production that was a compromise, neither fully his vision nor Michael's. Although it ran in London for three years, it never turned into a really big hit, and when the show came to Broadway in 1988, Trevor started from scratch with his own design concept, which utilized stagehands, inside onstage towers, who moved the pieces around the set. The show ran for only two months; even with all of that terrific music, including great pop songs like "I Know Him So Well" and "One Night in Bangkok," something about the show never did fully hang together, primarily, I feel, due to problems with the book.

Once Michael withdrew from the show in London, I had nothing further to do with it, and spent my time trying to support Michael as he dealt with his illness. He immediately began trying to gather information about the disease, but it was 1985 and everything was undertaken in the atmosphere of secrecy and mistrust that pervaded the treatment of this plague. People were hysterical, and there was such ignorance and intolerance that people literally did not want to touch anyone who had contracted the virus. Thank the gods that activists like Larry Kramer and organizations like Gay Men's Health Crisis (GMHC) and ACT UP led the fight to call attention to AIDS and educate the public and the government.

We began traveling all around the country to search out different doctors who spoke of potential life-saving treatments. We spent hours sitting in hotel rooms waiting for phone calls to confirm appointments which held no good news. One of those trips took us to Minneapolis to meet with a doctor who was experimenting with blood transfusions, and when the doctor said, "I need donations in order to pursue my work," Michael gave him a substantial amount of money—but there was no solution to be had. We also went to a cancer hospital in Houston, where we met with the head of infectious diseases who bluntly stated, "We have no cures. We simply don't yet have answers." It was a devastating time.

Experiments with AZT were just starting at the National Institutes of Health in Bethesda, Maryland, and Michael took part in a trial. It was a heartbreaking scene: a floor full of young men, all at different stages of the testing process, all dying of AIDS. Patients participating in the trial did not know if they were receiving a placebo or the actual drug, but when Michael was released to his home in East Hampton he began feeling better. We actually shared a few weeks of optimism that maybe he was responding to AZT, but he started to decline again, developing breathing problems and feeling progressively sicker.

While at the NIH, Michael had become friendly with a nurse who told him about a doctor in Tucson, Arizona, then investigating new treatments. Could he get himself to Tucson? He booked a flight, but his breathing issues grew so severe on the flight that an ambulance had to pick him up when he arrived. By now, he was so weak that he could not leave Tucson, so he set up a team of friends to help him at his rented home. Bob Herr, our secretary from the offices at 890 Broadway, stayed to help out with all of the details regarding his medical care, and Gene Pruitt, a close friend of Michael's, stayed with him as well. While Michael settled in Tucson, I split my time between New York and my home in Kent, Connecticut, checking in on *A Chorus Line* and visiting the road tour of *Dreamgirls*. Everywhere I went I was asked about Michael's health, and to every last person I simply lied, saying that Michael was having heart problems. That was the story he wanted disseminated and I wanted to fulfill my best friend's request.

It was at this time that I was asked to choreograph the upcoming London production of *Follies*. *Follies* had never had a major West End production, but by the mid 1980s, Cameron Mackintosh, who had started his extraordinary run of success as producer of *Cats*, *Les Miz*, and *Phantom*, was looking for another show to challenge and excite him, and he thought the time was ripe for a London production of *Follies*. He asked me to choreograph the show—and I instantly said no.

Cameron persisted. Steve Sondheim called. I knew they wanted someone who could recreate the showstopping "Who's That Woman" number—after all, Sondheim himself had called it (along with the opening of *Company*) the best number he'd ever seen in a Broadway musical. I said I wasn't interested in revisiting the same show. We had delivered a glorious show back in 1971, but it had failed at the box office and that memory remained very painful.

Besides, Michael was failing, and my head was just not in a place to think about work. I flew back to Tucson once more to see my friend. It was devastating—he looked so weak, so thin, and old. He was still smoking his Marlboros, but all of his volcanic energy had vanished. I mentioned the London *Follies* to him; I could tell he didn't want to talk about it because he was completely preoccupied with his health, as anyone would have been. But, he looked at me and said: "Do the show. You know it. It's time you went out on your own."

I flew back to New York but I was torn, ambivalent about choreographing a show about ambivalence. How could we possibly capture the magic of that show again? I was worried about Michael and thought a year off would do me good. I had been working nonstop: *Dreamgirls* had opened in 1981, and between the Broadway run, the national tour, and the continuous checking in on *A Chorus Line*, I had been on an unending treadmill. With Michael failing, it all seemed a bit overwhelming, but when Peter said, "Michael is giving you a final gift—accept it," and Cameron and Steve phoned again, I said, "Okay, I'll do it." I had followed Michael's typically emphatic advice—"Make sure they pay you what you're worth"—and had my friend and lawyer, John Breglio, negotiate a generous contract. The deal was sealed, a fact which promptly made me nervous because now I had to deliver.

Off to London I flew.

CHAPTER SIXTEEN

OUT ON MY OWN

I WAS IN THE CAR HEADING TO THE AIRPORT WHEN THE NEWS OF THE Challenger disaster came on the radio. It was so tragic, so awful, and I thought to myself, "Is this an omen?" The world seemed upside down, which is why it was such a relief to arrive in London, start meetings with Cameron and director Mike Ockrent, and find an instant rapport with both men. I was impressed by Cameron from the first. I had never met anyone so upbeat and enthusiastic about the theatre, and he possessed an unequalled love of show business. Even before *Follies* rehearsals began, he said to me, "I want you to choreograph *Miss Saigon*." I replied, "You don't know me—how do you know you want me?" In typical Cameron fashion, he said, "I know."

I replied, "We'll see."

Guess who won.

This was to be a new *Follies*, one more upbeat in tone. James Goldman was determined to make book changes in order to make the show more audience-friendly, and with this directive in mind, we set to work; Mike Ockrent's charge to us: "Brits love shows about class distinction, but this show is about American angst."

It was the time leading up to rehearsals that was hardest for me, but once we began rehearsals I felt challenged but comfortable. Cameron left me alone on *Follies*, trusting me to deliver the goods, and my respect for him grew daily. I was also fortunate to have surrounded myself with great assistants: Maggie Goodwin, a terrific woman with extraordinary energy, was a great help in teaching steps, and I was happy to work with her again on *Miss Saigon*, *Martin Guerre*, and *Sunset Boulevard*. Jerry Mitchell, who had been involved with *Scandal* and has now gone on to be one of our top director/choreographers, was another of my assistants; I had first met Jerry when he was hired to be a replacement in one of our *Chorus Line* tours. A tall, affable guy with a boundless enthusiasm and energy that make you smile when you talk to him, I knew right from the beginning that he would make it. His love for the theatre and his ideas and passion are first-rate. He's a talented man whom I grew to love, and on *Follies*, his positive attitude always helped boost the energy in the rehearsal room.

Peter took a leave from his job in television and was also in London with me, proving to be a major help. While he never had a great deal of formal dance training, when I was ready to show a completed number, I could always rely upon his eye for a sharp analysis. This production of *Follies* was the first time we actually worked together, and I'd bounce ideas off of him, conferring repeatedly throughout the rehearsal process. He approached the sequences from a cerebral, rather than dance point of view, and he was right on the money. He was so sharp from a dramaturgical point of view that both James Goldman and Mike Ockrent grew to really like and trust him.

Having Peter with me made this time in London a completely new experience. When I first worked there on *Promises, Promises* and *Company*, I felt lonely, confused, and isolated—I didn't even understand the monetary system! By 1987, however, the currency system had changed, there was a structure to my personal life, and I was in this great city to choreograph on my own.

A big reason why I ultimately said yes to the show was because Steve had written four new songs for this production, a fact which gave me fresh choreographic possibilities. The show would now include the songs "Country House," "Social Dancing," and most notably, two new Follies numbers for the leading characters of Phyllis and Ben: "Ah, But Underneath," a striptease pastiche for the repressed Phyllis; and a big production number, "Make the Most of Your Music" for her husband Ben, the financial tycoon. "Make the Most of Your Music" would be the climactic song of the evening, and one definitely more upbeat than Ben's concluding number from the original, a nervous breakdown in song ironically entitled "Live, Laugh, Love."

The original set had been a Tony Award-winning masterpiece by Boris Aronson, but for London, James Goldman kept insisting to our set designer Maria Bjornson (the award-winning set and costume designer for Andrew Lloyd Webber's *Phantom of the Opera*): "I don't want anything like Boris Aronson's set. I want it realistic, not poetic." Maria ultimately came up with a series of scaffolds covered in plastic, a look which reflected the true state of a theatre about to be torn down. The design worked, but it sure wasn't easy to dance around. Maria also designed the costumes, which differed greatly from Florence Klotz's originals; Florence's gowns told you everything you needed to know about the characters' economic background and personal taste. Maria, on the other hand, had asked the London actresses what they would feel most comfortable wearing, and that simple query caused great difficulties, because those actresses wanted to look good, even if their choices were wrong for the character. The resulting problems were only corrected when the replacement cast took over one year into the run.

The great Diana Rigg was set to play the Alexis Smith role of Phyllis, and the multitalented Julia McKenzie took on the Dorothy Collins role of Sally. I especially enjoyed working with Julia; she is a first-rate singer, actress and director, and it gave me a chance to further refine Sally's Follies number "Losing My Mind." Julia was performing the show on a bigger "Loveland" set in London, so we worked on adjusting her gestures accordingly, and she sang the song beautifully.

David Healy, a warm, lovable man, would play sad sack loser Buddy Plummer, and in the end, I actually think "Buddy's Blues," his "Loveland" number, worked better in London than it had in New York. Daniel Massey played the John McMartin role of the successful diplomat/financier Ben, but he was, to put it bluntly, a huge pain in the ass. He questioned and challenged everything repeatedly, until all the momentum would vanish from the rehearsal room.

Rounding out the principals was Dolores Gray, the MGM musical star who was cast as Carlotta Campion, the Hollywood siren who sings the showstopping "I'm Still Here." Dolores was a true throwback to the era of the glamorous Hollywood studio system, and she traveled in a style reminiscent of those 1940s glamour girls, arriving in London surrounded by dozens of trunks. I was going to put her into the "Who's That Woman" mirror number, but she had put on some weight and was costumed in a bright pink dress, which meant that if she was dancing in the number, the entire audience would be looking only at the pink dress. Leaving her out was the right decision for the show, but Dolores was not happy, announcing "I'm taking my voice and going back to America." She stayed, of course, and sang the hell out of "I'm Still Here," receiving a three-minute ovation on opening night. She still had the pipes, and then some.

One year into the run, Dolores was replaced by Eartha Kitt, whom the audience also adored. Eartha was a big talent, and an even bigger character. She arrived for rehearsal with black and blue marks on her face—she had been pushing her car up a hill at her home in Connecticut and it got out of control, rolling backwards and hitting her in the face. Eartha was not interested in normal rehearsal room chitchat, but instead would ask me: "What do you think of Nelson Mandela getting out of prison?" She kept live doves in her dressing room, not always in a cage—you opened that door at your own peril. Eartha was strange, but gifted and powerful.

We had a good team, but it was also a very difficult personal time for me. I was on the phone to Michael every day, but the conversations were strained. He was dying, and you don't ask someone in that situation, "How are you?" We both knew the answer. I kept talk about the show to a minimum; talking about it in detail would just have reminded him of the original production from sixteen years earlier when he was vibrant and healthy.

I was forty-nine at the time of the London *Follies* and was relieved to be in London because it allowed me to escape the necessity of fielding endless questions about Michael and his health. When the news came from Phoenix that he had passed away, I was glad to be away from New York; I didn't have to walk through the middle of Times Square assaulted by the *New York Post* banner headline announcing his death. In the end, it was both a shock and a sad relief when Cameron came into rehearsal on July 2, 1987, quietly laid a hand on my shoulder and said, "Michael's gone." I took a walk around the neighborhood, cried, and then went back to work, which was the best possible thing I could have done. When I returned from London, we took a couple of months to organize a memorial service for Michael, which was held, fittingly, on the stage of the Shubert Theatre, where *A Chorus Line* was still running.

During technical rehearsals in London, the set wasn't working properly, and when we got those glitches worked out and started previews, the show seemed good to me, but not great. The opening number, "Beautiful Girls," Steve's brilliant pastiche of Irving Berlin's "A Pretty Girl is Like a Melody," just did not have the magic or theatricality it should have had. I was pleased by some of my work but critical of other parts—the way I usually am.

For the first time, I was now the sole choreographer of a major musical. Yes, I recreated Michael's ingenious choreography for "Who's That

Woman?" but the four new songs gave me opportunities to stretch my-self, reaffirming the lesson I always keep in mind: it's not about the dance steps—those are a dime a dozen. It's really all about how you tell the story, how you push the plot forward through the movement.

We opened on July 21, 1987, to solid reviews, and the show ran until February 4, 1989. During the run, when Eartha replaced Dolores Gray, and Millicent Martin replaced Diana Rigg, we were able to fix some of the problems. The show still divided audiences, but time seemed to have caught up with it, and more people realized the poetry of the piece, and just how brilliant Steve's and Jim's work is.

Follies remains a very complicated musical, because the show's creators were doing nothing less than attempting to reconcile who we thought we were in our youth with who we become in our middle age. It's really an examination of how youthful ideals collide with the difficult realities we all face years later, so audiences who enter the theatre expecting a splashy lighthearted musical are often disappointed—even upset. It's not a show for everyone, but I'm so proud to have been associated with this iconic piece twice, and this production in London also afforded me my first opportunity to work with the extraordinary Cameron Mackintosh.

It's interesting for me to look back and realize that this personal break-through of working on my own came in London, not on Broadway. I had worked in London before, assisting Michael on *Promises, Promises*, *Company*, and *A Chorus Line*, so I was comfortable there; it seemed right that it provided the initial home for my solo work. In fact, I had one of the biggest thrills of my career in 1996 when I passed through Leicester Square and saw posters for three of my shows lined up next to one another: *Miss Saigon*, *Martin Guerre*, and *Sunset Boulevard*. In New York, I had *Miss Saigon* and *Sunset Boulevard* running at the same time, but I never have repeated that London trifecta on Broadway. I should have taken a picture but it doesn't matter—theatre is of the moment, and because it vanishes as soon as the curtain comes down, it's the memory that matters. That line up of posters provided me with one of my favorite professional memories.

I would spend a great deal more time in London working on *Martin Guerre* and *Sunset Boulevard* in the 1990s, but I suspect I might not have been involved in either one if it weren't for *Miss Saigon*, which opened in London in 1989. Cameron insisted that I choreograph that through-sung musical, and while I held the highest regard for him, when the show was explained to me I had one instantaneous thought: I'm going to stage musical numbers about communism and capitalism?!

It all couldn't have been further removed from the world of a Follies showgirl reunion, and that is precisely what appealed to me about it: the challenge.

I was in for quite a ride.

CHAPTER SEVENTEEN

MISS SAIGON

I LOVED THE BASIC IDEA BEHIND *MISS SAIGON* FROM THE START: *MADama Butterfly* updated to the Vietnam War seemed like it would provide a powerful, emotion-packed story, and with the *Les Miz* team of composer Claude-Michel Schönberg and lyricist Alain Boublil (additional lyrics and material by Richard Maltby Jr.) providing the score, I knew the work would be solidly professional. But—when I read the lyrics to "Morning of the Dragon," a militaristic number about the communist North Vietnamese taking over the entire country of Vietnam—

> The tiger we were stalking
> Walked on paper feet
> And in the clear white heat of dawn
> Was gone.

—I really did think: "What the hell am I supposed to do with this?!"

Cameron's original intention was to first produce *Miss Saigon* in America, not England. Given the great success of *Les Miz*, he thought Roger Stevens at the Opera House in Washington, DC, would jump at the idea, but to his surprise he found that Roger and others shied away from the subject of the Vietnam War. Potential directors also proved skittish about the subject matter, with the notable exception of Jerry Zaks, who by this time had won several Tony Awards and enjoyed great success directing the revival of *Anything Goes* with Patti LuPone at Lincoln Center. Jerry, a very talented man, was enthusiastic and did a lot of work on the structure of the show with Alain and Claude Michel.

At the same time, Cameron had still failed to find a theatre for the show in America, when he suddenly heard that David Merrick was finally going to close *42nd Street* at the Drury Lane Theatre in London. *42nd Street* had been chugging along on a very inexpensive theatre deal which made for a low break-even, allowing it to run for years even with the upper circle and balcony open only on weekends. The owners of the Drury Lane were desperate for a new show, so a deal was struck with Cameron, who was determined to use the theatre's enormous full stage.

I flew off to London for script meetings, and Jerry and I met with Claude Michel and Alain, as well as with Cameron and set designer John Napier. The meetings went well, and I returned home to wrap things up. The show was scheduled to open in September of 1989, and knowing that I would be living in London for three months, I wanted everything organized before I began living overseas. Fortunately, Peter's weekly show on USA Network, *Calliope*, was on hiatus, so he could again assist me in London.

While I was back in New York, Jerry began having misgivings about the show. I think he may have been uncomfortable with the London-centric nature of the production; the show was being produced in the UK, and Jerry wanted neither to uproot his family nor to be separated from them for months on end. Cameron informed me that Jerry had pulled out, asking me to now meet with Trevor Nunn. Trevor was a smart, accomplished man who was then riding the gigantic success of both *Cats* and *Les Miz*, as well as his remarkable run at the Royal Shakespeare Company. He had also been most generous in stepping forward when Michael had to withdraw from *Chess*.

Alain and Claude-Michel both admired Trevor's work but Trevor was extremely busy at the time, with *Chess* set to open on Broadway in April of 1988; he was also already slated to direct Andrew's new musical *Aspects of Love*. I do know that Cameron was concerned that the *Saigon* production period not repeat the major difficulties faced when the Broadway productions of *Starlight Express* and *Les Miserables* both began performances in March 1987 while utilizing the same creative teams; the resulting scheduling and production issues had caused major problems for both shows. Trevor and I spent a great social evening together talking about everything except *Miss Saigon*, but I think Cameron began to have doubts, and the next thing I knew, Cameron told me that Trevor was no longer directing *Miss Saigon*.

When Cameron returned to London without a director, he got in touch with Nick Hytner, whom he had originally wanted to direct *Follies* in 1987; Steve Sondheim had been uncertain that Nick, then only thirty-three, was ready to take on such an enormous show, although he did state he felt Nick would be a major star director in just a few more years. Cameron sent Nick the *Miss Saigon* material, albeit with Nick's proviso that he had no interest in doing a musical and would just give his opinion on the material itself. First thing Monday morning, Nick rang Cameron and told him that he had to direct the show or he would never forgive himself.

Nick was immensely creative and clearly about to become a major player in the industry. I flew back to London to meet with him, but a new problem arose, this time of my own making: right before flying back to London, I had been helping my mother clear vines at her cottage, and I had contracted poison ivy. And not just a small dose—I mean, covering-you-everywhere-with-huge-welts poison ivy. I was incredibly uncomfortable, and on the flight to London the bubbles began oozing fluid. By the time I landed, I was in agony, and with Cameron's help, got in touch with a physician everyone called "Dr. Footlights," because he treated so many performers. The problem was that poison ivy doesn't exist in London, but eventually the doctor figured out a medication that would work and I went off to meet with Nick. I barely remember that initial meeting—all I wanted to do was scratch my entire body in order to relieve the itching. But Nick and I connected and I was impressed by how clear his vision of the show was. I thought we would make a fine team.

We started casting the show, but it was difficult to find the right actors in London, because at that time the local Asian musical theatre acting pool was not deep. So, Nick, Cameron, Claude-Michel, and Alain flew to Manila, along with my assistant Maggie Goodwin, to continue casting the show. They purposely traveled to the Philippines because so much of the music there is westernized: the Spanish influence is prevalent and the vocal approach is American in style. The Filipino culture was definitely more simpatico with the aims of musical theatre than were those of other Asian countries. We found a great deal of talent in Manila, including eighteen-year-old Lea Salonga who would play the lead role of Kim. She was sensational at her initial audition.

Simon Bowman and Claire Moore were signed to play Chris, the American soldier at the heart of the love triangle, and Ellen, his wife, but the biggest casting coup lay in signing Jonathan Pryce for the leading role of the sleazy pimp known as The Engineer.

At the very first meeting between Nick, Cameron, and the authors, Nick had raised the idea of Jonathan as The Engineer, and Alain responded very enthusiastically—"if he can sing." Having recently seen Jonathan's terrific performance in *The Seagull*, Cameron was very excited as well, and was also able to tell Nick, Alain, and Claude-Michel that Jonathan and he had met just the year before to discuss the possibility of his taking over from Michael Crawford in *The Phantom of the Opera*—he knew Jonathan could sing. (Jonathan had not signed for *Phantom* because he landed the lead in the film *Brazil*.) Although the Caucasian Jonathan would be playing the role of the Eurasian Engineer, there was no controversy about his casting at the time. That tumult lay down the road in New York City.

Peter joined me in London, and we lived together at Cameron's home. Though he was not my first assistant—Maggie Goodwin held that job—he was instrumental during the production period in terms of creating ideas and providing feedback. Each morning, Nick Hytner would arrive to pick me up for the drive to rehearsal. The daily commute provided me with a handle on what Nick was thinking about the show, allowing us to develop an easygoing rapport. That time with Nick proved invaluable because I actually had not spent a huge amount of time on pre-production; I remained uncertain how I was going to stage the big numbers—imperialism and capitalism as the subject of songs did not exactly cry out for big Broadway dance routines. I had to let the rehearsal process evolve so that I understood how best to proceed. It was actually the opening "Dreamland" sequence in the bar which felt most natural, since the number centered around how best to present the young women while keeping the story moving forward. That was much more congenial territory simply because it fell along traditional lines. I had helped stage many musicals which began by introducing the women onstage—think of the "Beautiful Girls" opening number in *Follies*.

When it came time to actually stage the communist march "Morning of the Dragon," the problem lay in how to tell the audience that three years had now passed in the story. Nick came up with an easy, straightforward fix: banners stating "Third Anniversary of the Revolution."

It then became my challenge to keep the set filled with a constant flow of people coming downstage in parade-like fashion. We were playing the

Drury Lane Theatre, which possessed the biggest stage in the West End, and I had a company of fifty to fill John Napier's huge set; my solution was to stage the number with the cast marching downstage, exiting into the wings, circling around, and beginning the downstage march all over again. I didn't have a big dancing company because the numbers were more presentational in nature, but little by little I found solutions. I heard that one of the tenors was a trained acrobat, so I utilized his leaping and jumping ability to fill the space. I gave him a special entrance in which he would flip over and over as he progressed downstage—not an easy task on our severely raked stage. I had the girls wear tiger masks and carry red streamers, and decided to climax the number with a gun dance that would both serve the plot and keep the show moving forward.

The best remembered number in the show, "The American Dream," actually fell into place without a struggle. The key lay in getting Jonathan Pryce to dance. He wasn't trained as a dancer so I told him, "Let's just see what you can do—what you're comfortable with." Jonathan was game and went for broke while I kept it simple, providing steps that he could execute and that looked good on his body. The use of the onstage Cadillac came to me one night when I was watching television; there was an American TV show with a woman lounging sexily in the back of a limousine and I instantly thought, "That's it! That's the American Dream." It was Jonathan's brilliant idea to have The Engineer jump up on the Cadillac and hump it until orgasm. It was surreal and exciting at the same time.

Saigon also brought a really satisfying moment when it came time to stage the bows. As usual, the order would be chorus, lesser principals, and finally the leading principals, with Lea and Jonathan taking the last two solo bows. It was all straightforward, but I remembered hearing the story of a production of *The Wizard of Oz* where Toto received the final bow, and that provided me with a bit of inspiration: to give the final bow of the show to the little boy playing the role of Kim's (Lea Salonga) son, Tam. I decided to have Jonathan take his bow, point to the wings, and then have the little boy come running out. The first preview arrived, and when Tam came running out, the audience exploded! It was just the right touch of emotional release after the heavy dramatics that are so much a part of *Miss Saigon*. That final bow has never changed in the thirty years that have passed since the show first opened.

We had a remarkable production team working on the show. Bill Brohn turned in fantastic orchestrations that provided beautiful emotional undercurrents, and David Hersey did a stunning job with the lighting—lots of darkness and smoke, very atmospheric. John Napier's awesome set and Andreane Neofitou's costumes perfectly reflected the war-torn world of Saigon and Bangkok. We had a few scary moments with the set because the individual pieces were huge, but the design fit the show so beautifully that as we progressed towards previews I was feeling very positive about the show. The story was so strong that the emotional through-line really resonated; in fact, Cameron felt that at heart the show resembled *West Side Story* in both its direct emotional appeal and in the tale of star-crossed lovers as much as it did *Madama Butterfly*. Once previews began, audiences seemed to connect with the piece instantly.

We opened on September 20, 1989, and the reviews were terrific. I distinctly remember the very glamorous opening-night party that Cameron threw; we all walked from the Drury Lane Theatre to the Thames River, where boats took us to a beautifully decorated Asian-style building, the site of a giant bash that was in progress. As the positive reviews drifted in, everyone was in a good mood, no one more so than Cameron himself.

Very quickly we began prepping for a production to open in New York. Jonathan and Lea would be heading the Broadway company, but the rest of the cast would be new, and this time around I became even more heavily involved in casting the show. In fact, knowing that I wanted to use real dancers and multiple acrobats for the New York production, I began rethinking my entire show. I left the "Dreamland" sequence alone, but put in a great deal more work on "Morning of the Dragon." The Bangkok sequence also became a Broadway style number; instead of natives thronging the stage while selling fruits and vegetables, the number would now feature young women and pimps in different nightclubs selling their wares. I wanted it all to be tougher and grittier, and I even wanted to change "The American Dream," which had emerged as a true showstopper in London. I wanted to make it bigger and better, and with our terrific new cast I thought that was possible.

Maggie Goodwin had come to New York to help teach all of the choreography to the New York company; she was an incredible help, as was my newly hired American assistant, Jodi Moccia, who had also been involved in in *Scandal*. Jodi was going to learn the show, become resident choreographer, maintain the New York company, and recreate the musical staging for all the national tours. Maggie and Jodi became fast friends, which lightened my workload considerably.

We were getting ready to start technical rehearsals at the Broadway Theatre when some members of the Asian American community began protesting the fact that Jonathan Pryce was playing an Asian; in actuality, lyrics in the show refers to The Engineer as being Eurasian, but that fact was lost amidst the quickly growing controversy. We did make the decision to no longer have Jonathan use any prosthetics on his eyes, because their use could understandably be seen as offensive. I think we were all unprepared for the controversy, however, because, although England has a very sizeable Asian population, there had not been any protest over Jonathan's casting. (In point of fact, in the United States we never had a non-Asian play the role of The Engineer again.) But, once the protests started the press pounced on the story—we were the big new musical opening in town and the controversy sold papers. The result, of course, was that the protests grew in number and strength. There were headlines in the *New York Post*, and publicity most shows would dream about—but of the wrong type. There were protestors outside of the theatre on a daily basis, a fact which cast a pall over the mood inside of the theatre. In retrospect, I do certainly understand the validity of the protests, considering the lack of roles available to Asian American actors.

We certainly had a formidable cast. Besides Lea and Jonathan repeating their roles from London, we had Willy Falk, Hinton Battle, and Liz Callaway in leading roles. However, when coupled with the protests outside the theatre, some casting choices helped create dissent within the creative/producing team, and we were not as cohesive a unit as we had been in London. The situation was not helped by the fact that Nick Hytner and costume designer Andreane Neofitou came into some conflict, and Suzy Benzinger was brought in as a co-costume designer, with both women eventually receiving billing for their work.

The audience was responding really well during previews, and we drew a very heavy Asian audience, especially among the Filipino community, but the protests regarding Jonathan continued. Previews were actually bumpy, despite the fact that the show itself was now stronger. Everyone was feeling pressure, but Jonathan remained very stoic and focused. He just wanted to continue improving his performance, and by his example kept the company moving forward.

We previewed for just over two weeks and opened on April 11, 1991, to a critical reception quite similar to that accorded *Dreamgirls*; the television reviews were not great, but the out-of-town print reviews were strong, and most notably, Frank Rich in the *New York Times* posted a very positive review. In hindsight, I wonder if part of the negative reaction was due to *Miss Saigon* being the fourth of the "British Invasion" mega-musicals: after *Cats, Les Miserables*, and *The Phantom of the Opera*, there was certainly grumbling about the through-sung British appropriation of a distinctly American art form.

The backlash became particularly evident in the face of our main competition for the Tony Awards that season, the all-American musical *The Will Rogers Follies*, directed and choreographed by Tommy Tune. Here was a homegrown product, created by Tommy, Peter Stone, Betty Comden, and Adolph Green, all in celebration of that most American of performers, Will Rogers. Tommy once again did dazzling work—he remained an extraordinary showman—but the show struck me as an example of Tommy's showmanship triumphing over weak material: Will Rogers was a nice man who died in a plane crash at a young age. Where was the conflict?

Jonathan was awarded the Tony as Best Actor in a Musical, and Lea and Hinton both won as well, but *Will Rogers* captured the Tony Award for Best Musical, and I lost as Best Choreographer to Tommy. But *Will Rogers* ran for only two-plus years on Broadway, as opposed to *Saigon*'s ten-year run, a pattern that repeated itself on the road. Just as with *Dreamgirls* and *Nine*, the press wanted to create a big rivalry between the two shows, but I remained close to Tommy—we had known each other a long time, and I'm a great admirer of his talent. I just thought *Saigon* was, all in all, a better show.

After the New York City opening, *Miss Saigon* went global; Cameron sent out a national company, a bus-and-truck tour, and then mounted a Japanese company. I continued to make changes, and in Japan had a great time working with the Olympic athletes the producers brought in to enhance the acrobatics in the "Morning of the Dragon" number. Actually, my associate choreographer, Jodi Moccia, and the associate director, Mitchell Lemsky, put that production on its feet, and then Nick and I came in to oversee the final polish.

I lived in Tokyo for a month, which proved to be a fascinating but difficult experience, given the differences between our cultures; the Vietnam War was being reenacted onstage while the corporate sponsorship for the show offered a Mercedes Benz for sale in the lobby! Yet, different as the Japanese culture was, I grew to love it; the cast and crew were incredibly respectful of the creative team and executed any request without a word of negotiation.

The Tokyo company gave twelve performances per week, instead of the traditional eight, with the show divided among three different casts. Because of that triple casting, a performance note didn't always reach the right actor. If I saw something in the performance of Kim #1, she might not give another performance for three days, at which time she'd be playing with a different Engineer.

Cameron continued to mount the show around the world, and when it was booked for Stuttgart, a theatre was actually built for the show! Over to Germany I went for the launch, traveling to Holland as well. After that, my associates oversaw the foreign productions. I knew the show was in good hands with them, and also knew that no matter where the show played, it seemed to strike a chord. The story of a mother making sacrifices for her child proved universal, and when that basic human impulse was combined with a large-scale, often dazzling musical production, audiences were more than happy to take an emotional journey with us.

That global success was also due in large part to Cameron. He never stops thinking about his shows and that passion shows; he is smart, possesses great instincts, and remains a dynamo of incredible energy. I first met Cameron in 1985 when he said hello to Michael and me in Charlie's Restaurant, a theatre hangout on West Forty-fifth Street. He was in town for previews of Andrew Lloyd Webber's *Song and Dance*, and even in that brief exchange I could tell how passionate he was about the theatre. We have now been working together since the London production of *Follies* over thirty years ago, and he is the same now as when I first met him. His gleeful enjoyment of the work is infectious, and even when disappointments come his way, he never gets bogged down. He just keeps moving forward to the next day and the next show. He's a great producer and a wonderful friend to both me and Peter.

My work with Cameron had now ushered in the third phase of my career: after my years as a performer, and then the two decades spent working with Michael, I was now beginning a third act as part of the British musical theatre invasion. *A Chorus Line* had closed in New York in 1990 after what was a then record-breaking run, and the central role that show had played in my life was now taken over by *Miss Saigon*. I was kept busy with my work on the various international companies, but finally took time to relax at home and spend quality time with Peter. As a result, although I was offered a number of shows during the next two years, it was not until 1993 that I actually began work on a new show—a revue of Stephen Sondheim songs entitled *Putting It Together*. I was very happy to be working once again with Steve, and to celebrate his brilliant work we put together a cast that proved to be the talk of the town.

CHAPTER EIGHTEEN

PUTTING IT TOGETHER

PUTTING IT TOGETHER WAS CONCEIVED AND DIRECTED BY JULIA McKenzie, who had made such a memorable Sally in the London production of *Follies*. It was performed in a fringe theatre in London under Cameron's auspices, with a cast that included Diana Rigg and Clarke Peters. My associate Maggie Goodwin choreographed the show, which had a very successful limited run.

Shortly thereafter, in 1993, Cameron contacted me to ask if I'd be interested in choreographing a new production of the show. Cameron had been very good to me and I loved Steve's material so I thought, "Sure, I can do this and hopefully have a good time." Cameron contacted Lynne Meadow, the artistic director of Manhattan Theatre Club, to ask if she'd be interested in having the show in one of MTC's theatres and she immediately said yes. MTC's theatres are small, off-Broadway-style theatres, and the salaries match the size of the theatre, so when I hired Jerry Mitchell to be my assistant, I basically paid him all the money I made on the show.

Julia came to New York and we met several times to discuss her ideas for the show. I could immediately see that she had the show conceptualized in her head, that she wanted to string Steve's songs from various musicals together into a loose plot, centering around a party in a New York City penthouse apartment, hosted by a married couple who are entertaining three of their friends. Cameron then asked me if I could round up the *Chorus Line* team of designers—Robin Wagner, Theoni V. Aldredge, and Tharon Musser, all of whom said yes. I hadn't worked with Theoni, Tharon, or Robin since *Dreamgirls*, and it felt great to be reunited with my dear friends.

The younger characters in the show were cast quite easily—Rachel York (so terrific in *City of Angels*), Michael Rupert, who had won a Tony Award for his performance in the revival of *Sweet Charity*, and the playwright/ actor Chris Durang. We were contemplating who to cast as the older couple when out of the blue Cameron suggested Julie Andrews. Julie had been absent from the New York stage since her run in *Camelot* thirty years earlier, but much to our surprise and delight she said yes. I was in awe of Julie and shy around her: *My Fair Lady, Camelot, Mary Poppins, The Sound of Music, Victor/Victoria*—she was musical theatre royalty. She proved to be the ultimate professional—no diva airs, hard-working, and a delight to be around. The talented and handsome Stephen Collins was cast to play her husband, completing a dream cast, especially for off-Broadway.

The show was tough on the actors because the characters weren't on the page; there was no script per se, so they had to construct a character out of disparate songs that had been written for different shows over a near forty-year time span. Steve's songs are inextricably woven into the plot of his shows, and he does not care about writing a hit song if it doesn't serve the show. He is interested in character and plot development. It's what makes his songs so extraordinary, but what also made a revue of his songs so difficult.

At the start of rehearsals, there were the usual bumps as the actors found their way. Chris Durang was a talented performer, but he was having trouble adjusting his low-key ironic style to a revue level of performance, which requires very high energy. Rachel also had problems finding her character for the show, so I suggested, "Go look at some Goldie Hawn movies—those zany characters might help you," and fortunately they did.

We were playing in a very small theatre, but the public interest in the show was enormous because of Julie's return to the stage, so I made sure to give her a star's entrance at the top of the show. She appeared after Rachel, Chris, Michael, and Steven, and when she first came onstage the audience exploded: people were just so thrilled to see her onstage again. That affection extended to backstage as well; everyone was slightly in awe of her and on their best behavior—we all had a fantastic time. (I have a distinct memory of Theoni arriving at rehearsal, looking at Julie's red hair and fair skin, and proclaiming, "She'll wear periwinkle blue!" That unerring eye is what made Theoni such a great designer.)

Julie and I had several interesting conversations during the rehearsals and run of the show, and because by this time I had already committed to *Sunset Boulevard*, she asked me about the show; she was clearly interested in the casting. It's fun to think what *Sunset Boulevard* might have been like if Julie had ever played Norma Desmond. As it was, during *Putting It Together* Julie and her husband Blake Edwards had me up to their hotel suite and asked me to choreograph *Victor/Victoria*, which they were then planning as a stage musical. Flattered though I was to be asked, I had to turn down the offer because of the *Sunset Boulevard* production schedule.

Audiences seemed to be having a terrific time during previews, and because of Julie's return to the stage the run had sold out as soon as tickets went on sale, but we received mixed reviews, most of which basically asked, "What is it?" A revue? A quasi-book musical?" Audiences and critics were both a bit puzzled; they remembered the songs from other Sondheim musicals, but the context was entirely different. We played out our sold-out run and that was the end of *Putting It Together*—or so I thought.

Five years later, Cameron called me to say he wanted to resurrect the show for a run from October to December 1998 at the Mark Taper Forum in Los Angeles, only this time Carol Burnett would play the Julie Andrews role, with the other roles filled by Michael Nouri, John Barrowman, Susan Egan, and Bronson Pinchot. Eric Schaeffer was directing this production, and we also had a new design team: Bob Crowley, the award-winning British designer, would design the set, and Bob Mackie, who had designed Carol Burnett's television series, would design the costumes.

I had always loved Carol as a performer, but the regard I held for her did not seem to be mutual. I was, I think, too enthusiastic about her work; she reportedly doesn't like people to fawn. It turns her off, and because I was so effusive, she pulled back. She was, however, always pleasant, and her sense of humor was as keen as ever: not wanting to be interrupted by constant knocking on her dressing room door, she had her name taken off and in its place had a slider stating "Janitorial Services" installed! She also told very funny show-business stories; my favorite was her anecdote about being called in for retakes on the movie *Annie*, weeks after principal photography had ended. In the interim, she had undergone plastic surgery on her jaw, and when it came time for the retakes of a scene which required her to enter a closet, the end result was, in Carol's words, that she "entered the closet with one jaw, and exited with another." It's a funny story, but in the end we never really connected. There were other problems with the cast as well; Michael Nouri had difficulty learning his show and was ultimately replaced by John McCook, and Bronson's needs as a comic showboat slowed down the entire rehearsal process.

One very interesting aspect of working at the Taper is that the audience is handed review cards during previews; they write down their opinions as to what works and what doesn't, where they lost interest in the show and which parts really captured them. I had tried to hold on to the show I had choreographed in New York, but because the Taper was a thrust, not proscenium, stage, I was reworking several numbers, and actually reconceived several sequences as a result of those preview cards.

After all of the changes, we actually opened to very favorable reviews, and there was talk of a run on Broadway. Before such a production could materialize, however, at the invitation of our director Eric Schaeffer, I agreed to choreograph *Over and Over*, John Kander and Fred Ebb's musical adaptation of Thornton Wilder's *The Skin of Our Teeth*. I had enjoyed working with Eric on *Putting It Together*, and since the timing was just right I quickly said yes. Eric was directing the show at his Signature Theatre in Arlington, Virginia, and I was especially excited by the idea of working for the first time with the great composer/lyricist team of Kander and Ebb.

I had two wonderful assistants in Jodi Moccia and Marc Oka, and Patrick Vaccariello, a hugely talented guy with whom Peter and I have formed a deep friendship, was hired as the musical director. We enlisted a cast of first-rate Broadway veterans: David Garrison, Linda Emond, Bebe Neuwirth, Dorothy Loudon, and Mario Cantone, but rather quickly began to run into problems with the casting. Dorothy's part kept getting smaller and smaller and she quit. I had first worked with Bebe on *A Chorus Line*, where, as an eighteen-year-old, she had very successfully played the soon-to-be-thirty Sheila. She had a great stage presence, but wasn't quite right for the character of Sabina, the maid who tends to the Antrobus family throughout the millennia. Sabina is written as a warm, wry observer, whose humor keeps bubbling to the surface, but Bebe had a much steelier take on the character and it simply wasn't working. When those problems kept increasing, Eric and I went to New York and auditioned Sherie Rene Scott, who was funny and brought great warmth to the show. Eric let Bebe go and she was furious; her dismissal made all the newspapers, which was not the sort of publicity we had been hoping for.

We ran for two months at the Signature Theatre, but when we closed in February of 1999, that was the end of any first-class production of the show. When all was said and done, the material did not lend itself to the musical form; it was too episodic and whimsical in tone. I liked working with Eric, who always makes the process pleasant and upbeat, and of course was happy to collaborate with John and Fred. But with its fantastical plot, the show ultimately ended up as an interesting musical misfire.

I took some time to relax, occasionally checking on *Miss Saigon*, which was then in the ninth year of its run in New York as well as still running in London, but Cameron now contacted me to say that he was moving *Putting It Together* to Broadway. Carol would still be headlining the show, but George Hearn and Ruthie Henshall would be replacing John McCook and Susan Egan.

We were booked into the Ethel Barrymore Theatre on West Forty-seventh Street, but the show just didn't play as well as it had in Los Angeles. George Hearn is a terrific singing actor, but he had to get used to the unique style required by a revue, and there were scheduling changes as well; Carol did not play matinees, so Kathie Lee Gifford was hired to play those performances. I thought Kathie Lee was terrific; she was great to work with, a pal to everyone, and worked so very hard. We opened in November of 1999, but the reviews were not particularly good and business was lackluster. Cameron saw the handwriting on the wall and didn't put a lot of money into advertising; we lasted exactly three months, closing in February of 2000.

I was ready for a rest, and in hindsight, it's a good thing I had an extended break of over a year, because my next show was a huge and complicated one in every way: Andrew Lloyd Webber's musical adaptation of Billy Wilder's classic film *Sunset Boulevard*.

CHAPTER NINETEEN

SUNSET BOULEVARD:
THE MANSION HAS LANDED

ODDLY ENOUGH, I FIRST HEARD ABOUT *SUNSET BOULEVARD* THROUGH Cameron, who said to me, "You should do that show." Hearing this from Cameron, I just assumed he was going to produce the show with Andrew Lloyd Webber, repeating the partnerships they had formed on *Cats* and *Phantom of the Opera.* It was only when Andrew's people contacted my lawyer John Breglio to begin negotiations that I realized Cameron was not involved.

I had seen a videotape of the show's 1992 "tryout" at Andrew's country estate in Sydmonton, where it played in the chapel which Andrew has converted into a theatre. I thought Patti LuPone was sensational as the faded silent film star Norma Desmond, and that Kevin Anderson made a solid Joe Gillis, the down-on-his-luck screenwriter turned gigolo. I also loved Andrew's score and saw the possibilities for an interesting "film noir" musical. However, I also realized that the show contained little opportunity for dancing, so I had no problem in saying "no" to the lowball figure they offered me.

My philosophy was simple: I couldn't work for Andrew and get paid less than I did when working for Cameron on *Follies* and *Miss Saigon.* It wasn't fair to me or to Cameron. Given my stance, I fully expected Andrew to move on, but his team kept coming back with increasingly better offers. They finally agreed to the terms I wanted and I thought, "Uh-oh—now I have to do this show."

I flew to London to meet with the director, Trevor Nunn, as well as look at John Napier's set model. One look at John's model and I realized,

"This show is a monster." I had been thinking about a show with maybe fourteen people in the cast, all shadow and light, and instead I was looking at the model for what could prove to be the biggest set ever designed for a musical—the interior of Norma Desmond's baroque mansion. It was an incredible piece of work on John's part, but not what I expected. The funny thing is that lyricist Don Black also had the same original conception of a smaller show, but regardless of our first thoughts on the size of the show, I knew that our creative team was first-rate: Christopher Hampton (*Les Liaisons Dangereuses*) was writing the book, and Anthony Powell, a brilliant Oscar-winning costume designer, was in charge of creating Norma's look and the rest of the period clothes.

When I went back to the US, I spent a good amount of time hanging out with Patti LuPone. We had met years earlier and I was delighted to be at her 1988 wedding to Matt Johnston; they were married onstage at the Vivian Beaumont Theatre, where Patti was then starring in *Anything Goes*, and seeing Patti so happy as she got married in that glorious space had cemented our friendship even further. Peter and I were thrilled that Patti and Matt built a house in Kent, Connecticut, and watching their son Joshua grow up through the years has made us feel like one big family.

After the 1992 tryout of *Sunset Boulevard* at Sydmonton, Patti had been offered the role of Norma Desmond, but she was, understandably, becoming increasingly distressed as she read reports that Meryl Streep was being considered to play Norma and that Andrew had given Norma's two biggest numbers to Barbra Streisand for her upcoming *Back to Broadway* album. Patti was not being treated like the incoming leading lady of the show and was, naturally, dealing with a roller-coaster of emotions. I was sympathetic and supportive of my great pal.

Peter and I flew over to London to start rehearsals but it proved to be very slow going. Trevor seemed uninterested in any musical staging that I was going to undertake; we'd start rehearsal at 10 a.m., and at 5 p.m. he'd turn to me and say, "Is there anything you want to do?" I did like Trevor and certainly respected his creativity and intelligence, and after he staged the opening, which involved Joe Gillis's body floating in Norma's pool, I used that as my springboard for a flashback number entitled "Let's Have Lunch"; this sequence incorporated Joe and the full company in a lush musical number taking place on the back lot of Paramount Pictures, and by the time the show opened, we felt the entire sequence worked beautifully.

Working with Andrew was not easy, for the simple reason that he barely acknowledged me. It was difficult to figure out the right time to approach him, and when I needed sixteen extra bars of music for the opening sequence, I went to the musical supervisor David Caddick, who instantly told me, "Don't go to Andrew for that!" In other words, I couldn't even ask him for sixteen extra bars of music. It was all very strange.

Andrew and I never did develop any sort of real relationship: it was always on the surface and never collaborative. He was the composer, but he was also the show's lead producer, and our relationship as producer/choreographer was a far cry from what I had developed with Cameron. The fact that I was staying with Cameron during all of the *Sunset* auditions probably didn't help matters; when Andrew asked where I was staying and I told him at Cameron's, his face turned ashen.

My choreographic duties weren't extensive, but I was happy to be working with such a first-rate cast: Patti was terrific and singing better than ever, as were Kevin Anderson and Daniel Benzali, who was playing Max, Norma's butler. We finished our work in the rehearsal hall, moved into the theatre for technical rehearsals—and that's when the nightmare began. The stage of the Adelphi Theatre was small, but that set was immense. It was very difficult to make the set work properly, and at times the mansion would literally move onstage of its own accord, without any cues being called. This was driving all of us to distraction until someone figured out that cell phone calls being made within the theatre were setting the machinery in motion. It was scary and bizarre at the same time.

Technical rehearsals took so long that the start of previews was delayed, but when we finally began performances, audiences really responded. I was actually enjoying the show itself; I thought Andrew and Don's score was terrific, and the design of the show was extraordinary. But I felt that the show did not end properly. It all just sort of stopped—"That's it, the end"—with no strong emotional or musical button to the evening. As a result, audiences weren't responding as they should have at the end; they seemed bewildered and caught off guard.

We opened in July of 1993 to reviews that ranged from mixed to very favorable, and the London critics and audiences adored Patti. The problem lay in the fact that Frank Rich, writing in the *New York Times*, felt that Patti was miscast—that the role of Norma should have been played by someone older like Angela Lansbury or Shirley MacLaine. Patti, he felt, was too vital. Having read this, Andrew decided that even though Patti's contract called for her to recreate the role in New York, she would be replaced for the Broadway production.

It was Christopher Hampton who first suggested Glenn Close to play Norma. Andrew listened to the cast recording of *Barnum*, her one previous Broadway musical, and apparently felt that she could sing it well enough. I was not privy to any of the negotiations, but when Glenn was contacted to play the role she agreed. The plan was that she would open and play the show for six months in Los Angeles, and then headline the subsequent Broadway production.

Word of this casting got out instantly—it always does in the theatre—and when Patti heard that she was not going to open the show in New York City, she was devastated and embarrassed. She now had to play out the remainder of her one year London contract while the entire theatre-going public knew she was being bypassed for Broadway. She was understandably angry, but her attorney, John Breglio, negotiated a very big buyout for her and she played out her London contract like the pro she is. She was magnificent in the role, and although I've worked with a number of different Normas, all of whom brought unique qualities to the role, no one, absolutely no one, ever sang the score better.

As we quickly began casting the full Los Angeles production, we all felt we could improve the show. I particularly wanted to refine the complicated opening sequence, a task in which I was again aided immeasurably by my assistant Maggie Goodwin. After *Follies* and *Miss Saigon*, this was our third show together, and when we began rehearsals in Los Angeles, I brought her to the United States so that she could teach the show to my American assistant, Jodi Moccia. Maggie has a mind like a steel trap, and I had a great time with both women, just as I had on *Saigon*.

As I reworked the opening sequence, John Napier began to rethink the set. His new design featured a black-and-white palette, one which gave the entire show a more mysterious feel appropriate to Norma's strange, self-deluded world. This design change immediately helped, and also made the show easier to light.

At the same time, we also fixed several sections of the show, most notably the ending. Andrew had written new music and John Napier came up with the perfect button; once Norma shoots Joe and descends into madness, she would glide down the stairs until she was standing in front of a blown-up still of her youthful self, singing all the time while having her breakdown. In London, this had all been instrumental, cheating the audience of Norma's vocals. It was now touching, eerie, and pathetic all at the same time—exactly right.

Glenn payed Norma as a much older woman than had Patti, and she deliberately embraced a grotesque look: chalk-white skin with deep socketed eyes that made her appear both ghostly and purposefully ghastly. The fact that Joe Gillis (the excellent Alan Campbell) was now sleeping with Norma while she looked like that made it all into a kind of Grand Guignol evening. Glenn was wonderful in the show, but was always cool with me. I couldn't figure out exactly why there was such a distance, but there was. Nevertheless, I had tremendous respect for her.

The show was a big hit in Los Angeles, beginning its six month run of sold-out performances at the same time that Patti was replaced by Betty Buckley in London. John Barrowman was now playing Joe Gillis, which proved to be a nice bit of casting, and I was hanging out with Betty—going to movies, having dinner, we were two Americans in London. We developed a wonderful rapport, and one night at Orso, she asked me to critique her performance. I told her that she was doing a fine job, and singing the score well, but asked her to remember that it's melodrama: "Don't overthink it. Don't take the fun out of it"—before adding, "Don't you dare tell Trevor we've had this conversation." I wanted to help my new friend Betty, but those sorts of notes are the director's province.

The following Monday at rehearsals, Trevor motioned to me and said, "Bob, can I please see you?" I knew what was coming, but before he could say anything I laughed and said, "That bitch! She told you." Trevor smiled and told me that he was actually glad I had given her my note, that I had reduced the entire adjustment to one sentence. There was absolutely no problem; Betty, Trevor, and I all got along like gangbusters, and Betty was terrific in the role.

Glenn continued to play the role in Los Angeles, but plans already were well underway for her to star in the Broadway production, which meant that we needed to cast a new star for Los Angeles. Enter Faye Dunaway.

To my great dismay, I never actually got to see Faye rehearse. The plan called for David Caddick, Jodi Moccia, and our production stage manager Peter Lawrence, to oversee all of the early rehearsals with her, at which point I would fly out to join the rehearsals before performances began.

But—after several weeks of work—David Caddick put the kibosh on Faye because she simply couldn't sing the score. Which, of course, begs the question of why she was hired in the first place.

Because Faye had become a genuine movie star in the wake of *Bonnie and Clyde*, there was a great deal of press interest in her playing the role of Norma Desmond. Aside from a very few people in rehearsal, however, no one got to see her interpretation of the role. I'm so sorry I didn't, but I trust the report of my associate Jodi, who said that Faye was amazing in the book scenes, fully inhabiting the character with great power and range, but that when it came time for the singing, she was a fish out of water. When Faye was let go there was no time to find and rehearse a new star, so the end result was that a standing-room-only show in Los Angeles was shut down.

Broadway, however, loomed on the horizon, and with Glenn, Alan Campbell, and George Hearn heading the cast, we opened at the Minskoff Theatre in November of 1994. There was very little drama throughout tech rehearsals and previews, and we received solid reviews. We were positioned as the new hit musical of the season, a fact only slightly undercut by our status as the only big new musical of that entire season. *Sunset* subsequently won the Tony Award as Best Musical, and even though the show did not contain any extended dance numbers, I was nominated for a Tony Award as Best Choreographer—a nice bonus.

Both the New York and London companies settled in for long runs, with one Norma replacing another in smooth progression: Betty replaced Patti in London and then replaced Glenn on Broadway; Betty, in turn, was replaced by Elaine Paige, the West End diva making her New York stage debut. In London, Betty was succeeded by Petula Clark, who was quite good in the role. Eventually, Petula was replaced by Rita Moreno, the only Norma I never saw perform the show.

Clearly this was a star-driven vehicle, and the public always wanted to know who was playing Norma. When we sent out a national tour with Linda Balgord, a terrific performer but not a name, great as her performance was, we didn't sell tickets, and the tour closed after four months. In Australia, Norma was played by one of the leading ladies of their musical theatre, Debra Byrne, but she began missing performances, and when that word got out, ticket sales fell off. The most noteworthy part of the Australian production actually came in the casting of Joe Gillis, with the part being played by a then-unknown and remarkable Hugh Jackman.

In Germany, Norma was played by the pop vocalist Helen Schneider, who sang the score in fluent German and made the production into a moderate success, while in Toronto, Norma was played by Diahann Carroll. Diahann was a charmer, very warm, and I liked her a great deal. She really could act and sing the role. The problem lay in the small amounts of dancing she had to undertake. No matter how often we worked on the sequence where Norma dances the tango with Joe at the demented New Year's Eve party she throws for just the two of them, Diahann simply couldn't master the steps. She was up and down in the role; on her good nights, she was terrific, but on her off nights, she just wasn't on target. In the end, we didn't have a very successful run in Toronto, where we were produced by Garth Drabinsky shortly before he ran into all of his financial problems.

During all of these productions, I was still in touch with Patti. She was my great pal, and we sometimes discussed the show. It took Patti several years to fully recover from her treatment on *Sunset*, but fortunately she had gone back to work as soon as she returned to New York, starring in the Encores production of *Pal Joey* and in a one-woman show at the Walter Kerr Theatre on Broadway. Andrew Lloyd Webber may not have wanted her to star in *Sunset* on Broadway, but New York audiences loved Patti, a local girl (she grew up on Long Island) who had made it big. I had worked with another LuPone, her brother Bobby, when he played Zach in the original company of *A Chorus Line*, but it was Patti to whom I had grown really close during her run in the Lincoln Center production of *Anything Goes*. Her passion and sensitivity make her an artist of the first rank.

When I look back on *Sunset*—on the show itself, stripped of all the offstage drama—I think that after all of the fixes we made for the Los Angeles and New York companies, it had become a very compelling musical, one which made for a fascinating evening in the theatre. It was beautiful to look at—"amazing" is not too strong a word—and I admire Andrew's score, which I think is arguably his best.

It was not an easy show for me. I had few opportunities in terms of actual choreography, yet I had to provide dozens of pieces of musical staging to serve as connective tissue between the show's big numbers. We were not a particularly close creative team—definitely not warm and cuddly—but eventually Trevor and I became closer, and I liked lyricist Don Black a great deal. I was very touched that when I directed a West End revival of *A Chorus Line* in 2013, I received a beautiful note from Trevor on opening night, as well as an equally flattering one from my *Saigon* director, Nick Hytner. They are both stunning craftsmen and true gentlemen.

It was written into my contract that I had to be offered right of first refusal to choreograph any first-class production of *Sunset Boulevard*, but I was not involved with the very successful semi-staged concert version of the show for the English National Opera in 2016, with Glenn Close once again playing Norma. The show was well-received and moved to Broadway early in 2017. Stripped of the overwhelming physical production, the very strong bare bones of the show itself were able to shine through, and the months-long run at the Palace Theatre proved successful.

Even though it was not the happiest experience of my career, I'm glad I was a part of *Sunset Boulevard*. It proved to be a formidable piece of musical theatre history, but for me, it is now a firmly closed chapter from my past.

CHAPTER TWENTY

MARTIN GUERRE

WITH THE VARIOUS COMPANIES OF *SUNSET BOULEVARD* KEEPING ME very busy, I wasn't necessarily looking for another show, but in 1996 Cameron asked me to choreograph a new musical based upon the French film *The Return of Martin Guerre*. It's a fascinating story, loosely based upon an actual historical figure: in medieval France, the young Martin Guerre goes off to fight in a war and is killed in battle, whereupon a friend assumes his identity and returns to Martin's home village in that guise. I was intrigued by the story, and with Alain Boublil and Claude-Michel Schönberg writing the score, I said yes.

Alain and Claude-Michel had worked on the score for a long time, and hoped to interest Nick Hytner in directing. Nick read the script and gave them feedback, but ultimately passed on directing the show. Instead of Nick, Cameron hired Declan Donnellan to direct and Nick Ormerod to design the sets and costumes. At the time, Declan and Nick, who had founded the theatrical company Cheek by Jowl, were very hot and seemed like they would prove to be very interesting collaborators. Right from the start, however, one major problem immediately presented itself: Cameron felt that dancing would prove key to the show, while Declan stated that he visualized a virtually dance-free show. My response: "You guys fight it out and decide."

Cameron was definitely running the show, and I think he started the process a little too early: the show simply wasn't finished when the momentum of casting and rehearsals took on a life of its own. Cameron quickly set up dates for the start of rehearsal, the first preview, and opening, and brought in Edward Hardy and Stephen Clark to craft the English lyrics to the show, but as Claude-Michel and Alain continued to write, we got further and further behind schedule. We really weren't ready to go into rehearsal, but Cameron decided, "We'll go into rehearsal and work on the piece like it's a workshop."

That's just what we did, and Declan began experimenting with the show's structure; I sat in rehearsal watching while he tried to create the beginning of the piece. I had total respect for Declan's process, but we were moving at a snail's pace. Cameron finally took Declan to lunch and said, "Nothing's happening. We have to get going." Declan became upset, and threw the show to me for a day: "Here, you work on it." The problem was that I had nothing to work from. Just to complicate the situation, I was again living at Cameron's house during rehearsal; we'd have breakfast together every morning, where he'd tell me what information to pass along to Declan, and what improvements he wanted made. That's a tricky path for a choreographer to walk with a director, but I ultimately worked my way through it.

Finally, as we got further into rehearsals, I started to distill the story in order to figure out where I could create dance opportunities. I began work on two sequences: the opening number "Working on the Land," which featured peasants toiling in the field—the men shoveling and the women picking grapes; and the big "Welcome Home" number in which Martin Guerre arrives at his village, and he and his love interest Bertrande see each other for the first time. We decided that we would view their initial meeting as if through the eyes of the villagers, and I developed a big, stomping number that felt both right for the moment and expressive of the characters. "Welcome Home" seemed to work right from the beginning, in large part thanks to my terrific assistants Maggie Goodwin and Craig Revel Horwood (who is now a judge on the UK version of *Dancing with the Stars*). The number evolved almost like a tap number, but without the taps (which would have been strange in twelfth-century France). Instead, I decided that the company would be pounding the floor as in a period clog dance, the full village of peasants expressing their passions and personalities through movement (one of these peasants was a completely unknown seventeen-year-old James Corden who had exactly one line: "Roast the meat!"). Just as on *Follies*, *Sunset Boulevard*, and *Miss Saigon*, Peter was really my sounding board on *Martin Guerre*, and I knew I was on the right track with this "Welcome Home" number when, after the first full run-through of the entire number, he turned to me excitedly and said, "This might be your best work ever. I smell an Olivier Award!"

Getting the show onstage was like climbing a very steep mountain—and that was even without worrying about the second act sequence where I had to musicalize the Protestant rebellion. Between the Protestant rebellion and *Miss Saigon*'s "Morning of the Dragon" paean to communism, I was becoming a specialist in how to choreograph political ideologies!

It was now becoming clear that while *Martin Guerre* did work in fits and starts, fundamental issues were never fully resolved; in the film, Martin Guerre's wife is not sure whether the man returning to the village really is her husband or not, but in our musical version, it was clear from the start that she knows the man standing in front of her is not her husband. I asked Alain why he had changed this crucial plot element, which removed all suspense. His reply was a blunt: "I changed the plot because I didn't buy it the way it was."

We kept working on the show all through previews and opened on July 10, 1996, at the Prince Edward Theatre. The tradition in London is that you go to the ad agency the morning after opening to read all of the reviews and plan the ensuing advertising campaign. As everyone was reading the reviews—the majority were negative—it became clear that the one element that was consistently commended was the choreography. My reaction to this was simple: "This isn't good." I really didn't want my work praised if the work of everyone else was dismissed. It was an uncomfortable feeling.

Even after the show opened, we continued working, rewriting the book, adding new songs, and putting in a stronger ending. In fact, Cameron closed the show for four days in October in order to put in all the changes, reopening it on November 11, 1996, so that critics could review the new version. The show won the Olivier Award for Best Musical of the year, and I was honored to be awarded the Olivier for Best Choreography. The show ultimately ran for 675 performances, closing in February of 1998.

That is certainly a respectable run, but the plot remained so complicated that audiences never really were sure of exactly what was going on. Our cast was very talented, and the acting remained first-rate, but their musical abilities remained much less certain. The proposed Broadway version never did materialize, although two years later Cameron mounted a new production in the US that basically cut out all of the dancing. It was a confusing time for me—I received great notices, won the Olivier Award, and yet all of the dances were now cut. Fortunately, Cameron and I still laugh about it, and when the subject of *Martin Guerre* comes up I always ask him, "When are you putting the dancing back in?" In fact, I liked the basic storyline enough that for some time I toyed with the idea of expanding my work into a ballet, one which would use Claude-Michel's music and interweave the story, but the idea went on the back-burner and remains there.

To this day, I retain very mixed feelings about the show. I was proud of my work and thrilled to win the Olivier; I had won Tony Awards for *A Chorus Line* and *Ballroom*, but those were Michael's shows, while *Martin Guerre* was a solo effort. There was some very beautiful music in the score and as has always happened in my career, I find myself listening to the scores of these so-called "failures" more than I do the successes, in the process reminding myself of what I initially liked about the show. But we never fully solved the problems with the show's structure, and my frustration is perfectly summed up in the fact that while rehearsing *Martin Guerre*, I began smoking again.

CHAPTER TWENTY-ONE

HEY, MR. PRODUCER! AND *THE WITCHES OF EASTWICK*

CAMERON AND I HAD ONE MORE BIG ORIGINAL MUSICAL IN OUR FUTURE together, but first up was a two-night salute to Cameron's career entitled *Hey, Mr. Producer!* This was to be staged June 7 and 8, 1998, at the Lyceum Theatre in London as a benefit for the Royal National Institute of the Blind. Two nights, a compilation of Cameron's greatest hits—how much work could it be? As it turned out—a lot!

Julia McKenzie and I signed on as co-directors, which really meant being traffic cops for a very starry group of actors performing hit songs from the incredible list of Cameron's musicals: Julie Andrews, Jonathan Pryce, Julia McKenzie, Judi Dench, Lea Salonga, and Bernadette Peters, along with a dozen other performers, would be performing excerpts from *My Fair Lady*, *Miss Saigon*, *Follies*, *Phantom*, *Les Miz*, *Carousel*, *Anything Goes*, and *Little Shop of Horrors*, all in the presence of Queen Elizabeth II. There were several choreographers on hand to stage the individual numbers, so Julia and I concentrated on all of the exits and entrances, the transitions, and the overall pace and flow of the show.

There was a huge orchestra onstage, and as an extra added attraction, we scheduled onstage sequences featuring Stephen Sondheim and Andrew Lloyd Webber, both of whom Cameron had worked with extensively. Although Steve would appear in person during the evening, Andrew decided that he did not want to appear onstage, so I suggested to Cameron that we film Andrew's sequence and have Steve introduce it. Cameron liked the idea, so David Caddick (Andrew's musical supervisor on many of his shows) and I went to the studio to record Andrew's "scene." When we arrived, it was as if Andrew had never met me. There was no recognition whatsoever, even though *Sunset Boulevard* had opened only five years earlier. There's no way around it: Andrew's non-recognition hurt.

But that certainly didn't take away from my pleasure in the evening, which was a true cornucopia of riches: Act One featured thirty-three sequences, and Act Two, twenty-five, and this was not filler material. This was "All I Ask of You," "One Day More," "Broadway Baby"—you name the hit from Cameron's productions and it was on the stage of the Lyceum. I was particularly happy to have a wonderful reunion with Julie Andrews, who capped a terrific *My Fair Lady* sequence: Liz Robertson (Alan Jay Lerner's widow) sang "Wouldn't It Be Loverly," Jonathan Pryce sang "I've Grown Accustomed to Her Face," and then the audience heard an offstage voice saying the final lines from "My Fair Lady"—"I washed my face and hands before I come, I did." It was, of course, Julie, and when she appeared onstage the audience went berserk!

The only sequence I personally staged was the Sondheim tribute, and after all of the big production numbers, I thought the best approach was a simple one: we placed a grand piano onstage, there were stools for the performers, and each person had their moment in the spotlight: Judi Dench, Julia McKenzie, Lea Salonga, Millicent Martin, Maria Friedman, Ruthie Henshall, David Kernan, and Michael Ball performed a medley of Steve's songs. Steve looked at me with a smile and said: "I didn't realize you were a minimalist!"

The show ended with everyone singing "Old Friends" from *Merrily We Roll Along*, after which the cast lined up to shake hands with the queen. I had already enjoyed one encounter with British royalty when Princess Margaret came to see the original London production of *A Chorus Line*. Back in the 1970s, none of us had met with royalty before, so Michael Bennett called a rehearsal in order to make sure that the entire cast knew the correct protocol. It proved to be a very funny and memorable rehearsal, with me playing Princess Margaret. Michael led me down the receiving line, and in full royal character, I would compliment each of the performers, who would then murmur, "Thank you, ma'am," and bob a little head curtsy. After this introduction to royal protocol, it was very hard not to laugh when Princess Margaret herself walked down the receiving line that night. On the occasion of *Hey, Mr. Producer!*, however, we were all meeting Queen Elizabeth herself, and as it turned out, even before the cast met Her Majesty,

Julia, Cameron, and I were introduced to her during the interval. We were presented to the queen in the private room reserved for VIPs in each West End London theatre, and we all shook hands, receiving a few words of murmured royal greeting. The queen was charming—and friendly as hell!

Cameron and I next worked together on the Carol Burnett version of *Putting It Together*, which opened on Broadway in November of 1999, and it's worth noting that this was the only time in our thirty years of working together that Cameron and I had a major blowup. This dispute centered upon my contract, or should I say non-contract; the SDC (Stage Directors and Choreographers union) was pushing me hard to get it finalized, which forced me to push Cameron. Cameron became so angry that he didn't even come to the first preview of *Putting It Together*, and when we finally did meet up in person, he read me the Riot Act. In hindsight, he was basically right. We had built up a long relationship of mutual trust and friendship, yet I momentarily doubted that trust. I could have handled the situation better.

It was right around this time that Warner Bros. sent Cameron their entire catalogue of films and told him: "We're up for licensing any one of our properties which interests you." Cameron had produced a musical entitled *The Fix*, and had liked working with the composer/lyricist team of Dana Rowe and John Dempsey, so he gave the list of Warner Bros. properties to John and Dana to see if they were interested in musicalizing any of the material. *The Witches of Eastwick* was the one film they felt had potential as a musical, and work on the show immediately began.

As Dana and John were writing the score, Cameron approached me about choreographing the show, but I was still angry about our disagreement and said, "No, you ought to find someone else." But as we worked through our dispute, we mutually decided that Cameron would hire Stephen Mear as co-choreographer, a move I endorsed, not only because Stephen had been a dancer in *Follies*, but also because he was now a very talented choreographer in his own right, and a man I liked very much. Eric Schaeffer was set to direct, Bob Crowley would design, and John Dempsey would write the book in addition to the lyrics.

It certainly was an interesting and unusual idea for a musical, because the plot, based upon the novel of the same name by John Updike, centered upon three women friends in a small New England town who playfully and accidentally conjure up the Devil. There were plenty of sexual escapades, all of them centering upon wishes made and granted. It promised to be a lot of fun, and also promised a lot of flying. (In fact, Cameron wanted Eric Schaeffer and me, along with Cameron himself, to be the first trio to test the flying harnesses. When I realized that he was serious about this, I managed to instantly disappear.)

We cast Lucie Arnaz, Maria Friedman, and Joanna Riding as the three witches, and Ian McShane was signed to play the Devil. We also had the good fortune to hire Rosemary Ashe, the original Carlotta in *The Phantom of the Opera*, and the five leads all brought great camaraderie to the rehearsal room. Lucie did constantly question the staging and the script, but she was still a good egg. I enjoyed the rehearsals because Stephen Mear and I worked so well together, and it was actually Stephen who ended up doing most of the legwork in putting the numbers together. Although Dana and John were inexperienced when it came to big West End musicals, they were absolute pros, and by the time we began previews in June of 2000, the show not only looked great but also seemed to possess a lot of potential—it played like a good, old-fashioned musical comedy.

As always proves to be the case while putting big musicals together, we continued to make constant changes during previews. Songs came and went in the blink of an eye, the example I most strongly remember centering around the show's opening image of a boat crossing the stage; Cameron told Dana that he wanted underscoring for that piece of business, and Dana wasn't sure of exactly what the tone should be. I said to him, "Just write forty-five seconds of fabulous water music and don't worry about it—it'll get cut anyway." It was. So constant was the re-writing, re-ordering, and re-composing, that I think we threw out some material that actually was working.

We opened in July of 2000 (John Updike never did put in an appearance), and the reviews ranged from mixed to favorable. The three ladies fared well, receiving strong notices for their singing, dancing, acting, and—don't forget—their flying out over the heads of the audience. I did, however, think that Ian McShane was ultimately miscast in the show's key role. He's a first-rate actor, but possessed no musical theatre technique or flexibility, and it showed. Michael Crawford had been Cameron's first choice for the role and he would have been terrific, but he turned down the role. Pity.

One year into the run, we moved from the mammoth Drury Lane Theatre to the more intimate Prince of Wales, which helped the show immeasurably. Downsizing made me realize that the new, small-scale production constituted the show we should have had all along. By this time, we also had a new Devil; Earl Carpenter, who had been Ian's understudy, took over the role, and after months in the role, he was eventually replaced by Clarke Peters. We cut the song "Who's the Man" and replaced it with a rousing gospel number "The Glory of Me," and all of these changes helped the show a great deal. It's just too bad that we hadn't opened the show in that smaller version at the right theatre, but we still ran for fifteen months, closing in October of 2001.

Without even planning on it, I now took an extended break. There were still business matters to tend to, primarily requests regarding Michael's shows, which came first to John Breglio, the executor of Michael's estate. Given my position as Michael's closest artistic associate and one of his heirs, John would call me after receiving an inquiry and say: "I've had a request for a first-class company of *A Chorus Line*—what do you think?" When London producer Sonia Friedman called John about mounting the first-ever West End production of *Dreamgirls*, John called me, and I then spoke with Casey Nicholaw, the proposed director and choreographer. I loved Casey's work on *The Book of Mormon* and told him, "I hope it can work out"—which it ultimately did to great acclaim. John and I do not become involved with stock and amateur productions, but we've developed a smooth working relationship when the question of first-class productions of *A Chorus Line*, *Dreamgirls*, or even *Ballroom* arise. We come from the same place regarding these requests: we both want the integrity of Michael's great work to be preserved.

I continued to field questions regarding companies of *Saigon* and *Sunset*, but I wanted to spend more time with Peter, so I took a hiatus which lasted until 2005, when I received a game-changing phone call from John: would I take the leap and direct the first Broadway revival of *A Chorus Line*? Absolutely. Here was a challenge I couldn't refuse.

CHAPTER TWENTY-TWO

BACK ON THE LINE

BESIDES HANDLING ALL OF MY DEALS, JOHN AND I HAD BECOME GREAT friends while performing our joint duties overseeing the administration of Michael's work. After thinking about it for some time, he decided that the time was ripe for *A Chorus Line* to be revived on Broadway. Fifteen years had passed since the original production had closed in April of 1990, and John felt it was time for a new generation to see *A Chorus Line* on Broadway.

Because I was Michael's closest artistic associate, John felt strongly that he wanted me to direct the show's return to Broadway. His request, in fact, was emphatic: "You have to do it."

The initial conversations took place in 2005, with a targeted Broadway opening of fall 2006 after a tryout in San Francisco, and by this time, Marvin Hamlisch and I were the only members of the original creative time who were still alive: Michael, book writers Nick Dante and James Kirkwood, and lyricist Ed Kleban had all passed away. Ironically, Marvin had talked about a revival for years before it happened, saying things like: "Hire Dan Sullivan to direct it." But, once we started, Marvin was nothing but supportive, which meant a great deal to me.

The indomitable, original Connie Wong, Baayork Lee would be my partner in remounting the show and reproducing the original choreography. Baayork and I go a long way back—as of this writing, fifty years and counting! We first worked together on *Henry, Sweet Henry*, followed by *Promises, Promises, Seesaw*, loads of television, and finally *A Chorus Line*. She is always an invaluable asset to the show and is unstoppable. Further help came from our associate choreographer, Michael Gorman, who had actually been "on the line" as Bobby on Broadway, and not only knew the show step-by-step but brought a humor and intense dedication to recreating the musical numbers.

I asked Peter to come on board as associate director, ideal timing since he was ready to make a creative change after a successful twenty-year career directing and producing television, and we had worked together seamlessly in London on *Follies, Miss Saigon*, and *Sunset Boulevard*. He is very savvy about acting and can discuss text and character clearly and succinctly. I find him to be very astute in how he analyzes a play or the book of a musical.

It was our great good fortune that our friend Patrick Vaccariello signed on as musical director. He had conducted both Broadway revivals of *Cabaret*, the hit production of *Gypsy* starring Patti LuPone, Arthur Laurents's 2009 revival of *West Side Story*, and had served as Hugh Jackman's maestro on *The Boy from Oz* as well as his concerts. His musical artistry and taste is unsurpassed in my book, and his work on our revival (and its recording) is proof of his gifts.

We started scheduling auditions with casting director Jay Binder, and the open calls alone found literally hundreds of people turning out for a chance to stand on the line. Complicating the audition process was the fact that John had hired a documentary team to film the entire production period, and it took quite a bit of time to get used to cameras turning on the second we walked into the audition room. After several days, I was finally able to just forget about the cameras, and the finished documentary, entitled *Every Little Step*, does in fact capture my unguarded comments; I simply concentrated on the process, not the cameras.

We were actually able to see each of those hundreds of auditioning actors because we had the process down pat, with the maximum number of people seen in the allotted amount of time. It was certainly a casting challenge because of the indelible association between each role and the original cast member who played that character. Most of those talented performers actually were those characters (though some were composites), and they each carried the lifeblood of *A Chorus Line* in their DNA. But, as the auditions progressed, we were fortunate to get the triple-threat beauty Charlotte D'Amboise as Cassie; the sturdy Michael Berresse as Zach; Deidre Goodwin as a sassy yet vulnerable Shelia; the poignant Jason Tam playing Paul; the sexy, provocative Val of Jessica Lee Goldyn; Mara Davi, with a vocal gift to die for, as Maggie; as well as the rest of our stunning company. Together, they made *A Chorus Line* vital once again.

We did face a problem in finding the right theatre. At the time, the Shuberts had only the Schoenfeld Theatre available, and while it had a nice, intimate feel—the capacity was 500 seats less than at the Shubert Theatre where *A Chorus Line* originally played—the stage was shallow, and fewer seats made us a riskier commercial proposition. But—after consulting with set designer Robin Wagner, who said he could make it work creatively—we settled on the Schoenfeld, deciding to put the orchestra beneath the stage rather than in the pit, thereby gaining extra rows down front.

In addition to original set designer Robin Wagner, we asked Suzy Benzinger to reproduce Theoni's costumes, and the brilliant Natasha Katz came on board to recreate and enhance Tharon Musser's original lighting, while bringing it up to date in the face of the ever-expanding new technology.

On the first day of rehearsal, I had every one of the cast members talk about themselves—it broke the ice and served as a reminder of what the musical was really about. I was now at ease in my new role as director, and certainly knew the show inside out, to the point where I felt comfortable making tiny cuts in the show, including eliminating the birth years of the characters and substituting their ages. We had been told numerous times in early previews that new audiences were confused by characters stating they were born in the 1940s, and the text changes alleviated this problem.

We traveled to San Francisco for our tryout and were thrilled when the show was very well reviewed. Business got better and better every day, so we left San Francisco a big hit, riding a wave of momentum into New York City. The Schoenfeld Theatre felt right, and I loved what John had done with the front of the theatre, ensuring that the iconic look of the original production registered, but with an updated twist.

Previews began, and that's when problems with some of the cast began, with actors already starting to call in sick. In the old days, a star like Ethel Merman would have to have been on her deathbed to miss a performance. Now, however, some actors in the cast thought nothing about taking a night off, and when we gave a benefit performance for Lambda Legal, the LGBT legal organization with which Peter and I have had a long association, no fewer than three principals were out of the show that night. During previews. This situation unfortunately lasted throughout the run.

Nevertheless, audiences were responding well to the show, and I felt we were in good shape by the opening-night performance of October 5, 2006. I picked up the *New York Times* review late that night, read the first two paragraphs, and thought, "Uh-oh." Ben Brantley, the chief critic of the *Times*, had basically said that the first five minutes of the show were thrilling, but after that it was merely a recreation. We received many positive reviews and clearly were going to run, but we didn't receive the rapturous reviews we had in San Francisco. Business was very strong, however, and John had produced the show so smartly that by the fifth or sixth week of performances in New York, the show was into profit. We performed very strongly at the box office for the first year, only flagging in the second year when we replaced some of the cast.

We closed on August 17, 2008, but three months previously we had sent out a national tour. That tour opened on May 4 in Denver, playing very successfully for a full two years all around the country; even by the start of the tour, I felt that I had learned a huge amount. There I was, seventy years old but still learning on the job all the time—a very good feeling. I fixed casting problems and rethought a few of my directorial choices; it now felt so on target that by the time we opened in London in February of 2013—the first-ever revival of *Chorus Line* in the West End—I was extremely proud of the production. We had worked very hard on the London revival, and with Baayork overseeing the dance sequences, and Peter working with the actors on the book scenes, I could function as an editor—snipping here, refocusing there. It's a system which worked very well on both of the national tours as well as in London. By now, Baayork, Peter, Patrick, and I were functioning smoothly as a real team.

I had learned to take what the actors could bring to the roles, allow them to find their own interpretations, and then guide their work. I was happier with the London production than with the Broadway revival, and we received tremendous reviews thanks in large part to the terrific cast led by Scarlett Strallen, John Partridge, James T. Lane, and Leigh Zimmerman, who deservedly won the Olivier Award for her performance as Sheila. I felt, however, that the show was never sold properly. We were playing the Palladium, which is a very big theatre lying outside of the West End—it was too big a venue for *A Chorus Line*. The producers were not major powerhouse producers in the mold of Cameron Mackintosh, nor did they have the savvy of John Breglio.

Casting a show properly is incredibly important and many directors feel that their job is half done if they have assembled the right cast. For *A Chorus Line*, in particular, the actors have to bring their own impulses and personalities to the roles. I've learned that I shouldn't and couldn't create the role for them, but rather, simply guide them in the right direction.

In London, the biggest problem with the cast lay in the fact that England was part of the European Union, which meant that every cast member had four weeks of vacation a year—they had to take the time even if they did not want to. They were also granted four weeks of sick days, so the required total of two months of downtime ensured that once the show opened, it was rare to ever see the entire original cast together again onstage. With all that vacation and sick time, at some performances it was hard to muster enough actors to play the parts of the dancers cut during the opening audition. To give perspective: when *Miss Saigon* opened on Broadway in 1991, there were four swings in the cast. When the show opened in Germany, there were seventeen swings because of the required vacation and sick days.

Looking back on it now, I only wish I had directed and learned from other companies of the show before the Broadway revival, but directing these companies was an exhilarating experience, and I confess: I loved receiving director's billing.

CHAPTER TWENTY-THREE

SAIGON REDUX

IN 2013, CAMERON TOLD ME THAT HE WAS GOING TO REMOUNT *MISS Saigon* and asked me to be a part of his new production team. He had experienced great success with several revivals of *Les Miz*, and felt the time was right for another look at *Miss Saigon*, which he told me was his most heavily requested show for revival. But this production would be *Miss Saigon* with a difference, featuring a redesigned physical production that would fit into the smaller theatres that had proven incapable of housing the original, gargantuan set.

The production team would be different, from the director to the designers, so I was flattered to be one of only two members of the original production team asked to recreate their work (the other was Andreane Neofitou, the costume designer, who had to design literally hundreds of costumes; she was constantly refining her work, and always proved a joy to work with). The director was to be Laurence Connor, who had directed the revival of *Les Miz*, as well as Andrew Lloyd Webber's *School of Rock*; Cameron had discovered Laurence while he was in the cast of one of Cameron's shows, and was so impressed that he made Laurence his resident director. Laurence is smart, sensitive, kind, wonderful with actors, and thoroughly in charge at all times.

Cameron then hired Adrian Vaux to design a new, more streamlined production, and Adrian developed a design concept that did not rely as heavily on machinery as had the original. Because the show had been constantly tweaked in all of its various incarnations in the twenty-five years since the original production opened, Adrian could draw upon all of those elements to enhance his new design, with the actual scenic execution finalized and enhanced by Totie Driver and Matt Kinley.

From the start, I had one big asset for help with my own work: Geoffrey Garratt, Cameron's in-house choreographer, who had restaged the choreography for Cameron's various productions of *Oliver, Les Miz, Mary Poppins,* and *Miss Saigon.* I knew Geoffrey because he had been the dance captain of *Martin Guerre* and felt certain that I would feel very comfortable working with him. Even better, because he had been so involved with various productions of *Saigon,* he could display all of the adjustments made over the course of twenty-five years, and I could then pick and choose which bits I most wanted to utilize for this revival. Geoffrey was like a living archive of my work, yet brought his own collaborative vision to the material. He knew every one of the steps, yet always deferred to my position as the original musical stager. Working with him was an absolute dream; it made me feel as if I were working on a brand-new show.

When the first production of *Saigon* had been cast in London nearly thirty years earlier, I had not been present for the audition sessions; as a result, I was presented with a cast which featured singers, not dancers. I was able to exploit the skills of the one tenor who was an acrobat, but that still left me figuring out how to build large production numbers around non-dancers. The answer was to keep the choreography basic and to utilize props, such as the rifles in the gun dance. After that first London production, I was able to cast more and more dancers in each succeeding company, and by the time of the Japanese production, was able to hire no fewer than ten acrobats. In fact, after the Tokyo company opened, I went back to the other companies and inserted more acrobatics into the musical staging. On this revival, I was now able to hire very skilled acrobats who also happened to possess genuine skills as singers and dancers—"Morning of the Dragon" and "American Dream" began to take on deeper and more frightening shadings.

Just as with the original production, Cameron planned to open the revival in London, before eventually producing the show on Broadway. Mindful of the controversy surrounding Jonathan Pryce's casting, we were thrilled to cast Jon Jon Briones as The Engineer. Jon Jon, a native of the Philippines, had been part of the ensemble in the original London company, and the story of how he was cast for that production perfectly illustrates the necessity of grabbing any opportunity that comes your way in show business. Jon Jon had actually been helping run the original auditions in the Philippines, and at the very last minute said to us, "I've decided I'd like to tryout too." He did, and we cast him on the spot as a member of the ensemble.

The rest of the cast for this revival came from all over Asia: China, Japan, Thailand, Hong Kong, and Vietnam. Our casting director, Tara Rubin, had discovered the extraordinary Eva Noblezada, the young girl hired to play Kim, from a tape in which she sang with her high school choir. Eva is Filipino but born in the United States, and she wowed everyone on the spot—we had our leading lady, and one who equaled the stunning original, Lea Salonga.

Hong Kwang-Ho, who played the villainous Thuy, is Korean, and a major star in his home country, having been cast as the lead in the Korean productions of both *Les Miz* and *Phantom*. Kwang was handsome, could act, sang beautifully—and very much wanted the chance to work in England. We hired him even though he did not speak much English and had an interpreter with him throughout rehearsals. As the American GI Chris, Alistair Brammer knocked us out with his vocals and vulnerability, ensuring that we had a great cast from top to bottom.

Tech rehearsals began in April 2014, and I felt like I was a kid on a brand-new playground. Geoff and Laurence knew the new set better than I, so it was a pleasure to sit and figure out the new possibilities for choreography. Because the new set was not raked, the dancing proved much easier for everyone involved, and the entire tech period ran smoothly. When we began previews, every member of the production team was delighted right from the start—a rare occurrence. Cameron was present at every performance, suggesting, recommending, and maintaining control like the top flight producer he is. The audience response was terrific from the first performance on, and the reviews were solidly favorable; London reviewers often rate shows on a scale of one to five stars, and we received solid four- and five-star reviews.

A New York production was certainly hoped for right from the start, but it wasn't a fait accompli because we needed the right theatre to house what was still a massive physical production. It was decided that once again the Broadway Theatre was the only Shubert theatre that could comfortably house our production, and with a scheduled March 2017 start to performances in New York, Cameron shipped the actual London set to the US after the London revival closed following a run of two years.

It was decided that Jon Jon, Eva, and Alistair would repeat their roles on Broadway. The rest of the cast would be American. Everything seemed to be running right on schedule but midway through the casting process, while supervising *A Chorus Line* at the Hollywood Bowl, things were turned upside down when I found out that I had cancer of the tongue. I had the lesion removed at Yale New Haven Hospital and had to undergo thirty days of radiation therapy—five days per week for six straight weeks. I did not have radiation in New Haven because it would have meant commuting over an hour each way from my home, and the treatment was painful and intense enough without the stress of a heavily trafficked commute. Instead, I opted to undergo radiation in Fort Lauderdale, Florida, where Peter and I spend our winters. I finished the radiation in December, and made it back to New York in time for the start of rehearsals in January of 2017.

Working on the show was the best thing that could have happened to me. I was so busy that I had no time to think about my recovery, and I can honestly state that as a result I was happier working on this production than on any other show in my career. Not only did the work keep me busy, but Cameron surrounded me with Geoff, Ben Osborne, an Australian who had staged several productions of the show, and Jesse Robb, a Canadian who was to be our new resident choreographer. With these associates, I occasionally felt like Kay Thompson surrounded by the Williams Brothers! All credit to Cameron; hiring all of these associates cost him a great deal of money but he was protecting me, as well as the show.

Cameron was thrilled with this production, and I certainly was as well. We opened on March 23, 2017, received very positive reviews, and the show quickly settled in for a lucrative run before heading out on a national tour. Wherever the production, and whatever the venue, one thing remained constant: audiences loved the show, leaping to their feet without hesitation at the end of every performance. The show's major theme—the power of parental love—resonates no matter where the show plays.

CHAPTER TWENTY-FOUR

COMING FULL CIRCLE

I'VE HAD AN INCREDIBLE LIFE, ONE I NEVER COULD HAVE IMAGINED when I was a little boy, but it has recently struck me that in some ways I have come full circle: family was everything when I was growing up, and now that I'm winding down my professional life, it's family that remains paramount. My husband Peter is the single most important person in my life, and when I had my bout with cancer, Peter oversaw all of the care, coordinating the doctor appointments and hospital care. He's so perceptive and well-informed about health issues that I constantly tell him he would have made a great doctor. When I'm flooded with medical information it's difficult for me to sort through the thicket of words, but Peter digests all of the information. At the same time, on a professional level, he also remains the best critic of my work, the one person whose judgment I always rely upon.

It wasn't just the cancer that slowed me down for a bit: I've also had three back surgeries to deal with crushed discs. I first tried cortisone injections and nerve ablations as therapy, but it soon became clear that I needed to have a titanium rod inserted into my back. The first month of recovery after that operation was pure torture, and it took me six months before I felt like myself. Just as I did, however, another crushed disc surfaced, and I underwent a second spinal fusion. One thing I learned with the second operation was that the painkillers they prescribed made me feel worse than I ever did from the pain. I learned to find comfort in homeopathic remedies and they worked.

Two years later, the pain in my left hip became so unbearable that I had to have a hip replacement; with all the hardware in my body, I now literally set off alarms when I walk through airport security. These injuries can invariably be traced back to all those decades of dancing, not just on Broadway, but especially on the concrete surfaces found in television studios. I really do think we former hoofers understand what professional athletes go through while rehabbing from injuries. Peter's constant care is what has helped pull me through—I'm not sure how people living on their own manage. Peter and I committed to each other in 1985, and for over three decades now, it is he who has always been there for me.

Next to Peter, the person to whom I remain closest is my sister Laura, a remarkable woman who has remained incredibly vital well into her eighties. We talk at length once every week; not only was she a huge influence in my life by taking me to my first movies and plays, but I still trust her crucial acumen. When Laura says of a show, "I'd really like to see that again," I know that the play in question is first-rate.

She is also an extremely loving woman who not only raised her own children, but also took care of my mother in the last years of her life. My mother lived on for another twenty years after my father died, and while she lived in a cottage on our Connecticut property where I could look after her in the summer months, it was Laura who took care of her during the fall and winter. My mother lived until nearly age 100, and during the last four years of her life, it was my sister who bathed her, fed her, and watched over her.

It had proved necessary to place my older brother Jack in an assisted living facility, a situation which turned out to be so difficult that he only lived for six weeks after he moved there, but we were determined to keep my mother at home. As an immigrant, the concept of home was incredibly important to her well-being. When she passed away, I was sad but not devastated. It was time, and in her very devout way, she was ready to go, saying to me: "I know I'll be okay. God is waiting for me." It moved me a great deal when my sister told me that on the last day of my mother's life, she saw her reaching both hands up in the air—reaching for Heaven and her God.

Family holds center stage in my life, but one way or another I keep getting called back for one more go round in the theatre, and while I might start out dragging my feet a bit, in the end I am very happy to be back putting on another show. In the summer of 2016, *A Chorus Line* was staged at the Hollywood Bowl for three nights, and it turned out to be an absolutely thrilling experience. Baayork and Peter really rehearsed the show and put it on its feet, but I came in to supervise, and was incredibly happy with the final result. Once again, we had a top-notch cast: Mario Lopez, Sarah Bowden, Robert Fairchild, Krysta Rodriguez, and Sabrina Bryan.

I kept tinkering with little parts of the show because theatre shouldn't be cast in concrete, and you have to be alive to the changes in venue. The Hollywood Bowl concert was outdoors and had to start while it was still light outside—the cast could not sneak onstage during the opening blackout. In fact, we had to rehearse and light the show before the sun had set, so we couldn't even tell if the lighting was working until we watched the first performance; we ended up making fixes the day after the first performance. But that's part of the thrill—you continue to work on the show, refining it "bit by bit—piece-by-piece—only way to make a work of art" (to paraphrase Steve Sondheim).

Given the size of the Hollywood Bowl, we could utilize many more dancers in the opening audition sequence, and this time around I changed the finale by putting in two additional company bows. This idea had started in Tokyo because the producers had demanded it, explaining that this was what the Japanese audiences expected. Instead of the show fading out on an endlessly kicking chorus line, I inserted a full company bow. The orchestra then took a bow, after which the entire company, including the dancers cut during the scene of the first audition, took another bow. I think Michael would have liked that change; I can hear him say, "Keep the heat going." I wasn't breaking any "rules"—the show maintained its integrity. I was determined to retain a more old-fashioned type of company bow, one fully accompanied by musical underscoring, and the end result proved exciting for both the cast and audience.

A happy surprise occurred at the end of 2018 when Jack Viertel, the artistic director of City Center's Encores, asked John Breglio and me if we would consider doing a week-long run of *A Chorus Line* to celebrate City Center's seventy-fifth anniversary. We cast it with the best of the best from Broadway: consummate veterans like Robyn Hurder, Tony Yazbeck, Leigh Zimmerman, Jay Anthony Armstrong, and J. Elaine Marcos played alongside newcomers, and there was not a weak link in the cast of twenty-eight. I also had the opportunity to bring together the A-list of creative staff I depend upon: choreographer Baayork Lee and her associate Matthew Couvillon; music director Patrick Vaccariello; Peter as my associate director; as well as the incredible talents of Robin Wagner, overseeing his original set design; Ken Billington, adapting Tharon Musser's lighting; Michael McDonald, recreating and augmenting Theoni Aldridge's costumes; and Kai Harada, designing the pitch-perfect sound. The ecstatic audience reaction at every performance made City Center sound like it was home to a rock concert, and tickets on closing night were being offered at $1000 a pair in front of the theatre. It was one of those magical productions where all elements meshed to make Michael Bennett's masterpiece feel vital and brand-new. The respect and love that the cast felt for the show and for each other reinforced and underlined why, after sixty years, I still adore this unpredictable business, and it proved a great lesson in how the briefest of creative experiences—only seven performances—can often be the most rewarding.

I'm often asked how Broadway has changed in the fifty-plus years I've been working in theatre, and my instant answer is: economically. When *Promises, Promises* opened at the Shubert in 1968, the top ticket price was $8.80, and when *A Chorus Line* opened at the same theatre in 1975, the most expensive seats were $15. Nowadays, premium seats for *Hamilton* can cost $1,000 apiece and more. I understand that the practice of premium tickets started with *The Producers* in order to eliminate scalpers from the equation, but as the prices leap ever higher, Broadway is turning into an elitist art form. This hasn't stopped the industry from thriving, because audience members seem to have deep pockets when it comes to seeing the hottest new shows. But I worry that the audience isn't growing, just the grosses—that the same wealthy people are paying the ever-higher prices.

At the same time, the style of musicals has changed enormously in recent years, and after the end-of-millennium invasion of the British megamusicals like *Phantom*, *Cats*, and *Miss Saigon*, musicals in the twenty-first century are growing smaller in scale. *Dear Evan Hansen*, *Come From Away*, and *The Band's Visit* feature scaled-down physical productions and central characters you'd find in real life, rather than the larger-than-life characters found in many traditional musical comedies. It is hard to imagine a brand-new musical created in the mold of *Hello, Dolly!* ever coming to Broadway, but then, who knows? Thankfully, Broadway constantly surprises me.

Interests change, and styles of presentation continue to evolve; without question, the biggest change from when I was dancing in shows is the introduction of body mics. When we staged *A Chorus Line*, it was deliberately choreographed from foot mic to foot mic to foot mic. Nowadays every member of the cast wears a body mic, and whether it's because of rock music's influence, or because audiences are used to watching television at home with the volume raised on high, unfortunately most musicals now blast the audience out the back door. By way of contrast, Ethel Merman didn't need a body mic.

Peter and I travel, taking cruises with pals where we bring loads of books. I'm a lifelong reader of fun fiction—think John Grisham rather than *War and Peace*. We're lucky to have an amazing, close core of friends in New York and Connecticut (our "sewing circle") with whom we often share potluck dinners and Litchfield County restaurants. As Florida "snowbirds" in the winter, Fort Lauderdale is our perfect getaway, again with friends we adore. Stage work will continue to be on the horizon, but only work that we feel passionate about.

As a staunch Democrat, I keep abreast of the political scene, and one of the thrills of my life was when Peter and I met and spoke with President Obama at a fundraiser. Talk about charm, class, and charisma.

I never could have imagined the life I've led. When I went off to college, I never thought I'd be a professional dancer. I had a gift, but I did not have the usual early training. I honestly didn't think I'd end up dancing on Broadway, let alone for the likes of Jerome Robbins. When I met Michael during *West Side Story*, I certainly didn't have an inkling that our professional lives would be intertwined for twenty-five years, culminating in the groundbreaking *A Chorus Line*.

Choreographing on my own? Directing on Broadway? Even as a fifty-year-old man, I had no clue that I would have a full and very satisfying career after Michael, and that at one point I would have three shows running simultaneously in the West End. The chance to work with a genius like Stephen Sondheim, to work for Cameron, the best producer in the world—these are opportunities it would have been hard for me to even dream about.

Some of that success was luck, some due to talent, and quite a bit of it due to determination. We all have to keep plugging away, keep learning, and remain open to any and all influences and opportunities. When you see an open door, walk through it—find out what's on the other side. You can always return to a former life, changed but enlightened. But most of all: "move on" (Steve Sondheim again). Don't be afraid of change. It's the only constant in life.

It takes resilience to sustain a career, to deal with critics, actors, and collaborators—and I'm proud of sustaining for over half a century. It's just like Dizzy Gillespie said: the professional is the guy who can do it twice.

I'm content. Fortunate. And grateful to all who have helped me along the way.

Take it from a certified late bloomer: you never know what door will open next.

INDEX

ABOUT THE AUTHORS

Photo by Randy O'Rourke

BOB AVIAN (pictured above) is an award-winning Broadway choreographer and director, best known for his work on *A Chorus Line*, *Miss Saigon*, and *Sunset Boulevard*. He served as a lead producer on the hit Broadway production of *Dreamgirls*, and directed the New York and London revivals of *A Chorus Line*. He is a six-time Tony nominee, winning for *A Chorus Line* and *Ballroom*, and received the Olivier Award for his choreography on *Martin Guerre*.

TOM SANTOPIETRO is the author of seven books, including the best-selling *The Sound of Music Story*. He has worked for twenty-five years as the manager of over thirty Broadway shows.